IDOLS BEHIND ALTARS

ANITA BRENNER

HARCOURT, BRACE AND COMPANY

NEW YORK

N
6550
B7

24124

TO MY FATHER
ISIDORE BRENNER

NOTE

Essays printed previously in *The Nation*, *The Arts*, and *Creative Art* are included in *Idols Behind Altars* by courtesy of those publications.

ACKNOWLEDGMENT

If I were to thank in print and by name all the people to whom I am indebted for the materials of *Idols Behind Altars* I should have to begin with my nurse Serapia who told me what the comet before the revolution of 1910 signified, and I should have to include many dear friends whose middle names I have forgotten. However their valuable collaboration would have been less satisfactorily illustrated except for the sympathy and support of the former rector of the National University of Mexico, Dr. Alfonso Pruneda, who commissioned for the University an investigation of Mexican art, placing the author in charge. The two photographers who shared this commission, Edward Weston and Tina Modotti, are too well known and respected as masters of their craft to expect in *Idols Behind Altars* any acknowledgment less than deeply grateful, and artists about whom much of this book is written have been kind enough to sponsor it with interest and assistance.

ANITA BRENNER

CONTENTS

PART ONE

CHAPTER ONE

MEXICAN MESSIAH

An old prophecy current in Mexico announces that "When the chief temple of the Aztecs shall appear in the principal plaza of the city of Tenochtitlan, bearing upon it the sun, then shall the ancient people possess their ancient rights." In August, 1926, during the course of restoration and repair of the National Palace, in the main plaza of the capital, once Tenochtitlan, a monolith was brought to light. It is

2.   a model of the chief temple of the Aztecs, with a stone symbolic of the sun carved on its surface.

This is a curious piece of lore for 1926, but Mexico is a peculiar place. It is a fact that begins with the very contour of the land, torn into sudden transition, from the most luxuriant tropics to the grey, arid, rock-built heights around volcanoes. Mexico is made up of three planes: the hot lands, the cool or temperate, and the cold. They cut into and across each other so that you may stand on the top of a canyon and see snow on the mountain above you, while thousands of feet just under you, coffee and bananas grow. The dramatic and untimed juxtapositions of climates and landscapes are like the days, which everywhere go suddenly and without twilight, from white light into the night. And they are like the storms, short, powerful, saturating. Crops grow richly, disappear quickly. The land seems unfinished, and at the same time forever fixed.

Common to coast, canyon, desert and plateau, is a far horizon
of purple mountain chain, inescapable as the fear that perches
on the shoulder of the stranger. Most of the mountains are
volcanoes, many of them are alive and occasionally stir in their
sleep. Therefore they dominate in the making of that curious,
insistent uncertainty that is the essence of Mexican life, bound
up with the just as insistent sense of changelessness. They
dominate physically. The flat-topped volcanic pyramid is repeated over and over in different scale and material. In the
temples and observatories of pre-Hispanic structure; in squar-
ish colonial missions; in village houses, thatched with palms
where palms grow, and where stretches of lava girdle the
fields, walled with the same sombre rock. The Indian,
squatted, wrapped conically in his sarape, and his wife, swathed
in her rebozo, justify by their own architecture the ancient
custom of giving personal names to volcanoes.

Mountains, plants—ancient breeds, century plants, cacti,
maize and calabashes—and the people, all have a tense, animal vitality. The maguey grows spikes like claws on its grey-
green fibrous muscles; the maize is toothed; fruits and flesh are
of the same firm blood-filled texture; and the people state
facts and face them without sentimental or ethical apologia.
Who stays long enough cannot escape the demands of this
integrity. He may hate it, and feels impotent to scratch upon
it; or he loves it with passion. He is in both cases bound to it.
Women particularly find themselves tormented, and people
who cannot abandon the notions brought with them from
elsewhere.

With an intellectual axe to grind, this land which takes
such liberties with time and space, which jazzes the social scale,
which shifts into many faces, and is nevertheless a unit, becomes madness. The visitor's mind scurries from one interpretation to another, while his being goes to pieces or evolves

a new strength. He goes like the land to extremes, contracts a permanent faith like the Indian's, or a permanent doubt like the mestizo's; drinks himself to disease like most foreigners, or writes poetry, sings, paints pictures, like most natives. For the dust of Mexico on a human heart corrodes, precipitates. But with the dust of Mexico upon it, that heart can find no rest in any other land.

Without the need for translation or a story sequence, Mexico resolves itself harmoniously and powerfully as a great symphony or a great mural painting, consistent with itself, not as a nation in progress, but as a picture, with certain dominant themes, certain endlessly repeated forms and values in constantly different relationships, and always in the present, like the Aztec history-scrolls that were also calendars and books of creed.

II.

"Look around," says an ancient Mexican poet, "and wonder at this scene of many-colored houses . . . created and endowed with life. They make us who are miserable to see the light among the flowers and songs of the fertile fields, they cause us to see those things . . . created and endowed with life. They dwell in the place of spring, here within the broad fields, and only for our sakes does the turquoise water fall in broken drops on the surface of the lake. Where it gleams forth in fourfold rays, where the fragrant yellow flowers bud, there live the Mexicans, the youths."

Ever recurrent in Mexican thought, is this concern with the sheer fact of life. Life shifting from one form to another, and all still the same; movement defined by stops; light endlessly becoming darkness, plants and people of necessity dying, at a definite fixed point, to be reborn. Hence the constant considering of death, and hence the Mexican messiah.

The Mexican messiah began with the first sun and life-giver, in legend a most miserable and leprous brother of a family of gods, who was transformed in fire and thereafter climbed into the sky. The sun, the mountains, the gods, the heroes (of necessity martyrs), healers and rebels—this is the stuff of which the messiah is made. His form is multiple. There may be many of him at once. Always he is the same messiah, projection of divinity. Always he must die, always return. He is fundamentally an abstract principle, the function of which is to kindle, maintain, justify, embody and give life.

Texcatlipoca the perennially youthful Smoking Mirror, or Fiery Rock, was a mountain, the night wind, a jaguar, and was present, although essentially invisible, in the forms of priests and of people bearing his name or wearing garments like his. He was dramatically synthesized yearly in the living body of the most beautiful male captive, who was honored for the seasons' cycle and worshipped as the god. At the end of the year he died, to nourish the sun, which could thereby live and make the next year's crops spring up again. Quetzalcoatl the Plumed Serpent, was water, the south wind, reptile, bird, plants, doctor, teacher, astronomer, priest, king, and ordinary wise person. As king he taught the people agriculture and how to measure time and the stars. Then he sailed away in a white-winged boat, promising to return. As wind and serpent, priest and ordinary wise person, he was considered to be still present.

The Tepozton of Tepoztlan, a mountain village near the capital, is, as his name signifies, lord of the mountain on which his temple stands. He is also the ancient Ometochtli who helped to discover the fertile maguey with its bowl of intoxicant milk. He is each of the kings who ruled the village. He is the boy who today takes care of his ruined house. And he

3. MAGUEY

4. LEAD SOLDIERS FROM GUADALAJARA

is the man who yearly dresses in red and green and sings a triumphant defiant Aztec chant in the churchyard of Our Lady of Natividad, Catholic patroness of the pueblo and dweller at the foot of the Tepozton's mountain. He is the favorite son of this Lady, though when she first arrived he angrily blasted the crops as the wind, and as a deadly white worm at the roots of the maize. He appeared on the shoulder of his mountain as a great serpent and as lightning, as a jaguar with tremendous jaws and a horrible roar, as a radiant being with waving head-dress, riding the storm. The Tepozton "usually walks about the fields and attends to the crops and other matters of the people's welfare." He is then dressed as a peasant with a straw sombrero on his head. "Thus it is known that he is poor and one of us." When the rain is late he appears in dreams or out of them, clothed magnificently in red and green ribands and plumes, "and thus it is known that he is a god." He makes his wishes known. They are fulfilled, and it rains. During the revolution he helped the peasant rebels against the Federal soldiers. The Tepozton, like the Teutli of Milpa Alta, like the Lord of Chalma, like the long-haired mourning Malintzin, "is a powerful person; but what he has of bad he has of good, too." He, and all the deities, it is frequently asserted, "Sleep in the mountains. They sometimes stir. But some day they will awake, and shake, and pour forth lava and boiling water, a great and barbarous breath. Then the people will no longer carry burdens on their backs."

In Mexican mood the messiah is always accompanied by disaster: an earthquake, a conquest, a revolution, the sacrifice of a ruler; death and pain. Therefore all the prophecies which promise restoration are complemented by announcements of catastrophe. New life, the fires rekindled by the ancient Mexicans at the end of each fifty-two-year cycle, was made after the darkening of these fires, destruction of possessions, with the sense of impending obliteration. The cycles were not arranged in sequence. Each was a completely new beginning, repeating the days and events of the past, with the same names and the same coincident events. Thus the prophecies were as calendrical as the seasons. The martyr-messiah was dated.

The return of Quetzalcoatl was set for the end of a cycle that proved to be the last of the Aztec Empire. He was heralded by comets, earthquakes, sinister messengers. Moctezuma was warned that the end of his reign was near, and with it his own death. Then Cortez materialized the white and bearded—maize-like but un-Aztec—human form of the radiant Serpent. In the eighteenth century just before the War of Independence, two cultured Spanish gentlemen entered unannounced the hut of an Indian in a garden suburb of Mexico City, and surprised "a very old man squatting on his mat, with a pair of spectacles on his nose, studying a hieroglyph chart or picture-map." He quickly flicked it out of sight, but, urged and questioned, he explained that "he had been figuring out the time set for the end of the Spanish reign."

Netzahualcoyotl the Aztec poet king sang the two facets of the ever-continuous Mexican persuasion of which the messiah is the symbol.

"I foresaw, being a Mexican, that our rule began to be destroyed.

"I went forth weeping that it was to bow down and be destroyed.

"Let me not be angry that the grandeur of Mexico is about to be destroyed.

"The smoking stars gather together against it; the one who cares for flowers is about to be destroyed.

"He who cared for books wept, he wept for the beginning of the destruction."

Then in another poem he chants, "The darkness of the sepulchre is but a strengthening couch for the glorious sun, and the obscurity of the night but serves to reveal the brilliance of the stars. . ."

While on a different plane, another chanter echoes him: "The disdained and the slaves shall go forth with song; but in a little while their oppressors shall be seen in the fire, amid the howling of wolves."

It is the same persuasion still. There is a good deal of faith in these prophecies. Many of them come true, and in schedule. They circulate among the otherwise inarticulate, by word of mouth, in ballads, hymns, penny broadsides, by gesture almost. One hardly knows how, but the feeling is there. Sooner or later the mountains and the men produce corroboration. In the years when the revolution of 1910 was brewing, and just before the pot boiled over, although the dictator did not know it, the people spoke among themselves of what was soon to come. I remember being held up above a mob to watch the great glare of a comet in the sky, and the old woman who held me said: "It means war, death, misery, hunger and disease." Soon after that it rained ashes for a night and a day from a distant erupting volcano. The people said: "After this it will rain blood."

When Madero, political head of the turmoil that followed, rode triumphant into the capital, he was greeted by a wildly enthusiastic mass, black on the roofs and jammed in the windows. But that same day an earthquake in the city split a big building in half. It was said, and Madero knew it, that he was soon to die. Out in the mountains of Morelos, Zapata, with his brutal, passionate peasant troop, was clamoring for the ancient lands. In Yucatan Felipe Carrillo Puerto was teaching the Maya peons their constitutional rights. They died for it, as they both knew they would.

Then afterwards there arose in the mountains of the north a nameless Indian boy who was called the Miraculous Child Fidencio. The Miraculous Fidencio, insists a penny pamphlet as anonymous as a ballad, "Is not like the numberless witch-doctors, bone-setters, hypnotists and other such individuals who now and again rise up in Mexico, particularly in the fields. . . The chronicles of the eighteenth century speak of Tzantzen, a mountain Indian from Zacatecas, extraordinarily learned in the curative powers of herbs and plants. Towards the end of the War of Independence there arose the somewhat unreal figure of Sor Encarnación, a nun escaped from one of the convents to become the aid and comfort of the Mexican guerrilla men. It was said that he who drank of the fountain which had sprung miraculously from her touch was cured of all his ills, and his wounds turned to scars . . . In these last few years countless cure-people have arisen. Rutila, the little old woman of the Blue Water, in Guadalajara, who offered to resuscitate the governor. . . Maria Auxiliadora (Mary the Helper) a peasant woman of San Luis Potosí . . . Don Erasmo Mata, that facetious Don Erasmo who with equal affability foretold the end of the world and cured the sick by means of the magic feathers of his prophet game-cock. But Fidencio stands apart, a pure, serene, and humble figure, a generous Child who makes paralytics walk while he sings to them naïve ballads and chants, and gives out among the poor the gold and gifts of those in power."

Shortly after his appearance in 1928, Fidencio announced that he had not long to live. The nation must hasten to him to be healed, for he could give it only two years. A city sprang up in the desert around him, permanently inhabited by changing hundreds of beggars for sight, for speech, for movement, for life. It was called the Place of Pain. Many of the healed declared that the power of Fidencio rested in the brew he made by throwing into a great vat of running water, the gifts of flowers and fruit that came to him. Others said that this power came from the songs he sang. His favorite was a lyric about and to a Blue Lily of the Mountain. It is a song of love and can, one hears, make death easier, and quiet any pain. Most often it was said that Fidencio's power came from the Place of Pain itself. The tree under which he wept and prayed to be given the boon of healing became a shrine and an altar. Candles burned around it and supplicants knelt on its roots. But Fidencio would not have these explanations. He said: "Those who suffer have the Grace of God. By suffering, health is reached, and it is necessary that this should be so, because those who desire to be well, should be strengthened by sorrows and pain."

III.

The ancient Mexican concern with death which created the messiah, remains like the messiah an organic part of Mexican thought. As a motif in art it springs from before the Conquest, cuts through the colonial period and appears over and over today. There are skulls in monolith of lava, miniature of gold and crystal, mask of obsidian and jade; skulls carved on walls, moulded upon pots, traced on scrolls, woven into garments; formalized into hieroglyphs, given a skeleton and an occupation in figurines; filled out around whistles, savings-banks, rattles, bells, holiday masks and jewels; woodcut and etched on ballads; strung into drinking-shop decorations; made into candies and toys. The skull has many meanings in Mexican argot. It trails gods, clowns, devils and subsidiary bogies in Mexican lore. There is a national holiday for it.

The Day of the Dead was fixed by the missionary friars according to the Christian calendar, but it was a habit long be-

5. **RETURN OF THE DEAD**
Illustration for popular ballad, by Guadalupe Posada

fore. This holiday comes on the first and second of November. All Saints' Day is all adult ghosts' day, and All Souls' day belongs to the children. The spirits return according to their ages, on the first and second eve, to dine with their living relatives. The table is set on an altar. There are beans, chili, tortillas, rice, fruit, other daily dishes, and the specialties of the season: pumpkins baked with sugar-cane, pulque or a bluish maize-brew with a delicate sugar film, and Dead Mens' Bread. For the children, candy skulls, pastry coffins, ribs and thigh-bones made of chocolate and frosted sugar, tombstones, wreaths, and pretentious funerals.

The living do not eat of the feast until the dead have left. They sit up all night "with the little dead ones" (affectionate term for invisible human beings) as if at a wake—a Mexican wake; singing, praying, drinking, making a little love. And it is a wake, except that the prayers are said not for the dead, but to them. Everybody "weeps the bone" picnicking in the graveyards. The tombs are turned into banquet tables similar

to those at home. The food is put upon them, on banks of
flowers, heavy purple wild blossoms and the yellow pungent
cempoalxochitl, ancient and sacred bloom. Little flags fly from
the mounds; sometimes arcades and booths are raised over
them, as upon holiday canoes. The recently bereaved or the
especially punctilious really may shed a few tears for the
honoured "bone." But somehow these tears are like the flowers
and the skulls, simply part of the gesture. One's respected
relatives, who "have moved their sleeping mats" come to call.
They must be treated courteously. A ceremonious gaiety is
the proper tone.

Cosmopolitan Mexico City with its top layer of rice-powder
faces is supposed to believe that the dead are only dust. Yet,
carefully flavored with doubt, the cultured Mexican tells many
of the same tales the mule-driver has heard, tales of dead who
appear, hold converse and depart, but always with nothing
about them different from any other people. The Mexican
ghost is no ha'ant. He calls out quietly from the grave to
please tread lightly, as the earth is loose and drops unpleas-
antly upon him; or he inquires whether or no he may have a
fresh jar of water, as he has used the other all up?

And why do the dead come back? Just to say hello, usually.
Sometimes to see about a bit of business. The Mexican department of archeology excavated at a spot which was pointed
out to an Indian youth by the ghost of his ancestor, the prince
Xicotencatl—and found a buried temple. The director of the
national museum relates that once an Indian came to him and
stated that in a hill near his village, there lay an enormous
treasure, one of the many that, it is said, were hidden from the
lustful Spaniards. This Indian, an old man, said that he had
come on the advice of the village priest. Leaving his name and
address, he departed. Upon inquiry at the village the director
learned that, indeed, such a man was of the place, but had

been dead two years. The description given of the dead man fitted the visitor to the museum. He had been a charcoal burner. The hills where he had gathered wood were scoured for the supposed caché, but no treasure-cave was found. This is a story that the director tells with relish.

In Mexico City the at-home of November second becomes grotesquerie. Fashionable pastry-shops swing over French confections, this urgent sign: Buy Your Dead Men's Bread Here. They turn their shining sophisticated displays into ranks and pyramids of skulls, miniature and life-size and bigger than that, luscent white, or creamy, with maraschino cherries for eyes and syrupy grins on their mouths, and rows of fine gold teeth. The funerals are of expensive milk chocolate, the wreaths of tiny candied fruits—and though this wonderful array is for the baby ghosts, no child in the city but awakes demanding on this day "my funeral" or at the least "my skull."

The city cemeteries are as full of picnickers as the village graveyards. Automobiles and buses travel end on end all day, and in the cemetery itself there are lemonade stands, and tintype photographers making a splendid day on arm-in-arm lovers and family groups backed by a pretentious marble slab or a churrigueresque flower-arbor. Markets and parks fill out with the paraphernalia of carnival except that the eating-stands are delineated by an interminable row of enormous skulls, and are lighted by bier candles. Pottery, masks, figurines, sold at this fair are not the useful, ornamental objects of other holidays. The figurines which throughout the rest of the year are realistic version of people in all classes and professions, on Dead Men's Day appear stripped of worldly possessions such as flesh. The carpenter and the fruit-vendor, the priest and the scholar, the murderer, the poet and the prostitute, Don Juan and the president, the general, the cowboy, the sad Indian, the politician, the bullfighter, the aviator,

Who will drink of this the soul
The soul of dreams and of love?
With my lips I give—my life!

At the turning of the path
They broke the bowl of my heart.
The clear water of heaven dropped
Made a stream where it poured out.
The soul of my land laments
In the shade of an old tree
As Mary Magdalen wept
Her despair
Without friend.

Who will wash his pain with tears
With the water of my heart,
Who is there to weep with me?

Accordingly, consistent with itself only, Mexico may take
and reject people, ideas, forms. In the same century brown men
may dance to the round full beat of a tree-trunk drum, and
brown hands mould small idols or lay red flowers on the altar
of a stone face in the hills; and the same men dressed in denim
overalls buck Fords over the throats of volcanoes and eat sar-
dines packed in Seattle. What Mexico assimilates into its apparently contradictory countenance is ultimately made into
native mould. Throughout the four hundred years since the
Spanish conquest, the white layer at the top has steadily diminished, by death or flight, or by growing darker. Even the
government is much darker than it was twenty years ago. The
cupolas of colonial churches, topped with crosses, are like so
many tufted hills, which are also topped with crosses. Native
symbols are carved into these churches; saints are recarved out
of idols, and eventually recarved again so that they certainly
do not look European. Many teachings of the missionary friars
have become part of the mind of the Indians, but woven into
the life of the cities run the threads of old Indian beliefs.

Ladies of society practise Indian love charms. Their children, withal the silver spoon, know the monster man-headed bird called *nahual* and the Mexican witches, which are not the kind that ride on broomsticks. They travel on balls of fire and when not travelling, live next door as quietly and as courteously as anybody else. In the heart of the capital, rock serpents stare at the automobiles and street-cars that daily scramble past.

All these are native things because there was a need for them, or a sympathy with them. The inconsistencies, the things that Mexico rejects, are the false things, the impositions and artificial transplantations. They die by violence or neglect, be they people, ideas, or forms. And they leave husks, like the lavish marble and gilt National Theatre, now sinking from its own weight in the tender soil mistakenly chosen for it; and like the village of Chapingo, ready-made by a Minister of Agriculture caught by the romance of similar experiments successfully performed elsewhere.

The village of Chapingo, almost contemporaneous to the Place of Pain, was assembled on the model of an American factory-settlement, and was equipped with electric lights and modern sanitation. Peasants were paid, it is said, like moving-picture extras, to stage an inauguration, thrusting smiling heads out of neatly built windows into neatly planned front yards, for the benefit of the President, who promenaded down the *Calle del Trabajo* and through the *Avenida de la Producción,* stopping to admire the school building, the theatre, the co-operative store with its shelves all fitted together as out of a toy box.

But nobody stayed. Today Chapingo is deserted. Weeds fill the trim avenues, and field mice colonize the plank houses, which are beginning to blister under the lambent Mexican sun. At the gate lives the only inhabitant, the caretaker, in a house built of adobe, low-roofed, dim and cool inside, earthen-floored, and promiscuous with children and animals. Potted geraniums hang asymmetrically in the door and over the pig-pen. The family laundry droops from a lazy windmill. Inside, a sewing machine whirs seam after seam on loose white cotton garments. And on the highway to the capital, a permanently sculptured sign, carved for the inauguration, announces —and subtly explains—the village of Chapingo. It declares: "This is the co-operative village of Chapingo, which expects nothing and believes in nothing that it has not made with its hands."

V.

The need to live, creating with materials; the need to set in spiritual order, the physical world; the sense of fitness—these are components of an artist's passion, and these are the Mexican integrity. That is why Mexico cannot be measured by standards other than its own, which are like those of a picture; and why only as artists can Mexicans be intelligible. Any artist anywhere would partake of his peculiar disregard for values others cherish, and the profound importance they attach to things trivial elsewhere. Michael Angelo and Cézanne would hardly find their viewpoint other than normal, and would rejoice with them.

The man of this viewpoint thinks in relationships to the making of things. It may take a day or a year to complete the task, but if the thing made satisfies the maker, that is all that matters. Size and time do not. If he is not interested in the making, he will do it badly or not at all. If the thing to be made itself calls to him to make it, then he will do it better than anybody else, and it does not mean that this thing must be a vase or a figurine. If he thinks a law, a building, an idea or a picture are well made, or beautiful—largely the same to him—he will not query whether there is any more "ought" than that, whether it is valuable, comfortable, moral, or the reverse of these things to anybody else. He cannot understand any other conscientiousness than this. Actions to him are a matter of passion, or a matter of taste. And he settles concerns with himself always first, mostly by making some kind of tangible form in which his heart may be contained.

Therefore it is that nowhere as in Mexico has art been so organically a part of life, at one with the national ends and the national longings, fully the possession of each human unit, always the prime channel for the nation and for the unit. There has been no seeking of the prescription of beauty; the very want of it creates it. There has been no hothouse fostering of a response. It is so natural and spontaneous that the great mass of Mexican art—and this is constantly enormous —is anonymous. Mexico goes ever through the creative travail. If the stench of its discards hangs in the air, only people who are all nose sense nothing but the stench. It is a land that has lain naked and bleeding, a people that has lived in pain. But it is a strong, live body, so alive that it can go to the extremes of beauty and horror with the same zest. And it is a land that moves, a people not dead, nor now in resurrection, but constantly reborn.

Only a strong current of life, and a pure current of life, can flow into the three kinds of things that Mexico makes: beautiful things made collectively, by one hand reliving the work of a preceding hand, on an article of material use, like a bowl; beautiful things of spiritual use, made also collectively, like an idol, a church, or a series of murals, and enjoyed collectively; and beautiful things made by individuals, within these two traditions, and a synthesis of them, running into prime human factors; intelligible or rather potentially the possessions, of all the world.

6. THE SAD INDIAN
    Pastel by Francisco Goitia

The Mexican answer to life is life. His tradition is a function which a dead body cannot possess, which a live body possesses in proportion to its strength. That is why an artist is the most essentially alive, the most deeply unhappy, and the most profoundly happy of all men. And all men have this function. Only some are atrophied, and others are emasculated, while still others are enslaved or prostituted, or dead. That is why, being dominantly artist, Mexico has a messiah who dies, yet always lives; who has so many names and forms that he is never graspable in one; who has humility and strength, who kills and heals, blasts and kindles, suffers and rejoices. He is the image of his people. He is a dark master of himself, and prodigal to the rest of the world. The prophecy which bears him is a prophecy that needs no future, but is constantly fulfilled; that needs no faith but vision. It is the brown hand, color of the earth, shaping a round bowl color of the hand.

CHAPTER TWO

THE PYRAMID PLANTERS

 Visible civilization in the New World began with pottery and religion, supposedly twin growths of the agriculture which is said to have originated somewhere in the Mexican or more southern highlands. Art began, and continued, closely bound to religion. Such

7. integration is not greatly different from Old World tradition, nor is the religion itself, that is, the presumed oldest religion out of which later cults and art styles grew, fundamentally different from ancient beliefs of many agricultural peoples all over the world.

In Egypt, China, Mexico, the main concerns were matters of the soil, its fertility, the watering of it, and the crops. Therefore in these places the forms into which group emotions were moulded, as persuasions and as images, were forms derived from these concerns. In Egypt and in Mexico there was a Great Corn Mother, a young Corn God. The crops themselves were different, certainly. In Egypt it was barley, in Mexico it was maize. The animals associated with the earth, and dominant motifs in art, were also different. Yet so defined is the range of form that man can create, perhaps, or so similar the bent of human thought, that startling coincidences occur; they might be less remarkably accounted for by historical contact, across thousands of miles of sea, in canoes.

It is supposed that originally the ancient Americans migrated from Asia, but when and if more than once, no one can yet say. Enough is discovered to give a vista of several great civilizations arising in America across the span of thousands of years, out of their own beginnings. Coincidences of detail with the Old World are so tied to and interwoven with the native patterns, each of which is a unit and unique in the world, that these exciting similarities when looked at reasonably, must seem largely affinities, and not identities, with China, Egypt, Phœnicia, Etruria or whichever connection has been romantically attractive. Whatever its antecedents, ancient America stands on its own feet.

Some heritage from Asia; some gift of the land itself; some racial bent; these are the unknown quantities already present in the oldest objects known, which are the work of people who simply because they are the oldest known, have been put at the beginning. But these objects and the degree of civilization they indicate are by no means beginnings, in the crude scale of civilization we generally accept. Agriculture is with them, thousands of years back, and in more or less continuous stretches and spots over much of the continent. With agriculture, necessarily the group possessions and elaborations, tangible and intangible, called by the students of civilization, "culture". This is the basic American culture which is basic Maya, basic Peruvian, and basic Mexican.

Ancient Mexico therefore to be seen accurately, can be considered of a piece with the rest of America, and specifically with that part between Arizona and Panamá. Or it can be seen as a great number of little groups or bigger groups, each with a more or less defined style of living and point of view, constantly interchanging influences and materials across time and space; with some intimacy, from the Pueblo region to Central America. War, trade, migration, fusion, friendship, conquest, the spread of cults and crops, increased the material in common, and at the same time helped to determine the character of each people differently, since the spread and strength and special ingredients of the respective "contributing" neighbors varied. The processes which made groups live and grow as integrated groups were assuredly still going on when the Spaniards came. They took part in them. And the one great channel that carried inter-American thought and custom and style, served as the one real bridge with the Old World: the mutual interest in religion, and in its created forms.

The prime material of the ancient American plastic artists was clay, the first enduring record sculpture. Archaic Mexican sculpture, which dates back at least over two thousand years, is not perhaps the oldest made, but it is the oldest as yet found. It is terra cotta, supple figurines of old men sitting, and priestly men, and women symbolic of fertility; of animals suggesting the fruitful tropics—monkeys, parrots, crocodiles, jaguars, serpents, lizards, humming-birds, snails, fishes, frogs; of gourds, melons, squashes, pumpkin blossoms, maize; and shells, long and hollow, curved and spiral; and composites of all these—man-and-frog, man-and-bird, man-and-monkey, anthropomorphic animals and animalized men, human-headed birds and bird-faced human figures, men with talons and fangs; and combinations of animals—birds with jaguar claws, serpents with plumes.

Glimpses and hints of later beliefs and styles are here, cogs of the great civilizations, small parents of the great monolithic gods. This is art and religion personal, portable, fingerprinted still, solitary and yet the widest shared. But unless an "archaic" sculpture is found below ancient lava or in the earth under other remains known to be old, it is not safely "archaic." It could as easily, and as legitimately, have been made last night. On the shores of Chapala today, things similar in form to those of a thousand years ago, and iden-

8. ARCHAIC TERRA COTTA
Sculpture from Chupícuaro, Guanajuato

tical in idea, are ranged round the heads of the dead in their graves, and dropped in the shallows of the lake. Vividly-colored in the craft centers of Tlaquepaque, in central Mexico, and shining or dull black (the pigment sacred in straight descent from antiquity) on the southeast coast, these same plastic ideas are made into whistles and bells and savings-banks, along with newer forms such as madonnas and Spanish sheep.

For whatever the superstructure, whatever the epoch, the charted course of deepest Mexican thought comes back to this significant source. The habits of thought and objects index to them, on the theme of continuing life, incorporate back-wash forms of all the passing official abstracted and monu-mentalized creeds. The beliefs include fundamental roots of creeds, and folklore version of what was once, or still is, offi-cially dogma. The sculptures are images of the official deities, remade in forms that were their origin, or sanction.

The set of beliefs of which these things are symbols, is hardly a system, and not always articulate. It underlies all Mexican religions which have had a priesthood, including Christianity. It is not everywhere accompanied by rite; but always by the constant Indian attitude, which is the participation of the same stuff of being, with other lives not human.

Thinking men by processes of association, identified them-selves with the things they perceived. The needs and tastes of their group gave this a special emphasis. Because the main desire, which can approximately be understood as the desire to live, to make life, was closely bound up with the crops, this made an urgent faith in rebirth, in the new flowering of the crops after each season's death. The doubt, that they might not, and the pleasure in the fact that they did, made an ex-pression of this faith through ceremony, prayer and symbol, into an effort to control this flowering, and be a part of it.

Highly elaborated, and with a greater doubt, perhaps a strain of fear, this faith in the Aztecs concentrated their whole life, raised to a highest pitch their passion, toward keeping life going, making the rain come, and the sun rise again, and the maize grow, a process so mysterious and important that to gain life thus, they valued at the cost of life. The process and the form of their expression then became a prime value itself.

The crops did flower again, and the sun did rise each day; all things were constantly reborn. Thus symbols of this fact are often composite; not figures of one specific being, but simply and abstractly, of a living one. This viewpoint or conviction which with the Aztecs becomes the core of their days, goes into minor version and differentiated interpretations among their neighbours, their vassals, their descendants, and varies from the original roots with peoples hundreds of miles away from everything Aztec. The Zapotec on the east coast, and the Maya, and many another Indian, considers new-born children to have an animal counterpart. Death or injury to one means death or injury to the other. "My soul is a jaguar", he says. And here is a contemporary key to much ancient poetry. The Aztecs made of this belief an identification of each person's fate with an animal which was the calendrical sign of the day of his birth; which identification is no longer a literal belief so much as a mascot, a symbol, a name.

By constant flux concepts became in different places differently synthesized, associated, and monumentalized. The parrot, for his gift of speech, early was looked upon as a supernatural being and represented, symbolically, as a man-headed bird; this bird is widely in Mexico today a favourite body for sorcerers, and the symbol of sorcery. His name, *nahual,* means a being who takes many forms. In cultured Aztec circles *nahual* gave *nahualli,* wise man and poet, and *nahuatato,* speaker of many tongues. The Maya, to whom also the parrot was early sacred, kept it a parrot, made it the size of a façade on temples, changed its aspect to correspond to the size and shape of façades, and pulled its beak to the size of a tusk to make a gracious silhouette on cornices.

The Peruvian share of the ancient American set of symbols grew into pot-size, branched into realistic art and into portraiture. The Tarascan share, in southwest central Mexico, grew to armful size in burnished maroon, red, orange, terra cotta; but retained the "archaic" mood. It is a style sharply different from Aztec, though developed parallel to it and as its neighbour. It has a sympathetic cast of the far south, and is nevertheless Mexican unmistakably, withal elusive of definition. Religious sculpture it is surely, yet sensitively, discreetly human, in a subtle smiling agreeable way. Figures of animals of the region and of tradition—frogs, fishes, cheerful little ducks, and dogs; figures of people—a hag, a sturdy warrior, a woman combing a child's hair, another grinding maize, not exactly portraits, but group traditional types. Limbs are foreshortened and the head is elongated, to emphasize human and religious essentials of the body, in a manner similar to the "archaic" and yet with a special consciousness, more rounded out, more elastic, and also more compact; with a new logic, and a new meaning; an attitude to man that simply and nobly creates in his form, the dignity of a god.

The descendants of the people who apparently made these sculptures seem to have lived always the same lives they lead today, in Tzintzuntzan, "City of Humming Birds", and around it on the shores and islands of Lake Patzcuaro; simple, gentle fishermen's and peasant lives, wanting little, having no fears and no great gods that demanded human hearts until the Aztecs suggested it, and even then took life reluctantly. They speak a rippling, twittering language, and tell myths filled with small shining birds and light breezes, or sing them in a wistful, minor, fragile melody. They have always been famous for delicate trinketries—mosaics, lacquers, featherwork, filigree, and, since the conquest, blown glass. They are different from all the rest of Mexico in that they are not a sad people. They never "communicated with the stars", never felt the stir of great breathing mountains, nor the crash of tremendous storms, nor the fear of great aridity. Their fresh rounded land is sheltered, partly by hills and partly by surrounding lakes, and is always crisp of air and sweetly flowering.

It may be that because of these things the Tarascans made no great temples, no gods profound and tragic; for the great art of America, and the great thought, grew out of the cross-ing of many threads, and great pain. It grew out of hand-formed clay into cast, clay and metal; into less portable stone, then integrated to architecture, monolithic, tremendously be-yond life-size. It grew parallel to religion, and as religion. Belief and worship, constantly assimilating new ideas from other peoples, assimilated thereby new forms, and ultimately the new god and new form were merged with the old. When the older semi-personal habit became an official creed, with a learned priesthood; and social organization, growing more and more compact, made possible the work of many days, hands and minds on a single project, art was a thing of temples and frescos that could be seen miles away.

The temple was the pivot of the nation. The activities of the people were governed by consideration of the thing which was always biggest before their eyes. The temple was the complete and accurate symbol of the nation, and of its his-tory and method of life. It was ever made bigger, more and more amalgamated to itself, unified, sharply elaborated into character, intricately symbolic with superpositions and addi-tions. From broad base to flat or crested top, it was a setting of many sculptures and background for painted symbols and

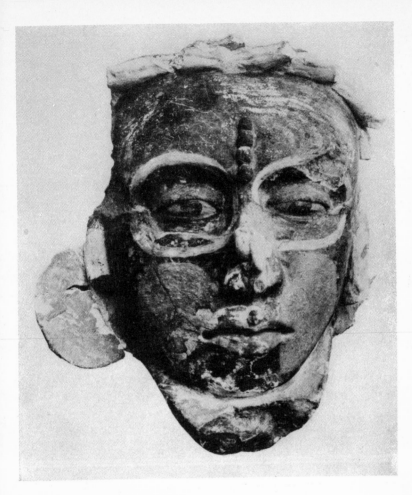

9. POLYCHROME MAYA SCULPTURE
   From Uxmal, Yucatan

10. PYRAMID OF THE SUN AT SAN JUAN TEOTIHUACAN
Pre-Aztec

11. SMILING HEAD, TERRA COTTA, TOTONAC

figures. Yet they were unified, consistently necessary to each other and to the structure, which was like a single sculpture, polychromed. It was always changing. Old statues were broken, recarved into new; old paintings covered by more and later layers. Whole buildings served suddenly as cornerstones —literally cornerstones—to new victorious altars. The course of creeds, events, and fashions was made to flow in stone.

II.

These achievements the monumental peoples, the great civilizations, held in common. They interchanged specific forms. Yet in the end the Maya sits and speculates, the Aztec is absorbed in adoration. The Aztec seeks the face of his god, and makes multiple masks for him; the Maya makes multiple masks for him, and puts a priestly, haughty mathematician behind them all. The Aztec empire falls by prophecy; the Maya ends in a cabalistic maze.

The Maya, oldest of American civilizations, begins in the plateaus and hollows of Central America. The material offered by the land, the temperature of it, necessarily had much to do with the ultimate organism. The first Maya Empire, already formed contemporary to Christ, flowered into classic harmony in the ensuing six centuries. Palenque, Holmul, Labna, Copan, Quirigua, Yaxchilan (a few of the discovered cities) suggest an easy, powerful, balanced way of living, based on agriculture, sufficient to itself, with no desire to conquer, in leisure integrating arts and sciences:—astronomy, architecture, mathematics, philosophy—calendrical systems accurate, as were not those of the Old World at the time—and much more, surely, that is lost to knowledge. The temples are crested and tall, elaborately friezed and faceted, truly an architecture that is frozen music. Walls and columns are by majestic procession sustained and compassed of painted and carved figures on soft white limestone or stucco, which lends itself to flow of line and finely finished surface.

The human beings in these scenes are visibly ancestors of the modern Mayas. The same wide, flat shoulders, slim incurving waists, superb legs, and the same profiles; high noses, cheeks flattened down from eye to chin triangularly, foreheads forced back (actually forced, in babyhood) as if sculptured to balance the head up, and high. The same spirit, too; aloof, sensuous, gracious, reasonable.

There was a great drouth, perhaps, or disease, or a push from the south, or new development to the north. The Old Maya Empire was gone about the year 600, and now it is swallowed by jungle. The high roads are layered with bush, the temples and observatories buried in leaves and trees and creviced by vines and burrowing things. Single niches and columns serve as altars and holy sites where before whole cities were never large enough for the same purpose. The portable heritage—science, religion, crafts, cultivated tastes— was part of the stuff out of which the New Maya Empire in Yucatan shaped itself during the next three centuries.

This civilization developed contemporary to the great pre-Aztec people of plateau Mexico, ever in closer touch with it, finally a subjugated part of it, in the end possessed by the Aztecs, last of all a portion of New Spain. At the time of the Spanish conquest Yucatan was "a place of white towers, whose glint could be seen from the ships . . . . temples rising tier on tier, with sculptured cornices. . . ." The capital was Chichen-Itzá, "City of the Sacred Well", which had been an outpost of the Old Maya Empire, like Uxmal, its neighbour and rival. Chichen-Itzá was Maya-Mexican. Here occurred a renaissance, with elements of pre-classic Old Maya, and ideas and forms brought from the north.

"Chichen-Itzá does not mean City of the Sacred Well at

all", says a Maya neighbour of its ruins. "Itzá is the people. And Chichen. . . . Suppose you started something you liked very much doing, and had to go away and leave it; and were always longing to come back, always wanting very badly to finish it. . . . That is *Chichen.*" And it is a city more than once rebuilt. Its heterogeneous wheel of styles connect it with different epochs, north and south. The hub is a happy welding and a distinct local flavour, in the famous Temple of the Warriors. There are temples crested and semi-crested, frankly Maya; pyramids elongated as if with a vestigial or incipient crest; a rounded spiral observatory similar to one in the Valley of Mexico; an intricately carved characteristic Maya structure; small charming chapels, elusive of identity; one elongated, truncated pyramid, with bas-reliefs, the Temple of the Jaguars, which sits over a ball-court, a religious playground that was also accustomed in Mexico. The Temple of the Warriors is a flat-topped pyramid, full of plumed serpents, but with un-Mexican studs and colonnades of columns girdling it about. In a corner underneath there is another temple. The polished deep red floor around it and between it and other buildings, has several layers; its murals peel back to ten and fifteen and more, repaintings.

Somehow all the feverish and powerful activity that this reflects, was ended. In the Valley of Mexico the pyramids are alive, and brood, and the people carve and paint and turbulently sing and fight. But in Chichen-Itzá the people mostly sit and think. They worship the old gods, and query each other, and the moon, how many of them there are. The land has the stillness of a stopped watch. It is a country of silhouette, with no twilight, no dawn, no half-shadows. Each colour, sky, earth, bush, is an absolute value, primary and contrasting or complementing, coming to an edge, not a blend, with the others. The surface is white and flat, mirrors the sun face to face and holds its own. The horizon is a bowl. There is no vegetation except low, sharp, acrid and electric brush, a few palms, and slender, small-limbed trees, branched taut as nerves. Cross-country, henequen plants irradiate in phalanxed rows, stiff and self-sufficient, shaped like super-artichokes. The layers of chalky earth are patched with red. They break through into great subterranean pools called *cenotes,* which are the sacred wells, ancient bowls of sacrifice, sinister oases arched to land-level with a lush tangle of tropical plants, feeding limp orchids and parrakeets.

A great painter whose name one does not know caught in the murals of a small chamber at the top of the Temple of the Jaguars, the moment that perhaps was decisive in Chichen-Itzá. The side walls of this chamber depict the life of the people. Here are boats, hunters, women, priests. On the main wall, facing the entrance, is a battle scene. The figures are about twelve inches high, except in the section directly

12.   DETAIL OF MURAL PAINTING
   From Temple of the Tigers, Chichen-Itzá, Yucatan

13. STYLIZATION OF SERPENT HEAD
   Colossal stone sculpture, Aztec

framed by the door, in which they are approximately triple this size, and this is logical, as they would be seen first from a greater distance. Only the first swift sketch is left in some parts of this painting. The chamber is dim and cool; the palette of the mural, likewise. It is made up of greens, blues, mauve, and some sienna, half-toned and shaded, by means of washes over other tones. The surface is fine stucco. The technical process is fresco, of remarkable skill. The general effect is quite different from murals and painted bas-reliefs on the outside of this temple, and of the Temple of the Warriors. These, obviously made to be seen at a great distance, and in hard white light, are composed like mosaics, with absolute values, in a kind of geometry of colour.

The battle scene is more than a battle. In the center, to the right, in the exact spot that is mathematical point of attraction to the eye, sits the god in his temple, perfectly still, served by incoming and outgoing priests, proceeding slowly. Above is an accurate and highly scientific pattern of swift-moving legs, with lances giving direction and balance. These are the soldiers, passionately outlined; giving motion fatigued and vigorous, with bodies leaping and bodies dying. A row of dwellings at the top cross-cut, give the human moment, and the normal rate of movement in all the turmoil. At the base of the panel are buildings with cupolas like European temples prophesied. Below, the sea. Some passing Aztec traveller or soldier scratched in one corner of this mural, a squat, angular figure; of the tall suave Maya warriors, a typically Mexican critique.

III.

This accidental juxtaposition of the two ideals of beauty cuts the last historical moment of the New Maya Empire into the surge of Mexican civilization, which had been growing for centuries, slowly gathering and claiming itself. Several great nuclei, with their tributary or planetary centers, at this moment held the central valleys and mesas between them. They traded, warred, intermarried, toward both coasts, but more to the south and east, the road to the Mayas.

Other Mexican nuclei dissimilar to those of the interior grew along the eastern coast, crossing with Maya strain, on perhaps bases of unusual distinction. These coast civilizations were approximately more saturated with Maya or with Mexican, according as the contact with each was closer. Nevertheless they are highly individual and some things about them and their style are especially strange. The Zapotecs, who send to market today amusing little black monkeys and madonnas made into bells, and the ancient fishes and frogs and birds, made then black clay gods and funeral urns at the most two and three feet high, but impressive as any monument, and loaded with complex and intricate symbolic detail; inversely, they built temples decorated by stone mosaic of unending, simple patterns such as those on the rims of bowls and the hems of women's garments.

Their neighbours the Totonacs made in clay and stone, sculpture abstract and pure, so beautifully balanced and executed that it could be any size. They eliminated intricacy from Maya forms, or adopted the least baroque, and gave elegance to Mexican forms, and remade both into figures clean and structural, with lines easy to the eye and hand. In view of their evident skill, and the tropical environment and nature of many articles traded in, they exercised admirable restraint; partly, perhaps, because of more sympathy with Mexican things, and surely also because of delicate taste. Apparently they were much pleased by masks for they cast many remarkable plaques, mostly of smiling faces.

The strongest Mexican civilization developed in the central valleys. Two cities were especially important: Cholula, to

date and since then, city of innumerable temples, and Teotihuacan, "Place of the Gods". Both were sacred places like Chichen-
Itzá and both were also consecrated chiefly to Quetzalcoatl the
Plumed Serpent. Smaller towns were much under their influence, as for example Tlaxcala, which, however, developed a
local pride and style and was later a bitter enemy and a vassal
of the Aztecs. Throughout to date, also a gathering place for
sorcerers and rain-makers and other wise people.

Teotihuacan was the center of many roads. Here lived a
numerous priesthood in subterranean dwellings paved, like the
city itself, in polished crimson tile. The walls were decorated
with painted friezes of calabash blossoms and sheaves of maize.
On walls and floors, channels were cut for constant trills of
running water, in which Mexicans always delight. Above the
ground is the citadel of altars, laid angularly and regularly
around a central platform, upon which the new fire of each
fifty-two-year cycle flamed first to the other altars and then
to the surrounding hills, the symbol of the birth of a new
sun or century, and the reassurance of life. The chief symbol
of this reassurance inhabits all the buildings. Great curved
stone bodies embrace the walls, give them movement, poise,
balance; fanged heads rise upright, thrust from the stones,
rise on coils; flank and hang on the stairways; accentuate,
remind, repeat, stamp indelibly the sense of the continued,
multiform, unchanging presence of Quetzalcoatl.

Here the Mexican calendar was discovered or adapted, and
elaborated. There was much study of the stars. Temples were
also places from which the stars could be clearly seen. Some
of them had little sunken pits at the top in which a man
might stand and see nothing but the heavens. Measurements
of one pyramid-temple obtain a theory that it was built not
architecturally, like Greek structures, but astronomically. That
is, the proportions are in accord with relationships between

the planets. There are inclined lines where straight would be supposed, by eyes accustomed to Greek derivates. The steps are placed in relation to corresponding steps asymmetrically, on deliberate tangent. What first looks like faulty architecture is pointed out as planetary geometry. The two magnificent pyramids of which this is one rise steadily, massively, dominating the landscape and the people who live in their shadows. On the soil around them, in the walls, beneath, and in the huts of the natives one finds clay figurines, rattles, bells, torsos, heads, snakes, to be dated with temerity. The only thing certain about them is that they are all made by the same kind of hands.

The barbarian Aztecs or *Mexica* filtered and swarmed to this region from the north, about the year 1000. They came with the confident insolence of a tribe following divine command, seeking "an eagle on a cactus with a serpent in its beak", and found that sign on an island in the middle of a lake, adjoining Teotihuacan. The Aztec eagle lit on the choice spot of the country. It is a place never too hot, never too cold, fertile, enjoying rain; floored with sculpturable stone, nurtured by rivers and lakes and a kind sun; dropping on one side to the sea, and the forests and fruits of the coast, on another raised to the sublime height of two great volcanoes, on a third breaking to warm rich sub-tropics, on a fourth stretching to the central plateau—land of mines, silver and gold and copper, jade and opals, hunting grounds and grain fields. A place easy to leave and hard to take, indeed a gracious sweep with brilliant stars at night.

The Aztec invaders called their predecessors *Toltecs,* which means craftsmen. They intermarried, fused, possessed the native culture, and gave it new impulse. They were originally or became eventually of the same tribal blood, and as far back as is known spoke the same language. Hence the pre-

Aztec and the Aztec civilizations are two aspects of one. But they are not the same. The god of the Toltecs and symbol of their life is a being who loves life, and all things growing, and peace, and enjoys measuring the days and inventing useful things. His successor is fierce, joyous, flies ever in the winds, has never enough of life. The eagle swallowed the serpent.

It seems natural that to the nomad, warring Aztecs the salient thing about the Toltecs should be their ability to do things with their hands, and their possession of many techniques. Though they had conquered the peaceful agriculturists and scholars, their admiration of these talents grew into veneration, and the Toltecs in Aztec legend become people who lived in a golden age, for which they sigh in poetry, and the return of which they prophesy. In that epoch:

"Quetzalcoatl as priest and king was present among men. He was white, large, bearded, powerful. He was so modest that he always wore his robes very long; so rich that he had palaces made of silver and precious stones; so industrious that he had invented the art of smelting, and of carving stones. He was very wise and prudent, as could be seen by the laws he had given to men. Above all, he led an austere and exemplary life. He hated war. When he wanted to publish a decree, he sent to the mountain of sounds a messenger whose voice could be heard three hundred miles. In his time the maize grew so abundantly that a single ear was a burden for one man, and the calabashes were as long as a human body. It was not necessary to dye the cotton, for it grew of many colors, and all other fruits and grains were of similar beauty and abundance. There was an incredible multitude of singing birds and quail."

Tenochtitlan, since then capital of Mexico and famous and beloved City of Palaces, was built on the island in the middle

of the lake. Four solid roads were fixed on swamp and water
to the mainland. The Aztecs took the shores about them, and
the kingdoms beyond them. By the time the Spaniards came
Tenochtitlan was the capital of an empire which consisted of
many cities and kingdoms more or less unwillingly tied by an
Aztec cord, all the way from the northern desert, east to the
sea and west to the ranges, south to the swamps and into the
Maya empire, and pushing to central America. The Aztecs
had become, within four centuries, the key people. They had
matured a nation with a defined and powerful character, moving over the face of the land and establishing between heterogeneous units a growing number of things in common, and
a growing sense of that unity which was a fierce and sacred
possession of these dominators. They played the decisive rôle in
the Spanish conquest. It was their tragedy that all of Mexico
was forced to mourn, and it is their vigor and peculiar
genius that is felt in the shaping of New Spain, and in the
present and future Mexico.

IV.

The Aztec empire was organized on a system of high central-
ization, mass production, and specialization. Labor was collective and adjusted to give the best of itself to their main desires.
The masses worked the land, whose yielding was made fruitful
by the activities of the artists and the priests. Except for captured slaves, society was organized into compact guilds by profession, based on older family craft groups. There were merchant guilds, and teacher's guilds; guilds of metal, jewel, and
feather workers, potters, weavers, dyers, painters, dancers,
architects, musicians, scribes. Every man must work. The father
said to his child at the coming of age: "Look for some craft,
or occupy yourself with agriculture . . . . the land is our

mother and must be cared for, and always requites our love.
Or carry the merchant's staff, or the warrior's shield and mask,
or do penitence in the temple, to become a priest. For where
has it been known that man live not by craft, but by nobility
alone?"

Every person could feel himself necessary to the state and to
the gods. Every child was told that he was so, in the course
of the long "reasonings" which formed much of his education.
Whenever the people met for civil or religious purposes, they
were reminded of it. The elected ruler addressed them thus,
by rote and with elaboration of his own: "You . . . . courageous and industrious men, fathers of the warriors, do you not
know that the kingdom and country has need of two eyes,
of two hands, of two feet? Do you not know it needs a father
and mother to wash it and clean it, and to wipe its tears when
it weeps? It also needs persons to carry out the commands of
those who rule, and these, the ministers of war and state, may
go to you wherever you happen to be, gathering herbs, cutting wood, or perhaps sowing, and will take you to the royal
seat. . . . The nation will take you for its countenance, its
ears, its mouth." The betrayer of the nation would suffer. He
might betray it by offence to the least of its subjects, since the
least was a symbol of all. Justice was therefore severe, and the
process of it delicately balanced and complex. Punishment was
scarcely tempered with mercy. "And though it be my brother,
and though it be my son, I shall seek him out and he shall die,
be he concealed in the mountain or crouching under a stone."
No wonder Aztec fathers killed their young sons who betrayed the gods to the Spanish friars!

Whatever his work, the craftsman was certain of response,
acceptance, a respected place. He followed the tradition and
style of his group. The groups worked together according to
national needs and styles. Since the nation and style was living,

therefore constantly changing, a strong imaginative artist had horizon room to make his personal version of the inherited images. Individual artists may have enjoyed a personal popularity, but as artists they were anonymous. Their work was always part of somebody else's. It was famous or beloved because the god, idea, or national emotion was vividly present in it. Doubtless this kind of recognition was found natural and satisfactory. Furthermore, this was a highly critical public. It knew when the obsidian was faultily ground, and at what point of fineness and by means of what adjusted planes and curves it must flash radiance from its black depths; and why a porous material, carved large, might present a surface evenly proportionate to the dense basalt or jade, carved small. This public knew sculpture with its fingers, and painting with its mind. Literally from the inside out, for each one worked at some craft according to parallel ideals.

Each work of art was deeply interesting to all; it was the most interesting thing there was. They were all therefore as insistent as the artist that the ultimate qualities of the image and of the material be rendered, and at one with each other. They had mechanical and spiritual rules of craft. The wise man was one who practised his craft by putting his thoughts into beautiful words. Everyone practised this art with pleasure. It is still looked upon as a duty and is much enjoyed. The bad potter was defined as a man who was clumsy and smeared the paint. The good metal worker measured his time and made the raw lump pure, and also "was careful to consider what animal it is that he may wish to imitate; how its being and its aspect must be represented. . . . For example, if he wishes to fashion a turtle, it must have a shell, in which it may move, under which the head looks out, and from which the four feet extend and move about. For that which is made must resemble the original and have life."

The man who was skilled in his craft, however great that skill, must not be overproud. This might spoil his concentration on being better than skillful, and, moreover, pride was not justified in a being so lowly that there was always a higher. The correct attitude was this: "When you are offered a task, note that this is to test you; therefore, do not accept at once, even though you may realize that you are more apt than another to undertake it. Excuse yourself until you are obliged to accept."

These were people who applied craftsmen's standards to everything in life. Pleasure in good quality and in good workmanship is echoed in the idiom of their etiquette, which was also their ethical code. "Do not lie," the father said to his child. "This is bad; for when you sin you spoil yourself, and you begin to die. It is as if you blurred the paintings of your deeds, and broke or threw filth on the pool or mirror of your soul." The young girl was admonished, at the moment when she "ceased to run and tumble on the ground, and began to exercise her reason," in the following manner:

"Do not adorn yourself profusely with overelaborate things, because this is a sign of little sense. . . . Neither must your garments be very poor, dirty, or torn, because these are the signs of people who are laughable. When you speak do not do so very fast and breathlessly, but little by little, and in measure; do not raise your voice, nor speak too low, but with a medium sound. Do not move much when you speak, nor when you greet, and do not speak through your nose, but let your words be honest and of good sound. Do not use strange words. When you walk do not go too fast nor too slow, for it is a sign of pride and pomp to go too slow, and too fast suggests disquiet and little surety. When it is necessary to jump over a puddle, do so in such a manner that you seem neither heavy, clumsy, nor overlight. On the street and in the roads do not carry your head hanging, nor yet must you raise it too high. That is a sign of bad breeding. You will go straight, and with your head slightly inclined."

They thought of themselves as things of craft: fine statues, or delicate and worthy instruments. They gave themselves the intense, impersonal attention due a good instrument or an excellent piece of land. They prized the perceptions their senses permitted, and therefore they cultivated their senses and made them constantly subtler. They practised temperance, and ground themselves to a finer edge by abstinence. The bride-groom was instructed: "Do not make much use of your wife, for if you do you will weaken and ruin yourself. Though she be your wife, and it is your own body, still it is fitting to be temperate, just as with a dish of food, which must be partaken of with sobriety."

Sobriety and discipline were practised for power, for accuracy, for ecstasy, for self-control in the sense of being able to use the self to attain always a greater skill at life, and thus a greater delight. They were as sure of themselves as of any instrument. But they must not be proud. The rich man spoke as if he were starving; this was to be polite. It has always been the national tone. The Indian host serves you with exquisite and intricate courtesy, meanwhile his refrain is apology for "crude and poor breeding."

The prime index to a man's value was humility; but this, too, must be practised as was fitting. Subjection to the gods must be complete, or be a lie; a crack in the mirror of the soul, and a smear on its image. But in his life a man must be conscious of his sovereignty, and practise gravity, and sit in dignity. The king might not jest after he was a king. The young man must not play pranks after he has attained his manhood. It was the static majesty of the gods which every man must reflect, as in turn that majesty, synthesis of power, was the reflection of himself.

V.

The Aztec ideal, the Aztec achievement, the peculiar genius that made a savage tribe sovereign of an empire, that made that empire commit suicide, and that persists unexhausted, is an impulse that none of the other peoples so much as the Aztecs had. This is an enormous restlessness, a joy in possession, not in the sense of acquisition but of control. The Aztecs attempted to conquer every people they came in contact with. They did not buy and sell or colonize to any degree the lands they attached. The tribute consisted often more of things unique than of things valuable—the sweetest flowers, the finest vases, a curiously-wrought jewel.

It was a search in everything, for the most that it could yield. The merchants (who were also missionaries) travelled far and brought back wonderful objects and stories. They travelled farther and farther and ran great dangers, and brought more and more mysterious accounts of their journeys. They became a sect, that travelled for the sake of travelling. The emperor was pleased by the stories they told, and the reports they made, and the gifts they brought. They became his favorites. They became his private and especial friends. The gods of the merchants acquired signal power. The warriors followed the paths the traders made. This was normal conquest. There were always new paths, and war was intensified to a delight in war for its own sake, for the joy of measuring strength against the strong, and bringing captives to the gods. The sacrifices first were flowers and perfumes, fruits and birds, like those of the Toltecs; then bigger animals; then children; at last the most beautiful and noblest captives. Out of the sacrifices grew a delight in the sheer rip of flesh and warmth of blood, and the reach for ecstasy in communion with divinity, by tasting the flesh that by sacrifice had become godly.

With the same impulse they adopted gods of their vassals, greedily adding to their own treasures of forms and ideas, as if exploring what truth beyond what they themselves had found, could the others discover. They cut the hardest stones with stone, deliberately chose to try their skill on gleaming easily flaked obsidian, and crystal, and jade. They made the biggest gods out of the biggest single rocks, images that would thwart death by long outlasting their makers. They went the range from these to the most delicate tracery of decoration, and fairy-fingered plume mosaic. They covered some statues incredibly with symbol and motif; others they kept to the barest structural planes. They practised temperance and then austerity, then penitence and then self-torture. They sat in silence many days, then danced and sang themselves to coma. They manufactured fine paper and tinted it carefully, then ripped it to bits on their altars. Their food was meagre, and elaborately spiced. They lived austerely as monks, and wrapped themselves in complex ceremony and etiquette. They spoke of themselves as mean, weak beings; and invented ceremonies to control the sun. They spoke continuously of death; and asserted that they were immortal, would live in song, could become gods. They felt themselves to be masters, and they were masters; and they aspired to perfect humility.

But nothing was ever perfect; nothing ultimate, nothing complete. They went to extremes, disciplined themselves to go beyond extremes, to control the extremes themselves. They met in everything infinity, and knew it. They were a sad, or a sadder people because of it. Their ancient questing anxiety for the ultimate is caught in a subtle story still told today. It is the story of an artist prince. "His name was Atonatiuh, which means Sun on the Water. He used to pass the nights contemplating the stars. He ate only herbs and plants. In the daytime he was always very sad. He went wandering over the mountains or he sat painting hieroglyphs, which was writing with pictures. Several times he sat down to paint the religion of the ancients. It was his craft to paint hieroglyphs. But still he was very sad, so once his slaves and courtiers went to the emperor and told him about it. He sent for Atonatiuh and said: 'Why are you so sad? I have allowed you to live in peace in your kingdom. I have heaped honours upon you. You have my highest regard and your paintings are in the Great Teo-calli. Your slaves and your people love and respect you. In the nights the stars tell you their secrets because you are so wise and good. Yet your people complain that they always see you thinking deeply. Tell me, why are you so sad? What do you want? What have you lost?'

"Atonatiuh answered: 'Great Emperor, I speak. Let me go through your kingdoms and find the answer to my question. What must I do to be happy?' . . . Atonatiuh started by going first to the Great Teocalli. He went to the high priest and said: 'I am authorized by the emperor to ask you the following question: What must I do to be happy?' "

" 'You must sacrifice many victims to the gods,' said this priest.

"Atonatiuh was not comforted. . . . He went away. He came to the foot of an ahuehuete tree and there saw a warrior who was sick. He was rolling upon the ground in terrible convulsions. Atonatiuh said: 'And what is life worth, if in one moment it can be destroyed?'

"He travelled on. . . . Near a maguey plant he saw a young Indian woman, dead. Two little children were sitting by her side and crying. 'And what is life worth if even the young and beautiful must give it up?' he said. He ordered that the children be taken to his palace, and travelled on. He was very wise. He could understand the language of the plants and animals. He asked a maguey plant: 'What must I do to be happy?'

" 'Oh,' said the maguey, 'You should produce a lot of pulque, like I do, so that men may drink it and quench their thirst and forget their sorrows.'

"Atonatiuh sat down in the shade of an ahuehuete tree and from there he gazed upon his beloved mountain the Ajusco. It was very blue and clean. In these moments the sun was about to hide. The afternoon was ending. The sun lighted the snow peaks of the volcanoes. 'You who know the secret of life,' said Atonatiuh, addressing the volcanoes, 'tell me, what must I do to be happy?'

"The giants answered him: 'You must throw lava and rock and fire upon men and afterwards cover your head with snow.'

"Atonatiuh bowed his head sadly. He looked at the ahuehuete tree. 'Tell me, what must I do to be happy?'

" 'You must shelter many birds in your branches to brighten the hours of the afternoon.'

"Two tears rolled from the cheeks of Atonatiuh. He walked a little more, stopped suddenly, before a willow tree. Upon a branch of it a snake was coiling itself to sleep. A sunbeam struck it and it was like an emerald or a sapphire moving in the wind. Atonatiuh said to the snake: 'What must I do to be happy?'

" 'Suck the honey from the flowers,' said the snake.

"Atonatiuh that night slept out in the wilderness without a roof over his head. After midnight he awoke, and he was rested. He looked at the stars, and he said: 'Stars of heaven, tell me, what must I do to be happy?' But the stars just kept on blinking and winking and did not answer him. In this mo-

ment of silence an owl sent forth its cry. . . He travelled
and travelled and at last turned back with no answer. When
he returned to his beloved Ajusco, the Spaniards were upon
it."

CHAPTER THREE

THE WHITE REDEEMERS

When Cortez planted his Spanish cross on the shores of Veracruz, messengers of Moctezuma were waiting to receive him. The Aztec king, since he first reigned, had often said to an intimate friend: "Care for my children as if they were your own. Love them as I have loved you. . . For there shall come those who shall subject all of you as slaves. In myself all the lordships, thrones, seats and tribunals that the ancient kings knew and enjoyed, shall be consumed. In myself who am Moctezuma, everything shall end." As he grew older in office, omens and supernatural voices marked nearer and nearer the end of the empire. Toward the last a messenger from the gods, and signs in the sky, sent scouts and sorcerers to the coast. Boats were sighted southward a year before the coming of Cortez. The white men came from the south and east, like Quetzalcoatl. The prophecy was fulfilled.

Moctezuma was more convinced of this than anyone in his kingdoms. His brother sceptically said: "Don't let into your house him who may turn you out of it." But to the king, precisely this was fate. And the king was supreme. He prepared for the holocaust. Four vassal kings carried his embassy to the port. One of them was Tepuztecatl, the Tepozton, another was called by the name of the oldest god. He was the chief. All four were garbed as gods. They took with them the garments and masks of Quetzalcoatl, in which they ar-

14.

rayed Cortez, and rich mantles, jewels, perfumes, flowers, many things of delicate confection, slaves to sacrifice, and bread with blood, "in case the newcomers desire this fare."

Cortez could not have behaved in these first encounters with more assurance and haughtiness if he had been Quetzalcoatl. He had metaphorically in his pocket an investiture that tallied with Moctezuma's gesture—in which there were surely some elements of Mexican politeness—offering him all the domain, for in 1493 Pope Alexander had decreed America "discovered and to be discovered . . . property of the Crown of Spain." Cortez had touched regions vanquished by Mexicans, so his first suggestion to the ambassadors who did him homage was that they engage in battle with some of his men. He wanted to see, he said, if it were really true that Mexicans were so fierce and so brave that each one could fight victoriously against ten. The ambassadors refused. They said it was not fitting. They were bound and flogged for this refusal. Cortez next demanded to see Moctezuma. The ambassadors said: "You have but just arrived and already you want to speak with him. Take these gifts which we bring in his name, and tell us wherein further we can serve you." The answer is classic. "Gold! For we suffer of a disease in the heart that only gold can cure."

"There were at this time," says a chronicle of the affair, "some Mexican painters there, who came among the delegates, copying on cotton cloths, which they had brought for this purpose, the ships and soldiers, the arms, artillery and horses and everything else in sight; from which variety of objects they made scenes of drawing and color not to be despised. Cortez heard of the work of these artists, and went out to see them, and was not a little surprised at their ability. But learning that they were recording information for Moctezuma to consult

. . . he thought that these figures had not enough movement to make known the courage of his soldiers.

"So he ordered them to arms, prepared the artillery and put his captains on horseback. First some galloped and afterwards they had a kind of skirmish and executed maneuvres of a battle. . . Seeing which, the Indians seemed astounded and as in a trance. Because they saw the fierce brutes ridden . . they thought about the courage of the men upon them. Then the artillery was put in action, and the thunder repeated and increased. Some of the Indians fell upon the ground, and others fled. The cleverest pretended admiration, to hide their fear. And after this it was seen that the painters were inventing new figures and characters with which to put down those things which they had seen and which were lacking in the scrolls."

Pictures of godlike beasts, and Spanish helmets to be filled with gold—these were the first accounts that the Aztec sovereign received of men whom he supposed to be gods, or emissaries of gods. Later came other pictures: Cortez greeted and banqueted, enveloped in clouds of incense and presented gifts, in all the vassal provinces, and with sinister enthusiasm in Tlaxcala, which was always at war with Tenochtitlan. Cortez with a native woman, the young Malintzin, drawn the same size as Cortez, and therefore, apparently important. She was. Somewhere on the way she had become guide and interpreter, and, for love of the Spaniard, she helped powerfully to bring about the downfall of her people. She realized the betrayal afterwards. Now she mourns by all the rivers and in all the mountains and helps revolutions whenever there are any.

Cortez sent accounts to the King of Spain which he hoped would produce the same effect as his tableau on the Mexican artists. He wanted both courts impressed with the courage and drive displayed by himself and his men. These were the marching orders:

"Let no man blaspheme against God, the Holy Virgin, or Her saints.

"Let no man quarrel with another, nor draw his sword, nor touch a weapon to wound him.

"Let no man gamble his weapons, nor his horses, nor any other accoutrement of battle.

"Let no man force a woman, on pain of death.

"Let no man take property or goods that does not belong to him, nor punish an Indian, unless he be his slave.

"Let no man scout or skirmish without permission of the general.

"Let no man capture Indians, nor sack their houses, without permission of the general.

"Let no man mistreat Indians. We must try instead to keep their friendship."

And here are representative extracts of his reports to the Crown of Spain: "I burned more than ten towns, of more than three thousand houses. . . And as we carried the Cross, and fought for our Faith and the service of His Highness, God granted us much victory. . . We therefore killed many of them without being greatly harmed ourselves. A little after midday, when their army was beginning to gather, we were already back in camp . . . victorious. . . After resting a little, I went out one night and before dawn fell on two towns, in which I killed many people. I did not burn the houses because I was afraid they would be seen by other towns which were near. At dawn I fell upon a large town, of more than twenty thousand dwellings. As I surprised them, they were unarmed. The women and children ran naked in the streets. And I fell upon them and caused them some loss and harm."

Mexico was accustomed to war, but not in quite this fashion. A prince of Tlaxcala, Xicotencatl, abandoned in the face of it religious obligations and the ancient duty of enmity to the Aztecs. He committed heresy and suicide by declaring war on Cortez, and sent the following reply to Spanish overtures for alliance and peace: "We will make peace . . by honoring the gods with your hearts." It was an answer provoked by Cortez' previous reception of a Tlaxcallan embassy: "I captured the fifty emissaries . . . and had their hands cut off." Shortly thereafter twenty Tlaxcallan warriors attacked a Spanish troop, and fought till all twenty were dead. In this skirmish four Spaniards were wounded. "We doctored their wounds," writes a captain of the troop, "with the grease of a fat Indian which we killed there."

As the Spaniards climbed to the plateau disquiet grew in Tenochtitlan. When the shortened distance made reports of their progress more detailed and frequent, Moctezuma closeted himself with the gods and repeated over and over: "These people are by destiny our lords." He answered his sceptical brother by leaving the royal palace, which he ordered prepared for Cortez. Nevertheless sorcerers were ordered to raise mystic barriers, and warriors went out to subdue the vassals, who were rebelliously increasing the strength of the whites. Gold and gifts were sent in quantities progressively larger, as the Spaniards came nearer; and it was subtly queried whether perhaps after all the gentlemen really needed to go to Tenochtitlan, to cure their hearts?

If the unusual ferocity and destructive bent displayed by the whites caused uneasiness in Tenochtitlan, these excesses are something of an index to the uneasiness that possessed the Spaniards, or at least their chief. They were not yet conquerors, already less than gods, still precariously guests. Numbers of brown people swelled their train continuously, making their few hundreds relatively smaller and smaller, and cutting off more effectively than even their lust for gold, a quick retreat to the ships. The dissent in Tlaxcala—the sacrifices—the bread with blood—nascent terror was scotched by terrorism. It was necessary to have Indian allies, it was indispensable for food and for protection and as the troop progressed, and the soldiers in it were correspondingly inflamed on easy loot, to do even the fighting. The Indians isolated the Spaniards and forced them ahead, and the Spaniards isolated Cortez and helped to determine his methods.

He could reach Tenochtitlan, and stay there, if he could frighten and bully thousands of Indians into submission, and keep his own men obeying orders; otherwise somebody, white or brown, would surely murder him. And he had to hurry because behind his ships there were others, and their captains were bent on the same adventure. There was dispute in the Spanish train. Some of the friars did not like so much blood. Some of the captains wanted more gold, and other loot. One of them writes: "Taking many Indians . . men and women, as slaves, Cortez branded them. In some places, the men were stabbed to death and the women only branded as slaves. . . . In Tepeaca, we said we were friends, and they came to receive us. Cortez separated the men . . about two thousand . . from the women and children (about four thousand). He had all the men killed and the women and children made slaves . . sold and distributed. . . At the branding . . all the pieces . . together with the royal fifth, were set apart, and then another fifth, for Cortez. The night before, when we put away the pieces, they had already taken and hidden the best women, for not one of the good ones appeared, and when they were distributed they gave us the old and worn. . . . This caused much murmuring against Cortez."

Feasting and quarreling the troop, become now a caravan, reached Cholula, city of Quetzalcoatl. It was a procession of native priests, carrying banners; friars with crosses, native worshippers with censers and flowers; native warriors girdled festively, though a little wary, and maybe the sceptics were puzzled; Cortez, somber in his steel armor, and Malintzin, serene and enamoured; Spaniards drunk, disputing and praying; dark ambassadors who had been flogged, still bound, and young women chained to each other; ranks of slaves bearing tribute and loot and supplies; and behind, flames, ashes, coyotes banqueting, gorged vultures circling. . .

Cholula received them in the customary native way, with "Priests, and choruses of boys and girls, singing, dancing and playing on instruments. . . The people brought bread and fowls, and took the guests to great salons, and that day and the next they feasted." On the third day the city could not, or did not provide enough food for more banqueting for such a great host. Cortez looked on this neglect as deliberate treason. He called all the inhabitants together, "and they came, nobles, warriors, populace, crowded in the great courtyard of the Temple of Quetzalcoatl unarmed . . with eager and happy faces, to hear what the white men would say. The Spaniards fell upon them, and killed them all. . . The people of Cholula despaired, and many of them took their own lives before the Spaniards could do so." Then Cholula was sacked, and the caravan proceeded to Tenochtitlan.

II.

Cortez entered Tenochtitlan over a gracious open bridge. He stopped to marvel. Here was a city with long-prowed canoes rippling along the thoroughfares, the fabled city which he had heard was made of gold and set with precious stones. Nobles and priests met him on the way with gifts, and elaborate speeches, and more gold; young people scattered flowers before him. Each step was a ceremony.

"Moctezuma," writes the Spaniard to his king, "took me by

the hand and led me to a great salon, and seated me upon a
rich dais. He told me to wait, and left, returning in a little while
with many and different jewels and objects of silver and gold,
and feather-work, and five or six thousand garments, very
rich and woven and worked in different ways. . . He sat
upon another dais, and spoke to me. These are some of the
things that one chronicle reports Moctezuma said:

" 'Most courageous general . . . all my courtiers and servants are witness to the satisfaction your happy arrival in the
city has caused me, and if to date I have seemed to look upon
it reluctantly, it has been only to agree with my subjects; for
your fame has increased and gone beyond the reasons for it,
and disturbed all minds. They have said that you were immortal gods, that you came mounted on fierce beasts of por-
tentous grandeur and ferocity, that you flung lightning with
which you shook the earth. Others have believed that you
were monsters cast from the bosom of the sea; that the thirst
for gold had made you desert your own country; that you were
slaves of pleasure, and that so great was your greed, each of
you ate as much as ten of my subjects. . .

"But their errors were corrected as soon as they became better
acquainted with you. It is now known that you are mortal
like all men, though somewhat different as to colour and
length of beard. We have seen that those famous fierce beasts
are like deer, somewhat fatter than ours; and that your
supposed lightnings are stone-throwers better constructed than
is usual, and which throw balls more noisily, and do more
harm, than ours. As to your personal traits, we are informed
by those who know you intimately, that you are humane, generous, that you bear patiently with evil, and that you do not
exercise severity except on those who arouse your anger by
hostility, and that you do not use arms except justly to defend
your persons.

" 'No doubt you also have corrected, or will correct, the false ideas that you may have formed of us from the praise and flattery of my subjects, or the malevolence of my enemies. They will have told you that I am one of the gods which are worshipped on this earth, and that I take when I wish the form of a lion, a tiger, or any other animal. But you see, (and he touched his bared arm) I am made of flesh and blood like all other mortals, though I am more noble than they by birth, and more powerful by reason of the position with which I am dignified. . . The people of Cempoala, who under your protection have disobeyed me, (though that rebellion will not go unpunished) will have told you that the walls and the roofs of my palace are golden. Your eyes can disprove it. This is one of my palaces, and you see that the walls are lime and stone, and the roofs wood. I do not deny that I possess great wealth, but my subjects exaggerate it. . . Some of them may also have complained of cruelty, and of tyranny, but they call tyranny my legitimate use of authority, and cruelty the necessary severity of justice. . . .

" 'Thus corrected on both sides the false ideas formed by false information, I accept the embassy of the great monarch who sends you, for given the signs we have seen in the heavens, and what we see in yourselves, it seems to us that the time is here and the prophecies of our ancestors will be fulfilled; it is announced in them that certain men somewhat different from ourselves would come from the east, and that in the end they would be lords of the land.' "

It is said that Cortez taught Moctezuma how to play dominos, and that in the course of their games they had many discussions about the future of the nation. Cortez asked for all the information that could be given. The size of each vassal region, and the distance it was away; what tribute it rendered and what tribute it could support. And where the gold came

15. SAINT JAMES
From chapel in Tupataro, Michoacan. Colonial

16. SCENE OF THE CONQUEST
From Sahagun Manuscript

from. He examined carefully all the city's fortifications, and asked that Moctezuma send for his underlords. Moctezuma likewise asked many questions about the products, and the king, and the political organization of Spain. "And Cortez, having satisfied these questions, undertook to speak of religion. He explained the unity of God, the Incarnate Word, the creation of the world, the severity of God's justice, the glory with which He rewards the just, and the eternal punishment of sinners. Then he discussed the rites of Christianity, and especially the sacrifice of Divine Mass, comparing it with the sacrifices practised by the Mexicans, and censured deeply the barbarous cruelty of offering up human victims, and partaking of their flesh.

Moctezuma answered that as to the creation of the world he was agreed; for the same things Cortez related they had heard from the lips of their ancestors . . as to the remainder, his ambassadors had informed him about the religion professed by the Spaniards. "I have no doubt," said he, "that the god you worship is good; but if he is good for Spain, our gods are likewise good for the Mexicans, as the experience of many centuries has shown. Do not trouble yourself, therefore, to persuade me to abandon their cult. As to the sacrifices, I cannot see why it is censurable to give to the gods men who, for their sins or because of their fate in war, are destined to die."

The Spanish guests had the freedom of the city. While Cortez conferred with the king, "They did not leave corner or chamber in which they did not go and search and overturn," Father Duran wrote. "And so they stumbled on a room where the women of Moctezuma, with their maids and serving wenches had gathered trembling and fearful of the Spaniards . . though some say that they were the maidens from the temples, who like nuns carried out vows . . and had hidden afraid of being violated or mistreated by the Spaniards . . who

had already begun to show how slight was their temperance."
And another chronicler comments: "There is no need to state
what was the fate of these maidens at the hands of the lascivious conquerors."

"The Spanish soldiers," writes Cortez, "sacked the royal
houses where they thought there might be treasure." Once
when a palace was thus looted, Cortez said to the king: "These
Christians are insatiable. They found some gold in that house,
and removed it. But do not take it to heart." Shortly the Indians became suspicious, Cortez says. "They did not come so
much as they had, and food for the horses and dogs began to
be scant . . so that some of the Spaniards had to go out
and search for supplies."

Very soon after, they became even more suspicious, for Moctezuma was suddenly put in chains. A Spanish captain says
that "the nobles of the court were so amazed that they wept,
and put thin cloths between the irons, so that they might
not touch his flesh. They did not dare take up their weapons
because they feared that it might mean death to their sovereign, whom they adored." Cortez put to death a son of Moctezuma and fifteen noble relatives, who arrived from the provinces at the time, and also some of the neighboring kings who
refused to bring more treasure.

Still Moctezuma suffered, stubborn and patient, in the Mexican manner. He told the people that he was staying with the
Spaniards because it pleased him to do so, that his personal
god countenanced this captivity; and ordered his vassals from
everywhere to levy tribute and do homage. "And think what
a great lord Moctezuma was," writes one of the soldiers, "that
even imprisoned the nobles obeyed him. He ordered and they
came, and in eight days they were all prisoners in the same
great chain. They brought silver, gold, and other things, so
marvellous, so strange and new, that no prince in the world

could have had a like store." Moctezuma himself gave another
splendid share, Cortez remarks. "Also marvellous things, so
many and of so many different kinds that I cannot name them
all." More houses were sacked and finally Cortez himself was
accused of having broken into the private treasures of the king
and carried away everything to his own lodging.

Tenochtitlan murmured. The day for a big religious festival
was approaching. Permission was asked of the guests to hold
this ceremony, and granted by Cortez. Just then a Spanish ship
was reported on the coast. Leaving the city in the hands of
Pedro de Alvarado, much less a diplomat than his chief, Cortez
departed hurriedly, taking gold with which to buy the soldiers
and lieutenants in the newly arrived ship, whatever the price;
to keep them away, or add them to his own troop.

On the day of the festival all the nobles and priests of the
kingdom gathered to worship and sacrifice in the temple of
Huitzilopochtli. "About one hundred were dancing and two
or three thousand watching. . . They were nude, but covered with precious stones and ornaments." The Spaniards
were posted in the doorways, but the Indians thought they
were likewise audience of the excitement. Suddenly they fell
on the unarmed natives, "And the first thing they did was to
cut off the heads and the hands of the musicians, and then
they began to slice heads, legs, arms . . and rip stomachs
open. . . Some of the heads were crushed . . people were
cut in half, thrown in heaps . . some crawled, their entrails
dragging, till they expired. . . Some jumped over the walls of
the courtyards, others went to the top of the temple, or fell
among the mangled corpses and pretended they were dead,
and thus a few escaped. . . So great was the flow of blood that
streams ran in the courtyard. . . And still the Spaniards followed them to the top of the temple and hunted for living
among the dead, . . it was a muck of intestines and blood . .

a horror . . and sad to see the flower of Mexican nobility treated in this manner, for most of it perished there . . and the Spaniards . . removed their ornaments."

III.

When Cortez returned successful from the coast, he wept. He was forced to slink to the island on one of the days that the Mexicans set in time of war for rest and armistice. His soldiers were barricaded in their royal lodgings. Alvarado was bruised by stones, and complaining to Moctezuma of the behaviour of his subjects. "Alas!" said that unhappy sovereign, "you have ruined yourselves, and ruined us also." Then Moctezuma was killed, the Spaniards said, by his own people, and the Indians said, by the white men. At all events there was no hostage, and Cuauhtemoc, a youthful relative of the king, led ferocious assault on the barricades. So the Spaniards planned departure.

By night and quietly, carrying their treasures, they began this decorous withdrawal. Someone gave the alarm and the warriors fell upon them and their allies. They fled so compactly that the bridge to the mainland broke, leaving a great many fugitives still in the city. Alvarado, says legend, leapt prodigiously over the canal; but he himself said that he crossed upon dead bodies, holding to mules and baggage. Many Spaniards crossed in the same manner. "We pushed the allies in front. . . They going first, with the baggage, were drowned . . and we passed over their bodies." Some Spaniards also were drowned because they would not trust their gold to the porters. "One . . who was carrying a chest of treasure . . under his arm . . and would not drop it . . when attacked fought with his sword in his right hand and the gold under his left arm . . and so perished." Cortez leaned against a great tree on the far side of the canal, and all through the night that has gone down by the name of *noche triste,* watched the terrible scramble. It was then he wept.

After these tears the conquest goes from Mexican hands to Spanish. The weird, fateful drama performed like a ritual breaks rhythm and becomes a gory, formless thing of fire and rape, disease and famine. "Suffering hunger and thirst, fever and fear of the pursuing Mexicans," the conquerors retreated. "One night, when hunger was very great, which the Tlaxcallans suffered with singular courage . . a Spaniard, tortured by these pangs . . opened a corpse and ate the liver." Death was loose, and raging in every form. "Among the Spaniards there was a negro sick with smallpox. This disease spread into an epidemic among the Indians, killing them off by the thousands . . especially since they had the custom of bathing daily, and . . they did it still . . at the height of the fever, and thus they died. . . And because they could not bury all the dead, they tore their dwellings down over them, and thus their houses became their graves."

In Tlaxcala Cortez set his allies to work on brigantines with which to besiege the Aztecs. Meanwhile detachments of Spaniards roamed over the land and laid it waste. In Texcoco, former domain of Netzahualcoyotl the poet king, "we found not even women and children remaining. . . We saw them leaving, from the top of the temple . . carrying their goods . . some to the mountains and others to the canals, which were full of canoes. . . We sacked the city but found nothing of value, since they had taken or hidden it all. . . We set fire to the most important palace . . and there were burned all the royal archives; all the chronicles of their ancient things; and also the other things which were like literature or stories . . were destroyed. . . The house was the finest wrought of all that were found in the land."

The siege of the capital was a last tragic synthesis of all that had come before. "It was long, over sixty days . . . and the defence heroic. . . . Even the old women swept dust from the roofs on the Spaniards, to blind them. . . The boys threw sticks and stones . . and shouted curses and insults they heard from their fathers. . . The crippled and lame, and those who could not climb on the roofs, prepared stones for the slings." The defenders said: "We shall let our nails grow, and when all our weapons are gone we shall claw our enemies." And while the fighting was going on, says a Spanish account of it, some soldiers "Found in a grave . . gold, about a thousand or five hundred pesos. . . Because the Spaniard never, even in time of war, forgets to busy himself."

With the help of "more than a hundred and fifty thousand" allies, the siege was broken at last. "It was decided to throw down the houses . . and fill up the canals, leaving everything razed with each step advanced. . . That which was water to make into land . . and for this work our allies . . brought many people and tools." The Aztecs were forced back into smaller and smaller sections of their island, fighting at every step. And at every step they hurled passionate comment. "Pull down the houses, you traitors," they yelled to the native allies. "You'll soon have the work of putting them up again!"

"In the part of the city that we first entered," writes one of the conquerors, "we found the roots and the bark of the trees all gnawed. . . Men and women, old and young, sick and wounded, were cramped in a place so small that they crowded each other. . . And were in the sun by day and exposed to the cold at night. . . Expecting death any moment. . . With no fresh water to drink and no bread to eat. . . They drank salt and stagnant water, ate rats and lizards, and the bark of the trees. . . And for this reason, many of them

sickened and died, and of the children, not one remained." And
Cortez adds: "The putrid water, the hunger and the bad odour
. . had caused so many deaths . . that there were over fifty
thousand corpses . . which they would not throw out of the
city . . nor even speak of them to each other . . lest we over-
hear and realize their plight. . . In those streets we found piles
of dead and walked upon them, for there was nowhere else
to step."

Fearing that before all the island was taken the survivors
would do as they vowed, and "burn and destroy the treasures,
and throw them in the canals," Cortez sent Indian nobles,
prisoners of war, to propose peace, Cuauhtemoc observed the
defenders' agreement that death be the fate of whoever spoke
of surrender. He and his warriors, and their women and their
old people were in the end forced to take to canoes; and then
he was captured. He begged for death. Cortez replied that he
would be treated as his noble lineage and personal courage
deserved, but, where was the rest of the gold? And with
familiar obstinacy and patience Cuauhtemoc begged for death.
Cortez thereupon ordered his feet anointed with oil, and
toasted on coals, which was done. It was done to several of the
captives. The rest of the scene figures since in national oratory.
One of the tortured groaned in the process, and Cuauhtemoc
remarked: "Do you think that I lie on a bed of roses?"

"The very stones cried out, so great was the pain in the
land," writes Father Duran. For Tenochtitlan was razed and
all its people slaves. "Cortez became ill of the odor of the dead,"
says another account. "The land and the water . . every
place was full of dead. . . And the Spaniards took more
gold, silver, feathers, Indians and other merchandise and plunder. . . And Cortez branded many men and women with
the brand of the king." Then he ordered a banquet in Coyoacan, just off the lake on the mainland. "And for this . . .

much wine came from a ship which had touched on the coast
.. and they had hogs which had been brought from Cuba.
... Some of the men, after the meal, jumped on the tables.
.. Others shouted that now they would have saddles of solid
gold... Some spearmen said that all their darts would
henceforth be made of gold... The few Spanish ladies who
were there came out to dance. On the following morning they
heard solemn mass and there was a procession; all took communion, and thanked God for the victory."

17. THE COYOACAN BANQUET
From Sahagun Manuscript

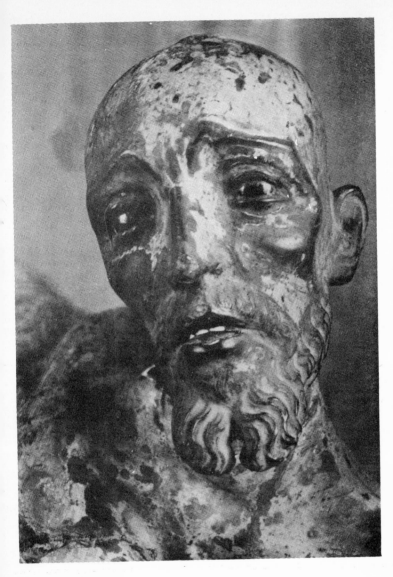

18. HEAD OF CHRIST
Wood sculpture, colonial

CHAPTER FOUR

CHURRIGUERESQUE

The thoughtless looting of the Conquest was followed by disparate struggles to divide the American chattels of Charles V with more decorum. The land was portioned out into fiefs called *encomiendas,* according less to extension of surface than to the size of the population upon it. A few villages were permitted, by royal grant, to keep their traditional communal plots. A few nobles were chartered free men. But the land as a whole was made vassal. It must pay tribute to the Spanish *encomendero* (who promptly derived a title from his fief); to the Church; to the State; to the Crown. The people must work for themselves, feed the monks and the friars who settled among them, help build churches, monasteries, and roads whenever required; and they were subject to labor in the mines.

19.

Gone the Aztec gold, with the fever burning higher than ever, the scramble was for the mines. Therefore labor was the valuable commodity of the moment. The Indian succeeded his gold, and preceded the soil and its products, as medium of exchange. The prevailing view was that "these are people without faith . . . and can indifferently be killed, captured, and their lands and possessions taken, and of this no one thinks in conscience." Fray Bartolomé de las Casas wrote that the Indians were people so often, and seemed so certain of it, that the Crown and the Vatican at last were convinced, and made

77

their opinion known in decrees. The Crown passed "Laws of Indies" designed to protect the natives. "But all the king's decrees, orders and desires," wrote Fray Bartolomé, "will never hold back, as they have not to date, the incurable and insatiable greed and ambition of the Spaniards."

"They all constitute themselves as kings in mind and state . . . while the natural kings of the land are slaves. . . Who before had ten or twenty thousand, or two and three hundred thousand subjects, now goes to the hill for wood, and the queen his wife, to the river for water; and the princes and dauphins, as much princes and dauphins as those of Castile . . dig, not with spades because they cannot afford them, but with burned sticks."

In Yucatan, Bishop Diego de Landa reported, "The Indians receive the yoke unwillingly. But the Spaniards have their towns well covered. . . There is never lacking among the natives some one to arouse them . . and for this they are cruelly punished. . . Some chief citizens of the town of Cupul were burned alive, others hanged. In Yobain, they took them and put them in a house with oil and set fire to the house and there they were burned alive. . . In another town called Verey, they hanged two Indian women, one of them a maiden, and for no other reason than that they were afraid the noble blood of the Spaniards might be mixed with theirs. . . . Two rebellious provinces were put down in such a way that having been full of people, they became the most desolate in all the land. . . They cut off the hands, arms, breasts, legs, of the women; others they threw in deep lakes with heavy gourds tied to their feet. They took them in chain gangs and if some did not go as fast as the others, they would cut off their hands where they stood in order not to trouble themselves with loosing them. . . They gave dagger thrusts to the children who . . did not keep up with their mothers."

The worst place was the mines. "It was ordered," one of the outraged monks protests, "that pregnant women or those recently in childbirth, were not to work. And so they left the old and the sick, the pregnant and in childbed, at home; but . . they were not able to work and needed their husbands and relatives. And so a village with twenty or thirty children under two or three years of age . . who could support it? When the Indians returned, they found all the children dead. If a mother took her child with her . . she could not feed it. . . . One could see many an infant tied like a little dog by one foot. . . And when the mother came to suckle the babe, the miner or overseer pulled it from her arms, and dashed it against the rocks."

"This is not the way to build and perpetuate the land," Fray Bartolomé insisted. "If the King wishes to have (not take) authority over the natural kings of the Indies, and if Spaniards wish to enter, and stay in the Indies, then whatever is done, ordered and disposed, should be for the benefit, not of the King nor of the Spaniards, but for the spiritual and temporal good of the Indians; and not on the point of a pin to their harm. . .

"To give the Indians to the Spaniards as has been done and as is still being done . . is to take the means for an end. So many thousands of miles depopulated . . thousands of people in this distribution perished . . . I have set forth these destructions . . . to kings and princes and their counsels; thousands of times I have said that they are all tyrants, and nothing has been done to prove the contrary, except to constrain me, and oblige me to retract what I have said. . . And then when a Councillor sees these things, and is horrified by the blood and lust about him, I am reproached for not discharging the duty upon me . . . to care for these souls. . . Oh, could he but see the things which for sixty years have presented themselves to my corporate eyes, and vanished."

But Fray Bartolomé was considered by solid people a demagogue and a dangerous radical. His economic doctrines nearly brought excommunication upon him. He went so far as to question the right of the Crown in America. And that, it was pointed out, was divinely established by Papal Bull. Some idealists on the other side of the water stood by him and believed what he said, and some enemies of the favorites who had the biggest grants helped the general agitation. It hardly went beyond agitation. The decrees were carefully filed; the troublesome friars were soon enriched, or died of a broken heart, like Fray Bartolomé.

He willed his adopted people a prophecy: "Who would undeceive our good Catholic princes, would make them understand that they own not so much as twelve cents in the Indies, that they can keep with a clear conscience. . . Sixty years and one more they have robbed and tyrannized over these innocent people, and forty the Emperor reigns in Castile, and he never has remedied except by patches, the dreams of the tyrants who dream for their own benefit. . . I am certain that God will take these Indies from the King of Spain. And what obligation have these unhappy, annihilated, impoverished beings, poorer of goods and possessions as never before in the universe, or in these Indies was known . . . to fill the needs of the kings, and uphold the Crown of Spain? Enough obligation they have to plead and weep to God for justice and for vengeance, and to the same Kings of Spain, by whose authority . . . they have been destroyed."

One other argument for mercy was advanced. It seemed more reasonable than the De las Casas theories. It was, indeed, demonstrable every day. "Then will the land have peace," an impassioned monk suggests bitterly, "when there are no more Indians to distribute, nor slaves to brand, nor burden-bearers to load . . . for the Spaniards, after using their Indians, care better for their dogs . . . and it is a common thing to hear, I

He observes that every time he discovered a rich vein he knew it beforehand because he heard noises in the ground, and voices.

Pintao has also been an overseer of Indian workmen on a landed estate, and though he surely did not, like the *enco-menderos* his predecessors, behead the natives, nor sack their homes, nor brand them, nor rape their women, nor, perhaps, even starve, beat or cruelly maltreat them like most of his contemporary colleagues, nevertheless his viewpoint is theirs, and his evaluation of the Indian one absolutely necessary if single fortunes are to come from his toil. Pintao is the conquistador repeated. There is no unkindness to him in the colonial arrangement of which subsequent systems are largely variants. In his view the conquest which brings Christianity to the Indian is a blessing. The native is either a man with a pack, or a soul.

The world of Pintao is the dear and friendly, closed and complete place of a Christian who is also a simple man. Man is Adam, central being in a garden made for his welfare and contentment. He is the keystone of the arch of creation, everything is subservient to him, and he is subservient to the angels, Mary, and the Trinity. Human notions are of no importance, because when worthy they coincide with the will of God. Whatever pain, sorrow or loss may come, there is no surprise and no fear, and no rebellion. Pintao is a happy man.

This is quite evident in his sculpture. He takes pleasure in his work and is certain of the complete rightness of it. His compositions are closed and built up in plastic hierarchy. Each thing exists fully in its own place. His ideas are a religious duty, and his expression of them is religious praise. He sees his materials as the craftsman does, which is an attitude sober and conscientious and happy like his faith. He explores his materials and examines them, and respects them. He never

develops a subject or composition independently of the particular wood on which it is carved. If he uses the same idea in
another material, it changes. He will not have—he bitterly
resents—photography of his work. It is unthinkable and shame-
ful to his mind that a thing of wood will be truly known and
loved if it is not known and loved as a thing of wood.

Pintao's work looks like something somebody stripped from
a church during the revolution. The movement and grain of
it is Mexican colonial, which style interests him as a style, but
apart from himself and not nearly so much as the difference
between a mahogany and a cedar. He does not study or imitate
Italian, Spanish, or Mexican primitives because he is one of
them. His work is the logical result of his position. The same
problems of craft, which include the same problems of spirit,
are solved by him with the same tools and materials. The
margin of difference between himself and the colonial artist
is not one of time, but of personal force.

In the twentieth century, with the mental and emotional
equipment of a craftsman some hundreds of years his predecessor, Pintao elsewhere would surely be an anachronism.
But were he not in Mexico he would not have that equipment. Here all styles are constantly being repeated; there is
primitive, renaissance, baroque, romanticism, impressionism,
cubism, classicism, realism, conscious and unconscious, all
simultaneously. A craftsman who would have been in place
three hundred years before, is still quite comfortably adjusted.
There is no conflict with himself or his environment, as might
be the case were he working elsewhere in the same manner,
could such a possibility be forced. Nor does he give the shock
of the unexpected which might occur in such a case. If he is
an anachronism nobody is aware of it, and himself least of all.

Martinez Pintao has been associated with the men who at a
moment of national spiritual new expression, had a great urge

to make certain kinds of images. His do not look like theirs,
but look very well by the side of them. He is Mexican as were
the creole artists of the colonial period who considered themselves apart from any other tradition than that which they were
making. He came for gold with the dreams of a man tending
flocks on the hills, and after many years of putting his hands
in native soil and walking among volcanoes, he sees many people painting and carving and finds he prefers to join them. He
is the recurring apex where Mexican and European meet, and
make not chronological nor national, but artistic and human
terms.

V.

When in 1910 Mexico celebrated with much champagne its
hundredth anniversary as an independent nation, it was decreed that all Indians who were found in the streets of the
capital were to be corralled until the festival was over, "that
they may not offend the eyes of our guests with their ridiculous and immoral aspect". This was at the end of the Diaz
period, which called itself the Age of Reason.

Pope Paul III had decreed in 1537 that from a religious viewpoint Indians were people. But since 1867 the State had not
subscribed to Papal views. Its mind was now engrossed with
the rationalist doctrines that had served their purpose in France
some fifty years before, and impressed with the idea and the
theory of prosperity. Its soul—it disclaimed one.

Since 1810 when Hidalgo, a parish priest, had tolled independence from Spain, the State had been on a racketing search
for another mother. Twice it had been an Empire. First, the
emperor was the post-independence culmination of glittering,
arrogant, Midas New Spain. The second time he was imported
from France. The liberal, progressive, reasonable prince was
greeted impishly by prophets who sang less poetically than

their ancestors the usual statement about the duration of
Mexican kingdoms:

> So you're here, Maximilian!
> And now that you came
> What's left of what have you, my brother
> Is going to remain.

Between the first and second empires there had been government by bishops and landowners, creoles and mestizos who
felt Spanish; and governments of provincial people, also creoles and mestizos, who were self-conscious of not being Spanish, hated the city people, and sought to be something else
than Spanish because the city people claimed that affiliation.
Immediately after the prophecy about Maximilian was fulfilled
by a firing squad there was an heroic attempt to establish
democracy, headed by Juarez, a heavily Indian mestizo patriot
who fought government by the old absentee owners. He split
the Church from the State, and hoped to reconcile the aristo-
crats and the resentful smaller proprietors under a Constitution modelled somewhat after that of the United States by
himself and people who would emulate republican France.
He wanted government by institutions, and government by
institutions did come about after his death, but it was government by institutions such as the army and the police.

This method was perfected by General Porfirio Diaz, who
ushered rationalism and positivism to the national scene by an
armed rebellion which he said was the last. He also perfected
and systematized a continuous outrage of the Indian's relationship to his land. In this period land rose in value because
foreign investors wanted to build railroads on it, and prospect
for silver, tin, and copper, and explore for oil. Though it lay
fallow it was valuable. Everybody wanted a clear title and
neat, large boundaries. If there was a fringe of Indian maize-

24. CHRIST IN THE GARDEN OF OLIVES
Woodcarving by Manuel Martinez Pintao. Modern

25. ANGEL
Stone sculpture, date unknown

fields around an estate, as there nearly always was, it was
gathered in by "moving the *mojonera*", the boundary post.
The peasants automatically became peons, or migrated. If the
estate adjoined a large and untitled stretch, and the government was a friend of the vested neighbour, as was usually the
case, the Indians became part of the forged title or were
exported to "colonize" estates far to the north or far to the
south of them, at an average of twenty-five dollars a head.
The tobacco plantations in the tropical Valley of Death in
Oaxaca were fertile from the labour of plateau Indians, and
the henequen fields of Yucatan prospered on Yaquis from
the northern sierras and plains, and sugar planters in Cuba
bought, at bargain rates, the encumbering Yucatecan Mayas.
Rebellious people were put in the army, or in jail, or shot, if
they were so rebellious that they assessed the price of a bullet.

The estates which were cultivated were administered preferably by Spanish foremen, because Spaniards were considered
better than anyone else "at getting the most out of the peons".
The owners had long since moved to Paris. They lived diony-
sian or epicurean lives on fortunes grown out of coffee, sugar,
cattle, and pulque, the only product sold at home. There was
never enough maize. Often the foremen grew wealthy enough
to buy the estate they administered, and in this case the peons
went with the soil. They were bound by a debt in the estate
books which was never paid. The life of a peon on one of
these estates was much like that of a peon on any other estate,
and this could not be more monotonous than the multiple
accounts of it. It was a dead level of misery, a horizon so low
that the most fantastic barbarity of an imaginative overseer
could not make a noticeable gulch in it. It was of submarine
horror, still, black, silent.

There was prosperity. The State rode the rickety chariot of
New Spain, which was no more golden but gilded; and tried

to convince itself by scientific arguments that this chariot was a locomotive. Possibly General Diaz and his cultured score of reasonable men (to be a positivist was a political accolade) supposed themselves patriots. They were assured of it for thirty years by distinguished visitors and by those of their own countrymen who, having lived in the great cities of the western world, or having read a great many books in French, could be considered authorities on the subject. And after thirty years anybody would be convinced. Furthermore, Mexico had a respectable international visiting card—credit, and bonds at 97%—and was laying boulevards. The capital was called "Little Paris", acquired a post office with bronze ornaments that came from Venice, many Louis XV palaces, gilt and marble monuments to progress and independence in the detestable style of such monuments everywhere. Every little town had a snug garrison, a good jail, and a grillwork bandstand in the plaza, where on Sundays the local band—military or militarizing—played Sousa marches and Verdi.

It was correct to buy bibelots and landscapes in France, if one would spend one's money that way. The ladies if they wished could choose the picture or figure of a saint for the *hacienda* chapel, and the ladies chose the prettiest ones they could find, along with their Paris wardrobes. The gentlemen had portraits painted in which they looked distinguished and thoughtful. Their sons studied medicine and law; if they insisted, music in Germany and architecture in Italy and France. The problems of the nation (recurrent every four years) were considered to be chiefly political.

In the Fine Arts Academy, students made dancing nymphs for bedrooms and recast Greek casts. The only surviving names are Velasco and Clausell. Velasco did landscape in the realistic nineteenth century French manner, with amazing detail and colour so clear and true and luminous that he was accused of using a magnifying glass, a microscope, and a prism. Clausell, later, and after the revolution, painted landscape with a similar zeal for colour but solved his problems as he understood was being done in France. The result is Mexican impressionism, which has grown into a school.

Outside the Academy Guadalupe Posada anonymously laughed and wept and created an art by himself, illustrating ballads. Other anonymous people painted miracles on tin or cardboard and hung them with prayers in their favourite shrines. Or murals in the city streets, on the walls of *pulquerias* with names which, if any one had read them, would have meant arrest of the owner on charge of heresy to the prevailing creed. The painter could not have been arrested. Nobody knew who he was. And nobody looked at the paintings, anyhow, except to deprecate them to guests, if the guests looked at them.

By 1910 all the anonymous people were dreadfully bored with making a good name for themselves at a meaningless distance. The ardent hands of builders, occupied with nothing that they could see, or imagine to be a concern of theirs, hung flaccid and, toying nervously with tissue paper and gunpowder, made firecrackers called judases, effigies dressed in tophat and morning trousers, or uniforms and brass buttons, which they exploded gleefully at the end of the week before "the Resurrection of Our Lord". They sang plaintively the death of "our beloved general". They could not very well build if no one wanted them to do so, or if they were being dragged about on strange soils. They had no heart for much after their own field, though the title might have been only of love and long occupation, was written away from them. The nation was quiet. It wished it were dead. Presently it heaved a monumental sigh.

PART TWO

CHAPTER FIVE

EARTH, STRAW, AND FLESH

One night we squatted, four of us, two painters, a sandal vendor, and I, on a roof in Mexico City, counting the stars and making ballads. Presently a weaver, the usual Indian shadow in white, joined us. He set his sombrero carefully on the stones, greeted us, passed cigarettes. He showed only a polite interest in our verses, and waited for the end of a strophe to take his kinsman the sandal

26.

vendor a little to one side. Evidently it was something concerning the family. We were hardly aware that the two had withdrawn; we were in the middle of another rhyme when a fragment of the murmured conversation broke it. . . . "Yes, dead. . . ." we heard. "Well, I took part in a discussion under conditions which were not suitable."

"What happened?" we asked when he was gone.

"He just stabbed a man", was the answer. Then, delicately, "They disagreed on the agrarian policy".

One does not question the murder. The weaver is a fine, sound young man. He lives in a nearby village, and makes the best sarapes in the place. We have seen a good deal of him. We know he has skill, taste, judgment; moreover noble, delicate hands; and rare colour keys in his designs. Furthermore, he had been drinking. And the quarrel was over the proper division and holding of land.

He lives in a village which is a center of potters and weavers who own designs and techniques as family estates. It is one of the places which kept some of its fields even through the Diaz days, and which was a bubble-spot of the revolution. It is well known to be even violently interested in the new land laws. Its name used to be written with a glyph of a mountain —place of power and home of the essential spirit—with a pot on top. All of these things fit together and make that murder a natural event.

Our friend might as well have been a potter from Tonalá, another village that fights over land and functions around crafts, and whose families are each identified with a certain style and form and texture. They supply many other towns with ware. All of them use for common daily cooking, old pots, which are sometimes taken from caves, and are much older than they know; or old in the sense that it is the same form repeated, made today. In Tonalá one family makes the "queen", a large clay statue set on a hill, next to a crucifix which commemorates the conquest. Once the man who made the queen did not do it very well, it was thought, and so the statue was broken, but no one else made another. There is another family which specializes in figurines and miniature portraits. A member of this family makes wares very popular in the cities: erotic pairs hidden under naïve lids. You lift the hen from its nest, or remove the pulpit and the clothed torso of a priest, if you enjoy such groups. The little bodies are always pink and white and blond.

It is hard to explain why these picturesque details should make you accept a murder. It is not that the man is an Indian, and an artist. Quite true, it is fashionable now to be lyric and mystic and avidly hymnal about the Indian. Whatever he does, is justified by his sufferings, if you like, or because he is that way, if you prefer. If you believe with Priestley that "The age in which people walk and dress and talk beautifully and are unfailingly charming throughout the day's routine, has left barbarism far behind, and is truly civilized", you must consider the weaver's person and actions far beyond your own critique. But the murdered man was an Indian too. Your sentiment would blur your æsthetic logic.

If you accept that murder on an Indian basis, it seems as reasonable to you as love, or rain, or being hungry. The family of the murdered man, though it may retaliate, will say of the avenged that he was destined to die. The weaver himself would be much confused if, once you were informed that the conditions for discussion were not suitable and that the discussion was about land, you asked for more explanation. You should know that in the course of that discussion he had been greatly outraged.

Nobody will tell you in words wherein the outrage lay, an Indian least of all. He is like sculptured volcanic obsidian, of which you see mostly reflections. The Spaniard, the city Mexican, any foreigner, can describe him physically, note his way of living and his possessions and make of these observations a silhouette, an incomprehensible photograph; the live man stays in his own material. You live in his house; he makes ceremonious speeches and feeds you as much and as often as possible. Unless you ignorantly annoy him, you are aware that he keeps unaware of you. Over a stretch of time, this is terrifying. You may easily, by remarks or attitudes that seem trivial to you, suddenly bring his attention upon you. The causes are never clues in your mind to the sometimes impressive results.

Small things, if you stay long enough and are sensitive and not dogmatic, and patient and loving, cohere. Each is a symbol, a little finger that implies a hand and a body of the same colour, texture, pulse. They add up like ciphers in your conscience, and when you think of the Indian you think as he does of himself. You begin and end thoughts, emotions, behaviour, on a basis of the earth.

Land is the point of reference to all activity, the ancestral womb and vault, the material in which all life is contained and to be fashioned. It is a core, a fundamental source, of speculation and law and art. The missionaries discovered their converts praying to it every time they handled it, long after they were all shepherded in the Church. Wise Fray Bartolomé remarked, therefore, that unless the natives were given their fields, they could not be saved. It was supposed that he said this as an ultimate argument for treating the Indians as he thought they should be treated. The Spaniards could not conceive that he meant it literally; but he did.

An otherwise comic incident that occurred recently on the edge of the village of weavers, has come to be told as a kind of parable of this thing that Fray Bartolomé, so isolated, understood. God interfered with a foreigner for insulting His mud. This man, a successful American painter, had made the mistake of riding to the village in a large automobile, an enormous shining Packard much too heavy for the path only recently widened from a trail of Fords. It was the rainy season, on a Sunday. On the way back the Packard went impotent in the sticky, sliding stuff of its own tracks. Along came a dozen Indians, all in the nice clean conservative white that the friars designed four centuries ago. They surveyed the situation. The foreigner and his wife were nesting in the bushes and the chauffeur was praying to the Virgin and stroking a tire. The Indians pondered the scene and offered to help remove it, which they did, but by the time they had finished they were no longer clean, starched or white.

As they turned to go in one direction and the foreigners in the other, the American called them back abruptly, took out his purse, produced two, three—it was not more than three

pesos. Said one Indian: "Well, señor, if you are going to pay
us, we think three pesos is not much for twelve men".

"Insolence!" said the white man. "Three pesos are enough
for a bunch of dirty Indians!" Whereupon the Indians went
home to wash, and the white couple started briskly for the
automobile, but the lady slipped. She fell face down in the
dirt, her hands went in all the way to the wrist. She was wearing costly elaborate rings, which came off in the mud, and she
never recovered them.

II.

The place of power. That is the fundamental thing about
land. In accord with this, all the actual relationships, and the
customs and laws and beliefs have been developed. The god
is a mountain, a body or bulge of land, and a pool is an eye of
the land. Water and the sun espouse the land. And, since land
is the principal place of activity, the activity itself derives power
from it, and this in turn becomes transferred to all activity, so
that the kinship between a man and his land varies into the
kinships between the man and the seeds, the man and the
crops, the man and his pots, his mantles, his images. Here is
a seventeenth century poem for sowing calabashes: "I myself,
the orphan, the one and only God speaks to my magic uncle,
who was a leper once (the sun), I take my thigh and plant
it . . I take my head which is bound to my sister the flower . .
the twining flower. . . With her help I shall recover, I shall
fulfill all my needs, I, poor and unfortunate."

The same kinship is extended to all phenomena of activity.
All honour, from that of the simple man who actually sows and
plows, to that of the supernatural administrator of the forces
involved, lies in preserving this relationship. It sustains an intimacy between the man and his field like that with his mother,
his wife, his house. In many villages a field is acquired with

a wife, and in Milpa Alta, another nucleus of revolution, the transfer is a religious ceremony. The Catholic wedding goes off first, in a hurry, with giggles and jigging music. Then the couple is taken to a small hut newly built in the lee of the girl's house, furnished with a crucifix and a fresh petate. This is the bridal chamber and honeymoon home. The bride and groom kneel on the petate, and their parents stand closely over them and talk to them for a long time. They admonish and counsel in set speeches which they elaborate. Toward the end the old people repeat, weeping, the many already repeated applications of their passionate theme: "Here is your house, here is your heritage which you must work . . oh, care for it!" The hut is a symbol of the house they will have. It means a home and activity, and new life. And a house means a house and field.

The only recognized native law about possession of land is the ancient tenet sung by Netzahualcoyotl: "The land belongs to him who works it with his hands". Possession is thus like the inherited design and style in the potter's and weaver's family. It is a thing which does not exist, unless it is worked. It is a function. And it is the place where the function is performed. Occupation, in two senses of the word, describes the idea exactly.

Labor therefore is the only title to possession, and, because of the feeling toward its chief materials, a prime religious duty. Mystically, it is the thing which guarantees and makes real the existence of both the man and his materials. Substitute for a field a pot, a loom, and labour becomes also craft, or art. So the Catholic missionaries find the converts praying to their own hands, addressing their fingers as gods, "five solar disks all facing one way, capped with pearl shells, coming from a single source, father and mother of gods". For, as the prime essential between a man and his material is labor, and the

important thing in labour is skill, this means guarantee of
possession, power, and honour, ultimately based on ability.

It is courteous to address the corner shoemaker, any craftsman, as *maestro*. And how carefully skill is treasured! One
hears that when cheap imported dyes were first taken to a village on the southern coast, famous for its shell-fish Tyrian or
royal purples, the dyer who was caught using anilines, lost his
hands. I have seen an Indian mother lash her little daughter's
fingers with thorned twigs, because the child dropped a bowl.
The bowl was not broken, and the lashing was not vindictive-
ness or punishment, but "a lesson to the clumsiness in her
hands". She wants them to be like the hands which pat tortillas,
and are, in a very old metaphor, "the wings of a butterfly
lighting from flower to flower in a rich field."

Land, labour, gods, skill, and personal honour are indivisibly
linked, and further fixed to place. Dignity and sanctity sheathe
the deep native emotions crystallized in the symbol of the
town, clearest perhaps in that glyph of the mountain (which
is sometimes shaped like a vessel mouth-side down) with a
pot mouth-side up, on it. The god is a mountain, the man is
a pot. The names of the god, his instruments, the shape and
colour of his shields and masks, refer back to the functions of
making things, and through them, to the things themselves,
which are known by the places where they were made, and
are also themselves places. The god is a synthesis of all the
life, and all the power, in the town. The meeting place between
man and deity is the non-existent space between the bottom
of the pot and the top of the mountain. They are one.

III.

Working from the initial basis of man and earth, Aztec
thought developed law and religion to coincide, considering

place and labour fundamentals. The man who works the land, and is therefore closest to the sacredness of earth and labour, has the most religious guarantees, is the safest. Necessarily he stays in the same place, as likewise the potter, who enjoys similar honours. Conversely, the man who is farthest from labour needs to exercise himself much religiously, to keep his soul. Therefore the Aztec ruler was the humblest, most penitent of men. The trader, who in practice was most outside the religious unit of place and labour with the hands, because he made nothing, and moved, needed to labour greatly in spirit. He must be charged like a negative of the deity's positive, because only the deity moved as much as he. Even the warriors were better provided for, since their efforts were fitted into the general scheme of cultivation.

The trader could hardly be less than a sorcerer to be able to live outside the unit of place and labour. He was a kind of awesome outcast just before he left and on his return. Then, only a very high priest or king could be friendly with him without danger to his own soul. It is so much the same now that a great fair is always coupled with a religious pilgrimage to the shrine of powerful images.

More than literally, the trader was the man who went as far as an Aztec dared, because he owned a great many objects. It was wrong, it was criminal, to base honour or pride on objects. They were used or traded, worn or put away for holidays, but were looked upon as by-products. At the same time, since labour had gone into them, they contained life, and therefore much stored power. Too many surplus possessions must be balanced by humility. To wear a rich mantle required much honour. "Do not amass worldly riches nor heap up treasure", Netzahualcoyotl said; "for this will avail you nothing with death, rather will hinder you." And another poet agreed with him: "I seek neither vestment nor riches, my friend, but a song for a place of joy." Father Sahagun relates that if a rich man grew proud and insolent over his possessions, "the king became grieved", and the proud man was killed.

The trader made a ceremony of this national philosophy. Each time he returned to his own place, he would first deposit his pack in the house of a friend or relative, and then go to his home to pray, masked in sacred black paint, carrying a staff, his god and only symbol of power. When he deposited the pack, he disowned it vigorously, insisting that his possessions belonged to the king and kingdom, and that he was a poor and very humble mortal. When he started out again he strengthened himself by fasting and prayers in which he told himself that, being poor and mortal, the most miserable of beings, nothing could hurt him; that, really he owned nothing and therefore had nothing to lose. But, since he moved like a god and carried upon him the things of the land, he also prayed:

"Let no kind of pain, green pain, dark pain, offend me. Undertake and array with the hands and the feet of those who live with the gods, and you Lord, green and beaten, green and belayed, come to my aid, for I am the chosen magician and the God Quetzalcoatl, I am not just anyone. Sun and day, come to my aid, so that I may overtake and travel first the road you shall follow after, and you shall follow that path after, because before you reach the end I shall have passed and have travelled the plains and the streams and the breaches, which I shall discover, and I shall not be hurt by the unevenness of the soil or land, because I shall go over heaven itself, on heaven itself I shall travel."

Since objects, by a complex esoteric reasoning, were reduced to symbols, they could be owned completely, without reference to the ephemeral things themselves, and this completed the circle which enclosed everything within the human being.

Land and its products, all things, were contained in the hands, the head, the body, the blood, the inviolate spirit, linked to abstract god, activity, and fixed in a given place. However, though theoretically ignored, the objects were physical things, and some provision must be made in law and mind for them. The law and thought about property, actual movable property, have the precision of Indian movements; the elaborate exactness of Indian speech; the quality of arrangement in native designs, in which elements are grouped, each has a place and a margin of space, and the lines never cross. The feeling was vividly defined to me when I saw six important old men in a village expounding law to a small boy who held a broken coffee-berry branch in his hands. He had stolen it from a neighbour's patch. The fathers made long speeches to him, gravely, by turn. The child was being told in many combinations of words that the coffee-berry branch was out of place.

Father Sahagun tells a story about Moctezuma, "the wise and just", or rather about Moctezuma's mantle and a plebeian's maize, which is typically Indian behaviour and contains the Aztec theory of property. "Once Moctezuma was hunting birds alone in his summer gardens on the edge of the capital", the tale begins. He killed one, and then strolled away, enjoying himself, seeing the flowering maize. He noticed a lovely twin-ear on a stalk, and admired it so much that he cut it off. Then he took courage and entered the house of the owner to show it to him. . . No one was there. . . Watching from afar, the owner resolved to meet him accidentally on the path. . . . With a deep bow, he said: "Lord, how is it that you, being so powerful, take two ears of maize—*stolen?* How, when you made a law that stealing one ear, or its equivalent, meant death?"

"True", said Moctezuma. "That is my law."

27. DETAIL OF POLYCHROME CLAY STATUETTE
From Tlaquepaque, Jalisco. Modern

28. WOMAN COMBING HER HAIR
Painting on calabash, modern

"Then", said the gardener, "you break your own law?"

The emperor held out the maize, saying, "Take it back; it is yours."

"My lord, what I say I say not for the sake of the maize itself. Yours is my garden, myself, my wife and sons. . . I have spoken to make a good saying."

"No", Moctezuma replied, "if you won't have the maize, take then my mantle". (It was a blue jeweled net worth a treasure.) So much did the monarch insist that the poor Indian, deeply embarrassed, finally took the cape, saying, "Lord, I accept it, and shall put it away for you".

IV.

It was inconceivable to the Aztecs that the contracts between themselves and the things around them could be broken. When Tenochtitlan fell, the survivors began living the chant made in honour of Netzahualcoyotl: "Thy destiny shall snatch the sceptre from thy hand, thy moon shall wane, no longer wilt thou be strong and proud. . . The nobles of thy line, the province of thy might, children of noble parents, lacking thee as their lord, shall taste the bitterness of poverty. . . They shall call to mind how great was thy pomp, thy triumphs and victories, and bewailing the glory and majesty of the past, their tears will flow like the seas. . . These thy descendants who serve thy plume and crown, when thou art gone, shall forsake Culhuacan, and as exiles will increase their woes." One of the survivors sat in the ruins of the capital and grieved himself to death. The place where he sat is called after him still— *calle del indio triste*. The rest fled to the hills.

Then the Spaniards began driving them down, mostly to new towns, to teach them Christ and to make them work. This was difficult. It was incredible that the Spaniards could pull their roots; they would topple the universe. They thought that if they explained fully enough, the error would surely be righted, and that their wish and privilege to sit and ponder when they felt it necessary would be respected.

"They employ such enigmatic and metaphorical terms that it is difficult to understand them, or to translate their speech", wrote one missionary. He gathered that "They live differently from other nations . . . because of idolatries . . . and in order to speak with the devil more secretly. . . They hate very much to congregate, because they say they wish to live and die in the law, house, and land of their forefathers. . . They did not choose valleys, nor seacoasts, nor plains for towns. . . Those which they made, were in high places, severe and mountainous . . without order nor house by house; so that a town of a thousand people spread over four leagues. . . They said that they settled in such places . . . to strengthen themselves against the enemy, and they kept apart one from another because each had his maize field next to his house; and also in case of pestilence, in order not to take it from one another; and surely this was advice of the Devil. . .

"Now, due to the efforts of the missionaries, they are made to live together and in order . . . and if this could be done it would help greatly, as much for visiting them as to avert the idolatries, sodomisms, drunkenness, adulteries and murders that occur daily because they live so far apart. . . . Naturally they are enemies of the Spaniards, because these correct their vices or because they are so unlike them. Their houses are of adobe and so small that one can be made in a day. The doors and windows are very small. They contain nothing except a mat or petate, which is the bed. They like to make their houses on high, where they can see the turns of the rivers and streams. . . They speak little one with another . . . and visit each other rarely. They are much given to sitting on their haunches, silent and motionless, even for a whole day."

Even when they were driven, they refused to believe that they were being removed from their ancestral sources of power. When their occupations were changed they practiced the old ones also, anyway. They refuted the change, to themselves. One Texcocan noble, who was discovered putting these thoughts into words, was processed by the Holy Tribunal for heresy and rebellion. He was accused of proclaiming: "Who are these who disturb us and live upon us and whom we bear and who subject us? Here am I, lord of Texoco, and there is the lord of Mexico, and there is my nephew the lord of Tacuba, and the lord of Tula, we are all equals and content, and no one shall presume to be equal to us, for this is our land and our estate and our jewel and our possession, and the lordship is ours and belongs to us; and if anyone wants to do or say aught, let us laugh, oh! my brothers, I am angry and hurt! And sometimes we speak, the lords and my nephews, and we say, who comes to command us and subjugate us? Who is not our kinsman nor our blood, and deems himself equal; thinks there is no heart to feel it and know it, and here we are and no one shall mock us, and there are the lords our nephews and our brothers; oh, brothers! deem no one your equal among the lying, and have no one among us who follows and obeys the enemy."

To his apostate nephew he said: "I forbid you, I reprove and censure you; do not do as the Viceroy nor the Bishop nor the Provincial say, and you need not even mention them; for I also was reared in the church and house of God like yourself, but I do not live and do as you. Are you not feared and obeyed in Chiconantla? Have you not food and drink? What more do you want? It is not our craft to do as you do, and thus it was taught by our ancestors, that it is not good to enter in other lives, but rather to stay as they accustomed, grave and aloof, having no traffic with low people. . . In their time the plebeians did not sit on petates. . . Rest, and be still, for our nephews are born; who, being children, will teach them all". He was sentenced to exile in Spain for such opinions, and his estate was confiscated.

Thus, and by violence, the Indians were dispossessed and subdued. They resisted thereafter only negatively, with the invulnerable, characteristic, since then traditional gesture of ignoring the white. A century after the conquest the Indian still humbly, arrogantly, deliberately, is blind to his conquerors. The abyss is unbridged and widened, between Indian and white. The white feels it. He feels so consciously that he is still a visitor, that a creole historian, a native of Mexico City, described his dark countrymen as if he were writing travels.

"The modern Mexicans", he begins, "are of regular stature, from which they vary more over than under, and their limbs are nicely proportioned. They are well fleshed, have narrow foreheads, even, firm, clean and white teeth, thick, black, straight hair, scant beard, and are generally smooth of limb. They are olive skinned . . . and have robust constitutions. (It is harder to find one hunchback, cripple, or purblind man among a thousand Mexicans than among a hundred anywhere else.) The disagreeable colour, slightness of beard and coarseness of hair are balanced by the regularity and proportion of limb, so that they are nicely between ugly and beautiful. Their aspect neither offends nor pleases. Occasionally one sees white, and quite beautiful young women among them, whose beauty is heightened by the suavity of speech and manner, and the natural modesty in their countenances."

In the Diaz days, long after slavery has been legally discarded, an American journalist discovers them with horror. He saw "Gangs of men . . . at work in the fields . . ." in the

29. TORTILLERA

Terra cotta from Toluca. Modern

Oaxaca Death Valley tobacco plantations. "The men were the colour of the ground, and it struck me as strange as that they moved incessantly while the ground was still. Here and there among the moving shapes stood others—with long, lithe canes in their hands and sometimes swords and pistols in their belts. The first farm at which we stopped was San Juan del Rio. Crouching beside the porch of the building was a sick slave. One foot was swollen to twice its natural size and a dirty bandage was wrapped clumsily about it. "What's the matter with your foot?" I asked. "Blood poisoning from insect bites", replied the slave. "He'll have maggots in another day or two", the boss told us.

"Just before we crossed the river we spoke to an old man with a stump of a wrist who was working alone near the fence. 'How did you lose your hand? we asked. 'A foreman cut it off with a sword', was the reply. During my ride through the fields and along the roads that day I often wondered why some of those bloodless, toiling creatures did not cry out to us and say, 'Help us! For God's sake help us! We are being murdered!' Then I remembered that all men who pass this way are like their own bosses, and in answer to a cry they could expect nothing better than a mocking laugh, and perhaps a blow besides".

V.

"The Indians were bettered by the conquest in many ways", writes a Mexican historian, "for some acquired chickens, and others donkeys and hogs, and others bulls and cows, and other advantages. And they were harmed in many ways. Whereas before the conquest they drank, or rather they sipped chocolate, afterwards they drank nothing but maize *atole*—and chocolate was the least of their losses. The Spaniards brought horses, and they and those of their race rode upon them, but the Indians always went at heel. The Spaniards brought wheat, and they and the other whites ate bread; the Indians ate maize tortillas, these being healthy for the liver. The Spaniards brought the wool of sheep, but the Indians never slept on mattresses; they slept on the petate, which has the advantage of being so nice and cool. The Spaniards brought their pearls and precious stones, and we gave them ours. They brought us beasts of burden, and we gave them men of burden."

Men of burden. But the posture is native. Aztec picture books portray the same bent back, the same enormous load, triple the size of the man, even the same swift, regular small prints of feet on Mexican roads as now. Burden and material suffering as seen by the European was not their grievance, was not the thing they struggled against, is not their final key reason for revolution.

Immediately after the conquest, it might be said that reason for sorrow was fresh and evident. Yet their peculiar grief, because of their deeply rooted system and philosophy of possessions, is not the obvious one. They were at first surprised, even amused, by the Spanish greed for ornaments. Then they were shocked; and then outraged. They could not understand the literal European way of putting all possessions in the same category. And it was monstrous to consider land in the light of an object, a movable thing. Like bartering your own mother, and like denying the first and only real fixed fact. Their repudiation of the whole system of thought—if they could repudiate what they perhaps never have comprehended—their denial of it, in behaviour, has always made them seem mysterious beings.

Exile is the word for their fundamental dispossession, but exile in their sense. The sorcerers who in the colonial period wove busily from village to village, curing ills and griefs, reported when examined by priests, on discovery, "Two . . .

ills prevalent widely . . . *tlacolmiquiztli,* which means, ills caused by love and desire . . . in excess or lack of fulfillment . . . which last, they say, causes melancholy and sadness and they become thinner and thinner and waste away. . . And the other is *netepalhuiliztli,* which means, dependence on another, or rather, the ills caused by dependence. . . And there is one thing more, which is called loss or departure of the soul".

Of these sorrows they sickened and died. It was the last protest, the last retreat, "to the excellent place, the place of shards". This custom, of which one has heard abundantly, greatly shocked the American journalist when he was told of it among the Yaquis moved from their northern sierras, exiled to tropical Yucatan: "The Yaqui woman muttered, . . When the Yaqui men are beaten they die of shame . . . the men die of shame sometimes . . sometimes they die of their own will".

The Yaquis are not agricultural people. But the feeling is the same as that which the Aztecs rooted complexly in land and activity. It is an intangible, subtle, tremendously powerful, permanent emotion. Even described in terms of its reflections, it is not wholly graspable in words. Crudely, approximately, it might be called self-respect, self-possession, a spirit which values first, itself aloof and sufficient to itself. The ideal is integrity of soul.

The natives salvaged themselves because of the attitude habitual with them. Complete submission enclosed permanently a kernel of complete pride. Labour, once the source, became the price of this pride, so intense, so much the same sense of power almost innate, it is so old, that even the hacendados remarked it. They would say amusedly, and they still do (the few that are left) that "If you jest with a peon, he considers it an insult to him". Only the fields and the mountains father this aristocracy.

One can hardly measure this great pride, so great that it is ultimately, logically, complete humility. One is tempted to think that it could hardly have been preserved without the social system which produced it. Yet there were enough surface similarities between the old and the new position, or enough factors in the new position, to keep it at the native pitch, and to heighten and change and transmute it from the red flame of passion to the still, blue fire of pain.

Something menacing, an extra added meaning, seems almost readable in certain colonial religious appeals. Their symbolism appears accurately descriptive of the Indian's attitude to the stranger in his land. Whether this symbolism was thought out before or after the conquest, one can understand from it a little of how the Spaniard was made to fit into the native mental scheme; and a little of why he was spiritually consumed. Compactly insistent, a sorcerer would say to an ailing body, and to the instrument he used for "expelling" the illness:

"Now, what are you doing, killing the earth and the mud (the body) . . . Here I come to examine you and also the barbarian (the needle) the foreigner of the white entrails similar to ours, shall not find a corner he does not enter, and though you hide among rocks and behind shields, it will avail you nothing, for he shall destroy you. . . You will be better somewhere else . . . where there is cotton and maize like a house in abundance, where there are rugs and seats of authority, where there are bouquets and fine odours. Why wait here, where we can remain at the most three days. We will be better where I say, and more comfortable: (Go.) I follow, for I also suffer hunger and thirst. But how will you live in the house of an unhappy man where there is not even an obstacle to the wind, where it enters and leaves and freezes, where there is not even one object to stumble upon?"

30. DETAIL FROM PAINTED VASE
   By Amado Galván. Tonala, Jalisco

31. DANCER'S MASK
From Guerrero, modern. Wood

VI.

Because the Indians deliberately ignored their conquest they
have endured it as long as they have. Toward ownership of
land, the most important broken bond, the base or symbol of
their legitimate pride, they were forced to make one adjustment. When the king of Spain at last listened to Fray
Bartolomé, believed that this matter was as urgent as the friar
said, he attempted to act accordingly. Certain villages were
legally endowed with their communal fields, and some families with their small plots. Now a piece of paper being, to the
Spaniard, a satisfactory symbol of the right to have the land,
the Indians accepted the symbol. Thenceforth they insisted
persistently and repeatedly as only they can, on the "writings".

One has seen them so often in village courtrooms. They
appear in the door, remove their great sombreros with an
orderly, sober gesture, advance, and say to the clerk: "Excuse
the trouble, and the bad breeding, but I am sent and come to
suggest that you will disturb your mind and deign to consider
the little paper, and inquire and investigate the little signature."

There are village feuds two and three centuries old, over
the interpretation of a boundary perhaps purposely blurred in
the original title. Murders over land are reported in the newspapers in the same section, almost in the same language, as
"passional crimes". One finds a testament made in Teotihuacan
in 1672, written in Aztec, which reiterates through pages the
exact portion which each inheritor is to work, and the witnesses
sign thus:

"Gabriel Alvarez, in regard to the lands which are given us
we shall work them.

"Marcos Alvarez: No one shall take our lands of which we
are the possessors."

The tragedy of the thing clubs you when an hacendado tells you urbanely how he "moved the mojonera", the boundary-post including two villages which had water rights to a certain stream which he wanted for a certain portion of his thousands of bushels of maize. Feuds over land have often at the root a feud for water, and, when there is evil in the land, say the natives, water is scarce. The streams and the beautiful clouds sicken and waste away.

The initial violation of the conquest was repeated in the Diaz days. Multiple titles held since endowment by the Crown of Spain, were destroyed, stolen, or more frequently, disregarded by the big landowners who wanted to consolidate their estates. Violence and literally, exile, was again the method. Curiously, one of the laws which bulwarked the thievery of Diaz days was the edict issued in the Juarez laws of 1869, forbidding communal holdings. This was directed against religious communities and was used by Diaz to include Indian villages.

These violations bewildered the Indians. They felt as they had when, newly conquered and converted, they confessed transgression to the priest, and were absolved, and then were punished by the civil authorities anyhow. However, violation of the title, like violation of the original Aztec arrangement, might exist in the government archives, and still be nothing to the Indian. He was aware of it, he was forced to recognize it, only if he was moved. And it took him four hundred years to understand that this catastrophe could befall him; and that the white men were responsible. Not the gods.

Four hundred years of resentment; four hundred years of outrage; then the nail was brought home. The Indians were again driven down from the hills and from coast to coast. Some villages held out sullenly. But many, among them agricultural and craft centers, which had kept the old unity of god, craft, land, belief and attitude, were encroached upon. Everywhere there was drought. Everywhere people sickened and died.

Then came protest in theory from intellectuals here and there who had studied modern sociology. Exiled labourers returned from the far north, Texas and Arizona, with ideas about other kinds of protest. When Madero stumbled on the idea of offering land as a bait for votes, on a platform which proposed the reform of shortening presidential terms, to do away with dictatorship, he did not realize that he was offering the voters their very souls. They wedged him into the ballot-boxes withal Diaz police and ballot-guards, and sat him hard and suddenly on the presidential chair. The poor, amiable little man squirmed there and looked bewildered. Foreigners, landowners, city people, all the vested interests objected and quite easily pulled the fretted seat from under the diminutive saviour. The nation rose in a great dark wave to die.

VII.

A joke on the Mexican sometimes caricatured in the metropolitan press, pictures him suddenly rich, possessor of many bags of gold, on which he sits and cogitates. He communicates the fruit of his thought thus to his spouse: "Well, now I think we can buy a new petate". The story is double-edged, and has further point. He sits and meditates: and he gets himself a new petate.

A petate is the cheapest, most common, and oldest household possession. It is pictured in Aztec codices used exactly as it is today, as a throne, a seat of honour, and as an humble object of versatile and universal service. A reed mat, of coarse weave pleasant to the bare sole, of a sincere yellow colour agreeable to the eye; materially irreplaceable, spiritually an essential Mexican symbol. It is made of reeds that grew in the earth, by the side of water that feeds the earth, it is shaped by hands so deft with centuries of practice that it grows like a being.

Upon its homely surface the Indian baby emerges howling from his mother's womb, in the Aztec "hour of death". He cuts his teeth on a petate-bodied, faced, voiced, doll. He goes into the maize fields for the first time wearing a hat of petate weave and straw. He is quieted to sleep with a lullaby about the nahual, in the nursery the same old bird with a human head, flying on unique principles:

> "Oh mother, mother
> The nahual flew in
> His eyes were of cornmeal
> Petate his wings."

"Who was born on a petate", says a slighting creole proverb, "always carries the smell of the cane". It is a shrewd observation. For that odour, the unique, acrid, singularly sweet smell of *tule,* the petate reed, is in the woven mat from its green elastic youth to frayed old age. It mellows a bouquet of earth, water, maize, chili, sulphurous flowers, resin incense, flesh. It gives and takes from the people it lives with, companionably; pillows them from womb to wisdom; returns with them to the place from which they both came.

Spread out, a petate is cradle, curtain, bridal bed, bier; rolled, it is pillow, and hiding place for valuables such as rifles and gods. The petate is table and tablecloth for the beans and tortillas of the family. The basket in which, for dining, warm tortillas are dropped, warm from patting hands and clay hearth, is woven of fresh petate. A boy's first games are imitation bull-fights with a steer's head made of petate. He dances masked and fringed, on sandals with petate soles, laced in

32. INTERIOR OF NATIVE HOUSE
In Xochimilco

leather over his feet with a weave like that of the reed.
(Though now he sometimes substitutes leather for the
soles also. Very modernly, rubber from automobile tires,
which leaves a pattern in the dust, reminiscent of the
petate.)

You see the interminable grecque of petate weave, *petatillo,*
on pots, garments, walls, on sleepy children's cheeks early in
the morning. The imagery of thoughtful, sensitive people shuttles endlessly across this theme. The lingering guest
at baptismal, matrimonial, funeral, or any other feasts, is
"one who stays to pick up the petate". The usurer is slurred
for his bad manners in precisely the same phrase. A false alarm
is "a petate flare", much ado about nothing is "a shake of the
petate". (Only a fool is concerned.) The wealthy man "has his
little petates". Conversely, bad times are surely bad "when
there isn't a petate to fall dead on". Death itself is "a move of
the petate". A great man, a maker of things and of fates, a
person of ability and prestige, is *"the* petate man". The falsely
great, the insolent and boastful, is rebuked: "Bah! Those fleas
don't dance on *your* petate!"

Perforce there is a very old prayer to this important and
valueless thing: "Hearken now, my honoured mat, like a tiger;
with your mouth open in four directions; be with me, for you
also hunger and thirst. . . Hearken, now comes the fearful
one, who deceives the people and gives bad counsel. But what
can he harm me, who am an unfortunate and live with nothing on nothing in perpetual poverty?"

By its intimate kinship to daily and eternal things, the petate
is a perfect base for the national philosophy, a perfect frame for
the national image. It is place, craft, object. It rests on the
earth, in metaphor is interchanged with it. It is green, sere,
and gray. Life upon it, limited and controlled, is poverty made
productive, for it is life expressed in accord with the limita-

tion and control which are the laws of art. Here is the inviolate stronghold, the ultimate sanctuary, the meeting spot of land, being, and deity. With his elbows on his knees, owning nothing but this place, the wise man sits and hoards himself.

CHAPTER SIX

THE DARK MADONNA

Consider the Indian sitting. His knees are together, the soles of his feet rest lightly, but flat on the ground. His body curves, neither sunk nor extended, upon itself. Each part seems to want to join every other part. Earthbound and permanent, on the smallest possible space, packed close to himself; he has always, he and his gods, been sitting so. He is found buried so. Time, violence, even death, do not change this position. It is a profound index to the very visible, instantly felt certainty that the south side of the Rio Grande is very different from the north, and that Mexico is not a remnant of Spain.

Watch, then, this Indian kneeling, with unique unrigid stillness, for hours before an altar. His arms extend motionless, hands half open, thumb crossed over index finger. The face is set straight forward, the back is not curved. The neck appears. He is changed. His body is spent outward, is spread. Did the Spaniards do this? What does it mean?

Trace the story of the conquest. At the beginning and end, you find the Indian sitting in the same way, and it must indicate that he is living and thinking much as he always did. Was there a conquest? You find the mordant fundamental conflict over land. You know the ancient identity of land and sitting man; and of land and gods. What about the gods? Trace that story, and you find the channel in which, through

the four muffled centuries since Cortez, the nation, disintegrated, lived as a unit still. You find it flowing like a river,
solving its bewilderments and griefs, emerging.

Ultimately you find the Mexican Christ, a strange, impressive, living image, and a native one. Passion and resurrection.
The imported phrase is the current generic term for imported
miracle plays, both made native. It is the ancient theme. It
welds the old religion with the new forms. It is the mould
before and beyond Cortez, of native history. Every cycle and
every day, in the same, and in different forms, the great Mexican drama is consummate. If the new story with an old theme
was shaped differently; living the same story, the man assumed
another aspect; in his mystical sense, another mask. Is this a
conquest? Whose?

The race, the nation, is profoundly religious. It worships also
in Catholic churches. Whether or no it can be considered a
creature of the Church, only the Church can answer. Often
it has been doubted, but never fully questioned. Travellers and
historians almost unanimously are skeptical; friars and priests
voice bitterly frustration. Fray Bartolomé and Father Sahagun
immediately after the conquest; Fray Jacinto de la Serna and
his colleagues in the "investigation against idolaters" a hundred years later; Baron von Humboldt in the nineteenth century; Lumholtz recently, and other ethnologists today, record
similarly the thing that is written in the faces of lonely rural
priests. And nearly anyone in Mexico can add one episode of
an idol behind a cross.

The Mexican Christ rests on a hidden, significant base. Yet
religion is the conquest generally thought proof of conquest.
It is the only change the Spaniards really cared about making.
They baptized as they branded. The first, was a divine right
to the second. One might expect missionary zeal from the
priests who accompanied Cortez, but it is clear the soldiers

34. RITUAL DANCER FROM OAXACA
Black clay, modern

were also intent on the matter, and later, the traders, rulers, and intellectuals. Long before it was established from Rome that the Indians had savable souls, every Spaniard had his own passionate opinion on how best to effect conversion. It occupied consideration in every issue: political, economic, spiritual. Bernal Diaz del Castillo writes that in Tenochtitlan, "we placed, in a department of the major temple, apart from the idols, the image of Our Lady, and a Cross". Alvarado gave religion as the reason for the great massacre in this temple which he superintended. Cortez repeatedly called for more friars, and begged that they be pure and strong men, because, he said, the Mexicans were so accustomed to austere prelates, that the Christians must surpass them if they were to be convincing. Everyone took part in the experiment. Depending on inclination, he persuaded, cajoled, bribed, beat, and threatened into the credo.

Missionarying was widespread and constant, was ardent, the first hundred years of the colony. The interest of the Church shifted after, from souls to property, either because this seemed more important, or because the priests themselves were not of the character and energy once necessary even for residence in the land. If the Indians attended service it may have been considered sufficient. The task of real conversion dispirited any other conclusion. Furthermore the religious orders were all engaged in struggle with each other. The bishops spun intrigue. The city clergy held death-watch at noble beds and inherited thereby. The rural priesthood sipped chocolate and fattened, simple-mindedly worldly, or, resenting the position and spirit of its urban superior, brewed rebellion. Miguel Hidalgo, known as the Liberator, was a village priest. He very reasonably observed at the beginning of the nineteenth century, that New Spain was Mexico, so he promptly rang a bell and told his rural congregation that it was now free.

After the War of Independence the Church, which owned by this time half the national real estate, was perforce very busy insuring its interests with the newly-created federal powers. In 1857 a great political grapple occurred between Church and State. Independence from Spain had been achieved, after Hidalgo was quashed, by a throwback. Spain was becoming liberal, and the Church had therefore suddenly leant to home-rule. It wanted an emperor, first Iturbide and then Maximilian. It lost far more than had been gained, in the meteoric crash of Maximilian. It was forbidden by the Constitution of Juarez (who dreamt democracy) to own property or to teach religion in the schools, and restrictions were placed on ceremonies anywhere outside a temple. These restrictions, it is true, were never strictly observed after Juarez. But the theoretical passing of Church property into State hands cut into clerical autonomy and material activity, and thus diminished the number of priests and members of orders. Many convents and monasteries were completely emptied. The whole tone of religious endeavour changed through the end of the century, particularly in the positivistic Diaz days, from a national duty to a tolerable tradition.

From 1910 to 1920, during the worst of the armed revolution, church edifices were sacked by the populace and the guerrillas and army. A great migration of priests, monks, and nuns again took place. Now, if there are any religious communities they are secret. The buildings that housed hundreds shelter one, or crumble abandoned. In 1926 Calles precipitated a duel with the Church, because the State was prescribed to be no longer its ally and fellow-landowner. Acrid and violently, the Church locked its doors, protesting against the restated laws of 1857. It suspended services and sacraments, surely expecting mass revolt, which did not occur. All the people mourned, prescient of some disaster. Conducting their own spiritual activities, they knelt alone, and looked into customary space for their fate.

II.

The history of the Church is part of the superficial expression of a deep thing. It is in some aspects a dispute like that common to other nations in which the Church is landlord. But it is a quarrel uniquely Mexican in that more and more visibly the deciding factor appears in the apparently self-sufficient nature of native faith. Church, faith, and state, were one in ancient Mexico. They were also one in New Spain. The Crown was expelled, the state changed. The Church has been levelled to squabblings, and has long been pragmatically separate from the faith. The great majority, for whom católico is synonym of *cristiano,* and *cristiano* of human being, nevertheless know little of the hierarchy and care nothing for the Pope. At the most a village clings to or dreads its priest.

No more as in ancient Mexico, is the priest a part of the god. He is very clearly one thing, and the image another. This is a significant outcome of the only real conflict in religious Mexico which could be called religious conflict: the initial peaceless issue between two priesthoods, because of the native and Spanish idea that priest and god be integrated. To substitute the temple the Spaniards must substitute a priesthood. Systematically from arrival, army and priesthood were necessarily allied to destroy the native powers. As the state and the temple were one, to possess either was perforce to possess both; therefore to destroy both. The Catholic friars sabotaged the machinery by which the state revolved around the temple.

The Aztecs by no means rejected Spanish tutelaries. However it did not occur to them that these were meant as alternative to their own. In their minds all gods were the same.

Humiliated, the friars girdled up cassock, sang mass vehemently, and trotted forth in a hurry to decapitate multiple sculptures. To the Indians killing the gods meant natural violence, death to themselves, not from wrath of the gods, but by the universal feeling that harm to the image is harm to the man. They did not think that the murder was really accomplished, but the attempt was deadly trespass. Of course they objected. The native priests stood actually to lose their very existence. They and the nobles articulated the struggle.

A Texcocan chief argued the native side as follows: "What do the friars do? What do they say? What do you understand? See, the friars and priests, each has his way of doing penitence. The friars of Saint Francis have one way of doctrine, and one way of life, and one way of dress, and one way of prayer; and those of Saint Augustine have another way; and those of Saint Dominic another. And we see that, and we know that this is how it was before, among those who cared for our gods. Those of Mexico had one way of dress, and one way of prayer, and of sacrificing and fasting, and other places another. And each town had its kind of sacrifice, and its kind of prayer and offering. . . Let us therefore follow what our forefathers taught and did, and the way they lived, let us live."

In Tepoztlan it is understood that a delegation of Catholics met with the king and his priests in the house of the Tepozton. The Catholics jerked their thumbs at the stone image and said that it was a stone image and not a good god nor any kind of god at all. (Except a demon, they thought privately.) "You will see that if we throw it over the cliff, the image will break; and what kind of power has a god if he can be pitched over a cliff and broken?"

"Well, all right", said the Indians, but in many more words than three. Among themselves they thought it very silly of the priests to suppose that a broken image meant a powerless god.

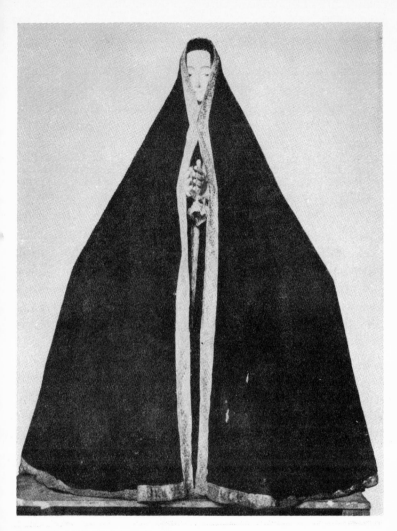

35. OUR LADY OF SOLEDAD
Oaxaca

The Tepozton was invulnerable, immovable as his mountain. But ravaging his picture was likely to make him angry, they pointed out. The priests insisted: "We will test him. If he breaks, you will have to admit he is no god. If he does not break, we will believe that he is a god and you can dance to him as you please". Beyond this scientific attitude they would not be escorted by any poet. So the Indians indulged them. They even helped to drag and push the monolith off its squat platform, down narrow, steep, smooth stairways blunted and scarred since then; and over the lip of the cliff. The god rolled and crashed like his thunder through the tremendous gash, and settled heavily quite whole, among the houses below.

Impatiently the Catholics sawed him in four. Each piece they made the cornerstone of a church. Then came a terrible time. "The Tepozton would be seen, now in the clouds, a fiery streak, now a great serpent, again a jaguar and sometimes a man. He entered white worms that gnawed the roots of the maize. No rain fell. The crops died." A truce was made at last, and since then the Tepozton is honoured on the holy day of the madonna whose church was one of those built on his body.

III.

One or two such episodes proved reasonable armistice impracticable. Mutual distrust, rival finesse, and the indescribable quiescence derived of permanence in this land, lined initial weapons in suave foils. Gesture of Spaniard like counter-gesture of native thenceforth averted reticently outward unseemly battle. "Since we found that in their ancient republic", says Father Sahagun, "they reared the boys and girls in the temples, and there disciplined and taught them about their gods and subjection to the state, we adopted that style of rearing them in our houses, and they slept in one which had

been built next to ours, where we taught them to rise at midnight, and to say matins to Our Lady, and the Hours of the
morning, and we even taught them to beat themselves and
pray. But as they did no physical labour, to which they had
been accustomed, and which their brimming sensuality requires, and as they ate better than they had accustomed . . .
they began to have sensual impulses, and to treat of lascivious
things, and so we had to take them out of our houses and we
sent them to stay with their fathers. . .

"We also tried making them into Religious . . . because
we thought then that they would be apt for ecclesiastical matters, and for the religious life. . . We invested with the habit
of St. Francis, two Indian youths, the most able and worthy
we had, who preached with great fervour the things of Our
Holy Catholic Faith. . . We thought therefore that, dressed
in the garments of our order, and adorned with the virtues of
our Holy Franciscan faith, if they preached with the same
zeal, they would do much spiritual good. . . . But we learned
by experience that they were not sufficient for the state, and
they were therefore divested of the habit, and never again has
an Indian been received in the bosom of this faith . . . nor
are they considered able even, for the priesthood.

"We furthermore attempted to settle all the newly married
near the monasteries, and had them come every day, and
taught them Christianity, and the way of matrimony, and this
was a good means of removing them from the infection of
idolatry, and other bad customs they might acquire from the
conversation of their fathers; but this lasted a short time only,
because they made it understood to most of the Religious, that
all the idolatry with its rites and ceremonies, was now so forgotten, that there was no reason for so much care, since now
they were all baptized and servants of the true God; and this
was most false as we have since seen, for even now idolatry is

by no means extirpated . . . nor many other evil customs, which might have been removed if the method had continued as begun, and if it were in all as in a few places. . . But now it is practically impossible to remedy the matter. . .

"We were greatly helped at first", he continues, "by the boys, both those we reared in the monasteries, and those we taught in the patios . . . and after they had been taught some time, one or two friars would accompany them, and they would go to a temple and destroy it in a few days, and thus there was left not even a sign of it, nor of any other buildings dedicated to idols. . . These boys also helped to extirpate the idolatrous rites that were carried on at night in the houses, and the drunkenness and ceremonies and other things done at night in honour of the idols, because in the daytime they would spy to see where it would be done that night, and in that hour sixty or seventy of them would go with one or two Religious, and they would arrest the idolaters, and take them to the monastery and punish them. And there . . . they made them do penitence, and taught them Christianity, and made them go to matins in the morning, and beat themselves, and this for some weeks, until they repented of what they had done, and departed, catechized and punished, and if they repeated the offense, and were caught, they were again punished. . .

"It is true that some of the boys who were reared in our houses, because they told us the things their fathers did, being baptized, . . were killed by their fathers, and even now when we discover that there are things to be reported and punished, and we speak of them in the pulpits, they begin to investigate to see who it was told of that which was reproved in the pulpit. And they nearly always find the person, and punish him quietly and hypocritically. . . They complain to us in secret, and make us swear not to tell what they tell us, and so we find that we must be silent, and leave to God the remedying of this business.

"And so now they sing, drink, and make their holidays when and where they please, and they sing their old chants that they had in the time of idolatry, not all but many of them, and no one understands what they say because these songs are very veiled . . . and if some of these were made after their conversion, which treat of the things of God and the saints, they are involved in many errors and heresies; and in the dances and ceremonies there are many of their ancient superstitions and idolatric rites; especially where there is no one who can understand them. . ."

IV.

The friars searched and prodded. Owning an idol made a native liable to severe punishment, even, as in one or two cases, sent him in exile to Inquisition prisons in Spain. Loss of the gift of speech, with appropriate countenance, was the Indian defense. The expression has been described more poetically in an old chant: "I am like a wild bird, my face is that of a Mexican".

Led by their chieftains and priests they hid the gods in habitual private places. They shifted them back to the original sources: pushed them into caves, dropped them in lakes, covered them in growing vines. They buried them deep in granaries and between bundles of maize in the fields. The little ones they rolled in petates, dropped in cooking-pots and baskets, put in crevices, tree-trunks, and the puddles of large stones. The men tucked them in their girdles and the women hung them between their breasts.

Frustrate, the missionaries tolled their iron bells and intoned mass before submissive, docile, amiable dark faces. The gods skulked sullenly in the hills and winds. And who can remove the wind? Native religion was sheared, pared, abstracted, driven back to the fundamental needs which formed it; to the living core; to earth level. Nascent, dormant, centuries passed. At one end the Cathedral and at the other, every day in all those centuries, the secret, powerful old men who travel from village to village teaching, elaborating, curing, making rain.

For a brief time after a hundred years, a few missionaries opened their eyes to the religion they had succeeded in making invisible; and again, more quickly, more hopelessly, closed them. Resentfully one concludes: "They flee not only the light and clearness of the truth; from sermons, and teachings of the Ministers, who can instruct and correct them; but they flee also even the light of the day, and gather together at night, at midnight, hiding from their own sons and relatives, and if some discover them, they inform them that they will suffer pain of death, from the gods . . . and that this what they do is good, because this is how their forefathers did; and left instructions to continue so, from mouth to mouth descendance, so that it would not be forgotten, but would be conserved. . . And all the pains they have suffered, and suffer, in one province or another, are not to be considered for censuring it. Though to be pitied, they do not atone thus. . . Indeed it all comes from their idolatries, and their reliance on superstitions; because though before they were idolaters, they were idolaters in a pagan land, but now they are idolaters in a holy land, which is dedicated to God, . . . and so our Lord sends them the fierce lions of hunger and pestilence which consume them, aand all the pains they suffer in their servitude are beyond a doubt, the just punishment of God."

Fray Jacinto de la Serna, who led the seventeenth century crusade against idolaters, observed accurately enough the na-

tive stubbornnesses. "We see that the idols are not forgotten, as
was believed", he says; "for they are so existent, that even
though the natives believe there is a God, they also believe
that the worldly things come by way of their idols. And thus
they plead with them as if they had them, and worship them,
and fear them more than the true God which has been
preached to them, and venerate them more. They ask them for
aid in their necessities, their crops, their undertakings, and put
in their sheaves of maize, and their bundles, an idol, or the
equivalent of an idol, or representative of it; believing that this
will increase and conserve these things. . . And there are teachers among them . . . who sell these idols . . . and tell them
that these give them prosperity . . . and though it may take a
great deal of work to make the crops grow, . . . they nevertheless believe that success is due to the idols, and it is the
same with misfortune. . . Therefore they . . . offer animals,
food, drink, and give thanks for good (which they think
they have received) and offer the blood of chickens and
animals. There are some who even go so far as to shed their
own blood, as was done in the old days, pricking their ears and
skins, in places not easily seen. . . Neither are the gods forgotten . . . among them the Sierra Nevada, which is near
the volcano, and where they said their gods lived. . . They
call the sierra Tonanacatepetl, which means mountain of source
of food; and also they worship the mountain of Toluca,
where they have sacrificed, and other high mountains, where
they had their ancient temples . . . and also the waters,
rivers, lakes, which they invoke when they sow or harvest . . . and also they invoke their gods in other under-
takings."

Even to the exact places, Fray Jacinto's "Handbook for Missionaries" could serve as a guidebook today. Three hundred
years are nothing because the mountains, the days, the sun, the

rain, the crops, and the people, are the same. When spring comes in Milpa Alta, the natural and the supernatural wise people sit in caves and banquet off young maize and tiny calabashes, and decide what is to be done with the tender shoots in the fields. I have been invited to these banquets but somehow I always arrived too early, or too late. There is a stone image about a foot high in the very patio of the church. Around it grow calabash blooms and geraniums. Frequently the leaves are smeared with dripped copal, native incense.

Near Toluca on a hilltop I came upon a tiny chapel made of piled *tepetate,* a volcanic rock. Before the opening hung a curtain fringe of stripped leaves from the heart of the maguey. Around were scattered bits of figurines, heads and torsos, all feminine. Nearby, there was an open packed circle, like a witches' ring, and in the center, traces of dead fires. On the bushes, the rocks, the ground, were drippings of wax and copal. The branches were tied with green and red yarn and ribbons, the colours of the nature spirits, and pieces of white cloth and lace. An old man who could hardly articulate Spanish interrupted the exploration when I entered the chapel and saw a large, squat cross with a face carved on it. He said: "What are you doing? It is dangerous to be here. Once a soldier came up and on the way down he slipped and broke his neck. So I will accompany you to protect you. Let us go." And we did. Later I learned what the cross signified.

I have gone on pilgrimages to make rain; met hail-makers who would not perform for me because they did not want to harm the crops just then. I have drummed gleefully on the Tepozton's tree-trunk teponaztle, and fished for idols on the shores of Chapala. But I am not exceptionally privileged. There are people who know better and bloodier tales. A strain of the sinister recurs; sinister to a foreigner, but to the native casual, once the conversation has been, by virtue of long con-

fidence, flexed to the casual. My own god-child was suggested
as an offering to a Woman in a water-hill, once when it would
not rain. "But", I protested to the mother, "Isn't this wrong,
isn't this against religion?"

"Oh, no", she answered, "it is a part of religion."

"But isn't it murder? Would you kill your own child?"

And she answered: "It is not murder at all. The child is
there and then it is gone, and you don't see it but it is still
there. It would even come to talk to you and tell you things,
afterward. Anyway, the woman in the water-hill says now
that she does not want children any more. She says that the
man who lays a water-pipe from her to the village must
give himself to her before she loosens up and he says he will."
We visited the water-hill; and I discovered that the Woman
dwelt in a pump!

A little of this I recounted to a German archæologist, rather
timidly. But he had found in woods and caves around the
chief shrine of Tlaloc, who was the great rain deity, curious
heaps of stones, newly built, with wreaths of flowers and ribbons, and sometimes small dead animals upon them. Flowers
and ribbons and food and animals are, I told him, also taken
to the Tepozton's house. Soberly enough this scientist added,
"I wish I knew how much truth there is in the Tlaloc stories
I have been hearing lately". He recalled the story of a German
who went to Tlaloc, accompanied by two guides, on the scent
of sacrifice stories.

"What is in the caves?" the Indians repeated his questions
easily. "Oh, nothing, señor. Pretty flowers."

"What do we do in the caves?" They blinked slowly and
scratched their heads. "Why, nothing, señor. We are poor and
must make the corn grow in the fields. We cannot play in the
caves."

"What is the big rock in the shape of a man?" "Why,

36. OUR LORD OF THE TREE
      Michoacan

señor, we don't know. Only the white people, educated like you, know about these things. They know everything. They in the United States, we have heard, are all educated and rich. They eat white bread. There are so many people that, it is said, soon the United States will go over into its neighbour, Russia, and take her lands."

"Russia is not next door to the United States? Why, señor, truly we wish we had schools so that we might know as much as you. But we are poor and ignorant little Indians, your servants, señor."

"Feasts in those caves? Oh, no!" They all laughed together at the idea. "Those are things of the ancients. All of that passed with the revolution."

The young man procured a horse, it is rumoured, and went alone to the Tlaloc mountains at whose foot lies the great stone monolith of that god. He gauged the time for the sacrifices basing himself on the chronicles of colonial friars. He never returned.

"A young fellow with pale eyes, señor?" they said to inquiries. "Why yes, señor, he passed our way. He told us that the United States was very rich and that soon they will take Russia to make more room."

"Where did he go, señor? *Pues,* we do not know. Over there. . ." and gestured a vague half-circle. "Over the mountains. . .

"Do you think, señor, that the Americans from the United States will come to take our lands, too?"

V.

Thus, the exiled deities. Then primevally (and magnificently ironical), they moved back to their places by the agency of the friars. The situation becomes as complex and coincident

as two mirrors reflecting each other's images. Friars and natives were so insulated and oblivious to each other that they
co-operated, thinking to conquer. Both first, with very widely
different ends in view, assembled heterogeneously idols and madonnas. Bernal Diaz del Castillo describes factually performing
the very thing of which later, when the Indians even perhaps
innocently, follow suit, Fray Geronimo de Mendieta com-
plains: "And among the idols and demons were to be found
also images of Christ Our Lord and of Our Lady, which the
Spaniards had given them, thinking that with these alone they
would be satisfied. But they, having a hundred gods, wanted a
hundred and one more, if more were given them."

Every time the friars razed a teocalli they had a church built
therewith. They buried idols and planted crosses on their
graves. And again the Indians, though this time surely not so
innocent, did precisely the same thing. Says Fray Geronimo,
rather upset by the discovery: "The friars had many crosses
made for them and placed in all the gates and entrances to
villages and upon some high hills. . . They would put their
idols under or behind the cross, making believe they adored the
cross but adoring really the figure of the demon they had
hidden there." Fray Jacinto de la Serna adds: "And in all
their idolatries, they were greatly helped by the fact that
many of the idols were placed as foundation stones, cornerstones and pillars of the Church, and in other houses to adorn
them, and what was done accidentally thus, to strengthen the
buildings, and the houses, and to adorn the streets . . . the
demon took advantage of, to greater deceive them, so that they
could say, that their gods were so strong, that they were put
as foundations and cornerstones of the temples; and those
that are in the houses, and the streets, in order to conserve
them; where therefore they committed idolatry, and served
them. . .

"And they brought the idols from the mountains, and the temples, to their houses and to the villages, and even to the churches, and though they saw them broken, and taken ignominiously, from some of the places where they had put them (whether casually, or maliciously, by the Indians who built the temples and the houses, and put them there so to honour them) they nevertheless continued to adore them, even in fragments.

"And to better hide their poison and deception," he adds, "they adore, mixing their idolatric rites with good and holy things, joining light to darkness, Christ with Belial, and revering Christ Our Lord and His Holy Mother and the saints whom some of them consider gods, at the same time that they adore the idols. Some of the evil ministers have tried to imitate the Holy Sacrament of the Eucharist with mushrooms from the mountains, eating them as in communion. . . In the village of Tautengo, also, there was an Indian who made them worship an idol on Tuesday, Wednesday and Thursday of Holy Week, and his daring was so great that he even placed this idol on Holy Thursday in the urn which holds the Holy Sacrament."

Dr. Thomas Gann describes the modern analogy among Yucatan Mayas, which holds for the Mexicans also, to the skirts of the metropolis. "To Christianity, not as a separate religion, but as a graft on that which they already practiced, they seem to have taken kindly from the first; and at the present day, . . . the sun god, the rain god, St. Lawrence, and Santa Clara may all be invoked in the same prayer, while the Cross is substituted in most of the ceremonies for the images of old gods, though many of the latter are called on by name."

A former director of the National Museum shrugs at these accounts and says: "Of course the Indians are not Christians.

Certainly they worship idols, inside and outside the churches. They do not understand anything of what the priests tell them, and they do not want to understand". And then he tells one of his startling stories, with relish that of a miraculous Lord, served by many devotees all over the state of Michoacan. His altar was always covered with offerings, candles burned on it innumerably, and pilgrims made a constant kneeling mass below it. Until once, when the ancient altar-piece cracked. In the course of repairs an idol nearly a yard high was found under the feet of the Christ. The idol was carted to a museum; whereupon promptly, devotion ceased.

But after all, whose is the victory when in a village of the state of Querétaro, where the people still make idols, a woman who possesses a fine little image wanted the additional sanctification of a priest's blessing on it? She was aware that with his knowledge, it would never be given. So she put the idol in a vase of flowers; and it was duly blessed.

VI.

Trafficking from church to mountain, the Indians elaborated their concealed rites with new and pretty ideas of the monks. Shrewdly, ecstatically they invented new names for old things and tunneled the whole theocracy back into prime position. Within a century there was a new pantheon. Impressively it is a Mexican conquest, native spiritual projections in European forms, and at the apex where the two most abstractly coincide, a redramatization of the mystic, universal story of Chrsit.

Coincidences also in detail between the two religious systems; the native habits of concealment, masking, and dramatization; the methods of substitution adopted by the friars, and the dramatic in Catholicism—these are factors that with even chemical accuracy, fused the new image. But the amazing process by which this fusion occurred is the great coincidence that the system adopted by the friars was the same as the native process of religious development, an exchange and transformation of dramatic plastic forms.

The word between Aztec and Spaniard was powerless. The first vehicle of conversion was perforce unaccompanied and unprotected by explanation. Father Sahagun spent a lifetime learning the native languages, beliefs, and rites, in order to describe his own in these terms. He recorded in words, and in great tomes of pictures made for him by the natives, as accurate and complete an Aztec panorama as any foreigner in his position and with his talents might have secured. But by the time he might have been able to use this lore, the complementation of images was long past control, and sadly he says: "It was necessary to turn over and know many ceremonies and rites of their idolatry and infidelity, and as we knew little of their tongue, we hardly ever were right, as we now see."

The friars substituted because the wise old Church had found already elsewhere that she could not always extirpate. They came endorsed in method by St. Augustine, and they followed it to the minutest visible detail. For example they substituted miracle plays for ceremonial rites, and so close were coincidences even in this that the constant personage, the medieval clown, found a clownish similarly sardonic counterpart already existent in the Mexican religious theatrical cast. Such miracles as the Lord of Chalma appearing in the place of Ostocotheotl the cave god were deliberately hailed. If the Lord of Chalma has continued the other's tradition, and is still a master of sorcery, who must be danced to, it is because no reason was ever clear in the crucifix itself, against such celebration; and objection was made after the priesthood had mentally shed medieval Spain.

On the native side, acceptance was aided by many religious

circumstances. White redeemers, bearded and powerful, had long been prophesied. There was a native feeling about dread sacred power in shed blood. The cross was bound up in pre-Hispanic esoteric lore; it was the symbol of the moving universe. Confession as a religious form was practiced. Baptism, considering the inherent sacredness of water, and customs of ceremonial bathing, was comprehensible. Communion was carried out in many ways, from abstract symbol of little cakes of maize, to the bloodiest rehearsal. There were native deities miraculously conceived, by a breath, a feather, a snake, a tongue of fire. There were gods portrayed with attributes of animals and plants. Hence, for example, the Catholic lamb, the dove, the serpent, the lion, the lily, the staff, were accepted easily in symbolic light. St. Joseph was called "the powerful old one" on account of his trader-pilgrim-sorcerer's staff. St. John was made a patron of running water. Immersion is a religious rite, and at least a national custom, on his holiday.

"What happened is", I am told in Milpa Alta, "that at the time of the Spaniards, idols went out of style, and saints came more into use". The new forms were intriguing. Nothing so impressive at first to the Indians as white men in shining armour on a horse. So perhaps the earliest most eagerly worshipped image was that of the conquerors' patron, St. James. Now, his cult is spread and ramified over the continent, south of the Rio Grande. In nearly every central Mexican village there is a dancing-group called "St. Jameses" which performs on most religious holidays. The theme of its plays and dance-dramas is the fight between Spaniards and Moors—the struggle between dark and white. Curiously, I have occasionally seen the Moorish captain carry a Mexican flag.

Fray Jacinto de la Serna condemned this worship, incomprehensibly to the natives. But it was dispiriting to discover that St. James had become a being who rode in storms, and

that "they fear him and hold him a worker of magic". At the
Eucharistic Congress of 1924, a rural priest complained that
the Indians in his region celebrated St. James' day profusely,
but that they also celebrated even more lavishly, a day for the
horse, "whom they call San Jacobo". In Michoacan, I came
upon an engaging St. James, dressed as an Indian in coarse
white with a little red blanket, instead of in the usual conquest
armour. On the steed hung many tiny silver horses, ex-votos
offered for the cure and recovery of its fleshly kin.

Saints and madonnas brought from Spain, took the names
of the places where they were fixed, and functions such as
making rain, curing sickness caused by the wind, stopping
floods and plagues. Shrines of certain patrons in the depths of
mines are kept illumined with poor wax candles, and decorated with the prettiest bits of shining quartz; this could be
European or native. But it is certainly native when shrines in
pulque fermenting-sheds are adorned with red and green
strips of paper and "crowns" from the white heart of the
maguey. There are many Christs with names such as the Lord
of Amecameca, the Lord of Chalma, the Lord of Izquimiquil-
pan, Christ of the Poor Lead Mines; saints like San Antonio
Itzcuintla and San Francisco Ecatepec; madonnas such as the
Lady of Zapopan, the Lady of Atzcapotzalco, the madonna of
Juchitan.

Some are more powerful and miraculous than others, depending on the prestige, wit, and devotion of their respective
zones. Images nuclei of pilgrimages are often "visited" by
smaller, less remarkable place-patrons, in the course of which
visit they derive glory and power. The Lord of Chalma is one
such regional core. The archæologist Dr. S. K. Lothrop writes
of a famous southerner, the Black Christ of Esquipulas near
the Guatemalan border: "The *verdadera imagen* is a black
wooden statue about five feet high. It is said to have been

carved by one Quirio Cataño in 1595. Soon after its completion miraculous cures were noted among those who prayed
before it, and its fame increased steadily until the end of the
nineteenth century. As many as a hundred thousand are said
annually to have visited the sanctuary until the Guatemalan
government imposed passport restrictions with which the poor
Indians were unable to cope. Today about 40,000 are said to
come—an extraordinary number when it is remembered that
all easy means of transportation end far away and that the
accommodations are of the crudest. In fact the journey must
kill as many as it cures, for the overcrowded town becomes a
vast latrine at pilgrimtide. . .

"Esquipulas is of interest because it attests the survival of a
pre-Spanish cult. As to the colour of the sacred image, black
in Middle America has been considered divine, sacred, and
holy from time immemorial . . . one readily comprehends
how avidly the Indians received the worship of a Black
Christ. . . The sanctuary is a little more than a day's journey from Asunción Mita, to which pilgrimage has been made
from ancient times. . . There are several indications that
the Indians even today do not regard this Esquipulas cult as
entirely Christian. . . Many of the minor offices of the sanctuary, such as sweeping and swinging censers, fall to the
charge of Quiché Indians, descendants of the ancient priesthood and nobility . . . Today in Nahuala no Christian priest
(or even a white man) is allowed to reside, and in Chichicas-
tenango a priest is tolerated only if he does not interfere with
native pagan ceremonies. . . Clearly these Indians, who have
little or nothing to do with the church at home, do not make
the long journey to Esquipulas because they regard the cult
as Christian."

VII.

In spite of the warring priesthoods, in spite of the feared and hated Spanishness of the new images; parallel to the under-current life of the ancient faiths and cults, the demonstrable mystery of acceptance, transformation, and new creation surged luminously to full expression. Somehow the interworking of imported form and native content awoke new devotion, which made a new native religion and a new Christian art.

Of this epic a dearest and complete witness is our Lady of Guadalupe, Dark Madonna of the Tepeyac, patroness of the nation. Guadalupe "arose" in the hills which had been shrine and dwelling of Tinonantzin or Tonantzin, ancient mother of deities, and her kin the Tlaloque, rain and nature beings. It is said that the Lady—and which of the two, Guadalupe or Tonantzin, is not clear, for it might be either, and it is both— wandered shocked and lost in these hills, homeless, in the first days of the colony.

> "For token she left,
> Under a wall
> A goblet of water,
> From her own canal.
>
> A very little pool
> Of rippling white water
> Belonged to Our Lady
> Our Guadalupana.
>
> For token she left
> In a ravine at night
> A crystal of oil
> Which was her only light."

One day she appeared to Juan Diego, a "very poor and humble Indian" on the hill of Tepeyac, and half wistful, half threatening, required sanctuary. Juan Diego went to the archbishop, who, knowing the native habit of having interviews with deities, suspiciously refused Guadalupe a home, until proof was given him that this was a Catholic miracle. Roses in mid-winter Our Lady of Guadalupe made bloom on the hill of Tepeyac for the doubting clergyman; and brilliantly confounded and converted him by appearing in image on the Indian's *ayate,* or carrying-net, in which the flowers were wrapped, precisely at the moment Juan Diego displayed his bouquet to the bishop.

> "The reverend bishop
> He refused to hear
> Until by her tokens
> She made the truth clear.
>
> The reverend bishop
> Is converted now
> Long live Guadalupe
> To you we all bow."

However Father Sahagun looked askance on Guadalupe's sudden popularity, and warningly wrote of her lowly origin. "Near the mountains there are three or four places where they used to offer most solemn sacrifices", he says, "and to which pilgrims came from distant lands. One of these is here in Mexico. It is a little hill called Tepeyac . . . now called Our Lady of Guadalupe. In this place they had a temple dedicated to the mother of the gods whom they called Tonantzin, which means 'our mother.' There they made many sacrifices in her honour . . . and men, women, and children attended the festivals. . . The assemblage was large in those days, and they would all say: 'Let us go to the feast of Tonantzin.' Now, the church built there is dedicated to Our Lady of Guadalupe, whom they also call Tonantzin, imitating the prelates, who called Our Lady the Mother of God, (in Aztec) Tonantzin. . . . And so they come to visit this Tonantzin from afar, as much as before; which devotion is suspicious, because everywhere there are many churches for Our Lady and they do not attend those; but they come from great distances here."

Guadalupe's life thus hung balanced against pure Catholic ideas, in the fervid days of New Spain. But when Father Hidalgo declared Independence, he did so under her banner. The Dark Madonna was given the burden of making Mexico no longer Spain. She and the Spanish Mary, Our Lady of Soledad, fought that war. Once or twice during the struggle the Spaniards tried and executed their divine adversary's image. Victory raised Tinonantzin to first devotion. Philosophically, Mexico then reconciled the Virgins, and the elegant Soledad became popular enough, at least in Mexico City and in the south, to understudy Guadalupe in her rôle of protectress of the poor, dark, ailing and humble. During the revolution both madonnas fought on the side of their ill-equipped worshippers, but more vividly and famously Guadalupe. She even surpassed, with her miracles and encouragement, Malinche, who rode on horseback and cast thunderbolts at the Government.

Countlessly, every day, Guadalupe is on the lips and in the thoughts of all Mexico. The peak of society and clergy, and the serfdom, share her. City and village, mountain and plain, north, south, and center, turn to her intensely. Her ballads are added by thousands; her shrines can never be numbered. She rides printed on cards in taxis, fastened to sombrero-crowns and saddles. She smiles behind glass in salons, painted on tin in the kitchen, carved into cradle-boards. She is reminisced and reaffirmed in plaster, marble, wood, stone, clay, cake, candy, cloth, tissue-paper; beaded, embroidered, baked. A pistol and a medallion of Guadalupe—this is any Mexican youth's birthright.

She has forced hospitality on the Church, as Mary, but she is also still Tinonantzin. The primitive and supposedly uncate-

chized sierra Tarahumare, invoke her clearest in native terms:
"Likewise do we beseech Our Lady of Guadalupe, she who
was created within the white clouds in the seven beautiful
heavens where sadly she doth appear. Hither she looketh in
all hours, beholding her children, how pitiful we appear in our
sinfulness. Hither she will look upon us who are her children
and will cast from us the heat. Then will no ill befall us, then
will the strangers who speak strange tongues not molest us.
With the heat will ye cast them aside. And she who is Our
Mother will watch over us and protect us in all hours."

Guadalupe's Mexico is the real nation. Juan Diego is its self-
portrait. He, the "poor, sad, humble Indian", resting his head
on the shoulders of the gentle and brown-skinned Virgin, is
emotionally the basis of native spiritual, daily assurance; is a
picture of a reason for living. She is the proof of the fundamental Mexican unity; and a definite, permanent, created
value. Tepeyac, on the edge of the capital, is more than the
religious focus of pre-Hispanic days. It is the Mexican navel.
Yearly, on the twelfth of December (which is in the season,
before the rains, when Tinonantzin was worshipped) as much
of the nation as can find a place, revisits Guadalupe at her
altars on the little hill and below it, drinks from her holy
well under its glittering majolica cover, eats little maize-cakes
called *gorditas de Guadalupe* in the church patios, and traffics
through the ribboned and flowered and tissue-paper fringed
streets of the holy Villa. The roads are dust by day and fire
by night; alive with decorated Fords, donkeys, mules, horses;
pilgrims walking, dancing, crawling, and on their knees—for
miles writing ecstasy in the soil. Recapitulating the tale, in
music, word, and verse, threading each rhyme faithfully on
an appeal that contains a declaration:

> "Favor your sons, oh Guadalupana
> Oh favor us your sons, Guadalupana."

Insisting over and over, varying, repeating, the initial miracle
which has mothered all her miracles:

"From Heaven descended
In triumph and splendor
To give us her favors
Guadalupe the Virgin.

Oh chosen Juan Diego
She appeared to your eyes
When you crossed the hill,
Of the Queen of the skies.

On your fine ayate,
She of the Indies
Left us her image
The Guadalupe Virgin.

Oh you are Guadalupe
White flower of olive
You appeared to us,
Once and for always."

Orchestras—flute, the tall drum *huehuetl,* the long flat drum
teponaztle, fill the cup of this valley with rhythm that rises,
endless, and winds like the ribbons and plumes of dancers,
around the gray-green mounds. The altars in chapels and
church are cut to spirals and columns by the moving "arches"
and banner-poles of dancers crowding close as they may to
Guadalupe. Clowns, devils, Spaniards, St. Jameses, Moors, mas-
querading animals and "foreign" feather-head-dressed Indians
rematerialize an American Middle Ages in the patios and
streets of the Villa.

Rattle, push, stamp, flash down with knee bent; rest only
if other circles are dancing; never permit crowd-chaos—even
this sweet-voiced crowd—to break the rhythm. Serenade the
madonna with the *mañanitas,* chant descendant from ancient
America, prerogative of the Mother, and prerogative, too, of
sweethearts and budding maidens on birthday mornings. Your

mothers before you, and your children after, simultaneously rejoice and grieve here; sing, fecund, dance, laugh, weep, eat, drink, love, in your sculptural ritual abandon. Hymn your greeting and your farewell; your presence; with a cry like an arrow.

VIII.

Guadalupe could very well be considered the mother of all other Mexican Christian images, because there is a family resemblance between them. None of them look like the original imported European models. Guadalupe is notably dark, and is clad like Tinonatzin, in the garb of Mexican heaven, "a blue mantle, dotted with stars like toasted maize grains". Our Lord of Chalma is the color of a mature tree. The Lord of the Little Maize Cane, whose cult is native to Michoacan, is made of maize-paste, a beautiful, light material generally of a shade between gold and bronze. This Christ is not a Lord Crucified. He sits bent over, as do so many other Mexican wise men, clay and flesh. In his hand he holds a fresh young stalk of maize. Under him an inscription, in a curious Indian-Spanish queries:

> "Does it not give you sadness
> To see me sitting like this
> With my hand upon my chin
> As if saying not a thing
> And yet speaking?"

Colonial critics who remarked the Indian saints marveled that the natives, "who are so skillful at copying and reproducing beautiful madonnas", should for themselves choose to model saints "monstrous, grotesque, and laughable." A pious lady, owner of a great estate, long after the colonial period, visited a native chapel, and was so shocked by the "ghastliness of their St. Anthony", that she substituted it with a new and prettier image. But the Indians refused to have anything to do with it. They brought no candles or flowers, and would not pray at the once popular shrine. They said the new Anthony was "pink and white and richly clothed, therefore a snob, a Spaniard, who won't listen to our prayers, while the other was poor and dark and humble, like ourselves, and will take our part in heaven".

Neither, however, do these images look like idols. Pre-Hispanic Mexican divinity, like pre-Hispanic Mexican art, was an abstract thing. The gods which Christian images supplanted were not beings, but complexes, dynamic, disintegrating, constantly reassembling groups of geometric forms and philosophic symbols and emotional associations. Each god had multiple forms and many symbols and attributes, many "masks". There were traditional moulds, but none rigid or constant, and rarely was one identified only with a certain deity. Worship was a longing, not to acquire the god's character and mode of life, (which was never defined) but rather an identification with some attribute or function of divinity. Thus an Aztec worshipper could pray, "I am the flower, I am the feather, I the drum and mirror of the gods. I am the song, I rain flowers, I rain songs".

Worship of Christian images meant worship, almost certainly for the first time, of the human form. Religious sculpture became therefore realistic. And so completely was religion made likewise realistic and human that, for example, Our Lady of La Salud, an image which appeared miraculously in a fishing canoe on Lake Patzcuaro, is said to be "Not like a Virgin at all; she is dark, like a real person, and perspires."

Being artists, the Indians became converts to new forms, and being powerful, honest artists, they created their own version of these forms. They disregarded their traditional highly stylized, complex moulds, and made primitive American images that belong with all other early Christian art. Conviction, and the artistic probity that never allows them to falsify material (they do not make clay look like bronze, nor cardboard into marble), determined the re-creation of their Christ. They interpreted Him in His own plastic and personal terms. They accentuated the blood, the horns, the wounds, the agony. But it is still Christ, supremely so. Who better than they to comprehend the symbol? They had a new martyrdom, and needed this new form. They made it their own so completely that they remade it brown.

37. MIRACULOUS APPARITION OF OUR LADY OF GUADALUPE
Illustration for ballad, by Guadalupe Posada

CHAPTER SEVEN

PAINTED MIRACLES

One of the few ideas that the medieval Spaniard and his Mexican contemporary might have discussed without too great misunderstanding, was the notion of miracles. The experiences of neither were limited by questions of origin, objective reality, physical possibility. The theological Spanish interpretation was, surely, different from the Mexican, and the attitude also was not identical. To the Spaniard, a miracle was a logical supernatural event; to the Mexican, it was natural.

In his mind all experience is pervaded with the feeling of contact with deity. So the glimpse of himself or a passing animal in a pool, the human echo of a parrot, a sudden contact of his foot or his eye on a remarkable colour or surface, can by the Mexican be considered a marvel. His mood need only be heightened to the spiritual, mental, and physical tension which focusses with delight or is impressed by a sight and sensation at any other moment perhaps irrelevant. Other poets feel and react in the same way, but they do not call the process a miracle. Doubtless neither did the ancient Mexican.

Miracles however were also a religious institution. Supernatural contacts were sought by the aid of fasting, singing, dancing, and intoxicants, among them pulque, the mescal button, and the jimson weed. Visions, songs, and special sensations such as flight were manifestations of unusual individual powers and were prophetic of successes in war, medicine, and other undertakings. Many of the visions were gorgeous new versions of beings and ideas common to the folk, others were personal so keenly that they might be called inventions.

From Spanish to Indian the traverse is clear in Juan Diego's encounters with Guadalupe. Hundreds of similar episodes the Church refused to recognize as miraculous or in all orthodoxy divine. The experiences of medieval saints find striking parallel often, and, like many medieval mystics, some natives who confessed such spiritual intimacies suffered at the hands of the Inquisition. The typical account of an Indian girl who was condemned for sorcery should have planted a very large question in the minds of her priestly examiners.

"This girl, Mariana, declared that . . . she had learned her charms and deceptions from her sister Mariana, and that this sister had . . . received it by revelation. . . That a youth appeared to her whom she thought an angel, and said to her, 'Do not grieve, for God gives you the boon of curing sores . . . boils . . . and smallpox . . . but if you do not use it you shall die.' After which the youth stayed and all of the night gave her a cross, driving nails into her hands, and that while she was upon the cross, the youth taught her how to cure, which was by means of seven exorcisms or invocations. . ."

It was difficult in any case to say where native sorcery and religious habit ended and divine intervention that could be endorsed by the Church, began. By encouraging devotion to miraculously appeared Christs and by preaching, as must have been done, with texts of the miracles of saints and madonnas, the missionaries sowed luxuriant crops. Many more miracles occurred than the friars were prepared to admit. If they were all authentic, they concluded, then heaven must be granting special dispensation to the converts, to make real Christians of them. Fray Bartolomé said as much, when he doubted that

Mexico would ever be saved, except by a miracle, and added "such as I hear has lately occurred in the state of Chiapas".

The Indian, who could converse with God daily, did not see why he should believe it only once a century or so. His viewpoint of the miracle as a normal thing is unaltered. It has been systematized into the Catholic process—invocation to a given agent, and performance by that agent, in response to the faith that produced invocation. It is an order of natural phenomena by mystic Catholic laws. Nevertheless the emphasis is peculiarly Mexican. It is on the fact of the miracle, and never, as might be the case among moralizing people, on the meritoriousness or piety of the person who witnessed or invoked it.

I have seen the darker and poorer among whom miracles are commonest show wonder, but I do not remember seeing surprise. I might if a miracle were questioned. I might if I inquired the pragmatic benefit of a miracle. I would likely be told that happenings, like some gods and saints, judged by immediate standards, "what they have of good they have of bad, too."

My friend the cook tells me: "I lost my pigs. I hunted everywhere up and down the street and around the town, but did not find them. Then I begged Our Lady of La Salud to find them, and went quietly home. There in front of my house were the pigs". She continues her exposition of the subject thus: "My little brother died by a beautiful miracle. Our Lady of Guadalupe came to see us. That is, she came to see him. He ran into the house one morning, all excited, and said that outside there was a lady in a blue mantle, and could she come in? When we went out we did not see anybody. He said that there she was, going down the road. The next day the same thing happened, and we did see a lady in a blue rebozo, but we thought it must be some neighbour. She went away before we could even say good morning to her. My little brother said that she had asked him if he would like to go with her, and he said that he would. The third time she came we saw just a bit of blue, shining and beautiful. Then my little brother died. That day, we smelled roses in the room."

The Mexican poet Nuñez y Dominguez more spectacularly, more a European, nourished like my cook and myself on the daily fruit of visions, writes with special enthusiasm of the miracle of the Virgen de las Angustias. This image belonged to the colonial Hospital del Amor de Dios and was there obscurely worshipped for the first hundred years of new Spain. In the seventeenth century it was to be buried, because of age and defect, along with others in a similar state. "One of the servants of the hospital", he says, "was especially attracted by it, and begged that it be given him, and after a few days displayed the Virgin nicely repaired and clothed. . . He said that she was much beloved in the house. . . . "

He and his wife began to note that in the mornings the Lady seemed mud bespattered, sometimes even splashed and wet. They would clean her up and in a few days she would be muddy again. One morning an Indian came to the house asking to see a lady who was dressed like a widow. He had been following her, he said, since six o'clock that morning, from San Cristobal, six leagues away, but he had not been able to overtake her. He had seen her before, several times, "holding the floodgate of a nearby lake with her shoulder, and since the gate was old and rotten it was dangerous, especially now as the season had been very rainy and the lagoon was full . . . and if it burst it would surely have flooded the city." He was told that no such lady as he described belonged in that house; but insisted so lengthily that he was told to look for himself. "And no sooner had he been allowed to enter than he pointed to the image of Our Lady and said that this was the person he meant."

39. OIL PAINTING
   The town of San Juan de los Lagos, Oaxaca, doing penance
   for the murder of two priests. Oil ex-voto, 1890

40. DETAIL FROM EX-VOTO
   Oil on tin. Modern

Possibly my cook and myself prefer the more familiar miracles of Our Lord of Chalma. One of them was performed for
a faithless wife. She and her lover were in the woods, when
the husband surprised them. The woman appealed to Our
Lord of Chalma. Immediately her lover turned into an altar
and the Lord himself appeared upon it. The furious husband
dropped his murderous machete and he and his wife kneeled
devoutly before the Christ. Another miracle of the Lord of
Chalma was the punishment of two people who offended this
Lord with their flesh on a pilgrimage to his shrine. They
violated the rule that the relationship between godparents and
real parents must always be spiritual; and therefore were
turned into immense rocks, which stand there now, "with
faces of people and eyes just as real". Two others, guilty of
the same sin, turned into a tree and a rock. The tree has long
hair and a navel mark on the trunk. This is the woman. The
man rolls forever making the pilgrimage, and never reaches
the holy atrium. You give him a pious kick on the way to help
him along. If he reaches the shrine he will be pardoned. When
he is, this will be another miracle.

One is tempted to go endlessly on with charming, horrible,
and memorable accounts of such episodes, and one would if
one were having a Mexican party, with Mexican leisure. One
would sing ballads of them, too. They would not be told specifically as miracles, but as stories. If the accounts were strung
on the thread of a title, they would have to be called as a
whole, "Miracles and Other Episodes".

Occasionally in print a self-conscious newspaper reporter
calls them superstitions. "The thief", writes one such sophisti-
cate in a Mexican daily, "is the most superstitious person in
the world. . . There are some, who from the earliest hours
of light, burn a candle to Saint Anthony to get his help.
Others tie a little image of this saint to a blackjack decorated

with flowers, and follow this practice for seven days in order to assure success to the coup of the week. . . But none so remarkable as Gash-in-the-Face. This man brought from his home in Guadalajara a charming idea. For a whole month he would beg alms among his friends until he gathered exactly enough to pay for a mass, which he then ordered sung, and heard with intense devotion, praying throughout seven credos on his knees. The result was, according to him, marvelous, for when he assaulted anybody, dagger in hand and at the turn of a corner, the victim saw him and also seven others, who were really the burglar's guardian angels."

The essential point about miracles is made in a ballad-hymn to Our Lady of San Juan de los Lagos, considered very miraculous and therefore synonymously, beautiful.

> From very imminent dangers
> You saved acrobatic performers
> Bull-fighters, many workmen
> Peaceful travellers and soldiers.
>
> You gave vision to the blind
> You saved from a fatal end
> A gentleman who was poisoned
> And called you from his deathbed.
>
> One woman escaped from drowning
> In a ship that rent asunder
> Because she uttered your name
> At the moment she went under.
>
> Another with faith was saved
> From horrible immolation
> Though the fire was unappeased
> And spread ashes and desolation.
>
> A great example you made
> Of an impious unbeliever
> Who just to amuse himself
> Went to your temple to see you.

With very evident scorn
He looked on your radiant light
And in that moment was punished
By being deprived of sight.

Then repenting he begged pardon
Very humbly did he pray
By faith to him were returned
The eyes that you took away.

II.

The habit of miracles having been common to every day and to every class, it was easily transferred to new theological dogma, and expressed in a new art. It is customary to tell and to sing these poetic events, as it always has been, but it is almost inevitable to paint them. The Indians learned to hang pictured experiences in the churches, and very little else, except how to use oils, to model with paint on a flat surface, and how, if they wished, to handle perspective.

So in Mexico nowadays the word miracle means the happening, and also the small painting which records it, in the shrine of the Christ, saint, or madonna with whom the event is associated. You may say, "I saw a little miracle", and mean that you saw an automobile miss a child which it was destined to kill, or that you were very ill with tuberculosis or a boil, and were cured; or that in the church in which you prayed, of the long horizontal and vertical rows of paintings describing such boons, one struck your fancy. "Saw" means that you passed through that moment. You lived whichever miracle you are recalling. This is the only way in which you may be aware that you did.

These very important documents are generally painted on ten-cent metal, usually tin. Canvas, being more expensive, is for very special miracles, or for particularly prosperous people.

Sometimes water colour and crayon is used on a sheet of wrapping paper or shoe-box cardboard. There are also occasional photographs of the person who received the boon, either incorporated to the painting, or as extra testimony. Hair, a bit of a garment, or a beloved rosary, may be supplied as further illustration. There are sculptured ex-votos, too, replicas of the stricken and saved members of the body, family, or herd. But most people prefer paintings. They seem to satisfy better than other vehicles the necessity of expressing kind thanks for the answer to a desperate prayer.

To see and to paint a miracle you should be able to recognize the combination of elements present in it. If you believe what you say when you pray, if you are ever moved to pray, you are vividly enough aware of miracles to think you can reproduce them. You consider that it would be terror not to have this conviction; whether because you paint or you pray, it would be difficult to decide.

Because both are national habits, you are blind indeed if in Mexico you have not "seen" at least one miracle. Hence the enormous sum of painted testimony in the churches, from colonial days to this morning. Mexican history, never adequately written, has been painted for saintly patronage. A collection of ex-votos from all over the country would give the lives, the thought, the happenings and concerns of each place and of all the people, and would give it more honestly than any narrative, more accurately than a most careful statistical survey.

From place to place and period to period, significantly, occupations, situations, official clothings, progress in caravan against a changeless endless background, vibrant of human trouble and of racial agonies throughout. Plagues, droughts, conflicts, are dated and described. The very emotion concurrent is charted, in kind and quality. In the quiet of miracles some years, the violence others; in the faith that makes them numberless. It is a moving record of a nation, a stethoscopic measure of its heart.

And a consistent record, evident in painter's language. The colonial period, of rich interiors and embroidered gowns; the end, and miracles of battles won from Spaniards. Later, the disappearance of embroideries, and a shifting of scene from rich interiors to chambers furnished with a bed only, and possibly furnished so only to portray the fact that someone was ill. Still later, prophetic resentments of caste: the rural villainous danger conceived wearing dark garments and shoes; the urban murderer seen swathed in a blanket and hatted in petate. Prophetic too, in the years between the beginning of democracy to the armed popular revolution, the number and kinds of miracles. The peasant who retained his land, painted the miracle of it. If he lost, was put in prison or the army or sent to a distant plantation, and ever escaped from any of these destinies, it was a miracle. In the city, people who after an accident or because of some contagious illness, were taken to a public hospital, painted a miracle when released.

If they were cured of any illness at all, they considered it a miracle. Necessarily, as this was almost the only therapy at their disposal. Workers in factories and mines were constantly painting miracles. During the revolution, any one who won a battle, or witnessed it and lived, painted a miracle as if he had escaped an earthquake. The civilian whose house was looted but whose life was spared (by his servants or friends of his servants) painted, or should have painted, that miracle. The soldier who, tired of looting at the risk of his life, deserted and was caught, but was not shot, painted a miracle. The peasants who held the hills against successive Federal governments after Diaz, filled the churches they sacked, with miracles. But earthquakes, plagues, revolutions, do not outnumber the afflictions common to all mankind. They heighten and make them deeply tragic; they, and the powerful landscape on which they occur.

III.

So many people painting so many things common to all develop a language. The artistic conventions of miracle-boards grow out of collective participation and interest in the craft. Nearly any one who can see a miracle, can paint it. But for those who have not the time or the paints, there is in every quarter where miracles occur, a professional miracle-artist whose rates are low, on account of mass production. The profession exists also, because the people, being much pleased with the artistic fashion introduced to them, and being conservative, adapted the occupation to national economics, as was their tradition. The mirale-artist is an extremely useful person in a Mexican community and is as much a contributing member of it as the butcher and the bricklayer.

His status is nearer that of the bricklayer than of the entertainer as whom other peoples treat their creators. He does not sign his name to the picture. He can hardly consider it his. He paints what he is told to paint, and often he is told precisely how. There is no probability of æsthetic dispute between himself and his patron, however, because they agree on the manner of portrayal. The concern of both is recording the idea. The painter satisfies his patron and himself on the ground of accuracy of description, and worthiness of it as a gift to his friend on the altar or in heaven. He is confident that what he is describing is real. He is giving a piece of news, in the intimate fashion of a letter home. The result is always a description without false- or overemphasis because there is no feeling that this was an extraordinary event. Nobody is try-

ing to "sell" anything. The picture is therefore the first thing
that a picture should be, and that is, convincing.

The mind that admits multiple possibilities in human events,
admits any form pictorially that will give the exact set of sights
and sensations that was experienced. The conventions develop,
grow, are not imposed. They grow in direct relation to the
subject and the public, divine and human. Since, furthermore,
collectively these people can speak as they think, in terms of
seeing and making, miracle-painting is a plastic and graphic
art, not a literature. The freedom for which modern artists
clamour exists here without clamour, and precisely, frequently,
in the forms clamoured about, though unconscious, or rather,
not thought-out as a theory of art before the particular picture
which demanded that particular form, was painted.

Diego Rivera, returning from Fauve Paris, was amazed into
much articulation by the range and æsthetic accuracy achieved.
He exclaimed: "The most unexpected analogies are suggested
in our spirit. The masters of the fourteenth century and the
beginning of the fifteenth, Henri Rousseau and to a certain
extent the orient, and the frescoes of Chichen-Itzá. . . In
reality, this is what is called the complete and natural work
of art; purity, faith in the reality of the marvelous, love and
lack of desire for material gain, teach everything; including
the aid of expression that is completely abstract, the "pure
painting" of the moderns. With these impulses everything
is accomplished . . . symphony of colour, gyratory volume,
ærial clarity, realized form, living in a transparent medium."

A miracle is a thing without chronology. A picture is therefore closer to its nature than a story. Even the written information about it on a margin below the painting, is not a sequence.
The name, the date, the place, the name of the saint or
madonna who performed the miracle, the vehicle of danger,
are stated as factors, in words, like a formula of the composi-

tion. There is no account of the antecedents or the less perti-
nent aftermath. A child swallowed a pin and was miraculously
saved: with the name, the date, the agency, appears the pin
itself, incredibly large, convincingly sharp. On a certain date
in a given place, Gonzalez the water-carrier, under the feet of
his stampeding mules; Jimenez impaled on the horns of a
bull; Maria Ruiz and her children, trapped by fire in the
family bed; Juan Rocha about to be shot by the Federals and
his wife "given up by the doctors"; these are the pictoric facts.
The only added text is a description of the act of painting, the
emotional mechanism of the thing: "I therefore devoutly dedi-
cate this."

This attitude of faith directly determines the manner, the
actual artistic style of the painting. It corresponds to the element which makes a painting into a miracle-board, that is,
the heavenly agency painted present, in a small space usually
above toward a corner. The little image represents æsthetically,
the postulate of all possibilities, the spiritual tangent. Pictorially, it is a plastic break with the visible facts of the physical
world. It establishes the reality of everything else in the picture, gives movement and significance to it, is an escape, or
rather a projection, beyond itself; accentuates by contrast the
human and the concrete; abstractly, links the subject to the
laws of art by a dynamic symmetry legitimate and real.

Diverse manners of reproducing miracles coincide similarly
in a visible, but with difficulty explicable way, with the nature
and kind of event. The picture can be realistic as you please, in
order to underline the magnitude of the miracle; or abstract
in principle, as for example when it is simply a portrait, or a
person kneeling, over an inscription like the following: "The
name of Juan Ramirez, his father and mother, remain engraved
at the feet of my patron the archangel Michael". Implications
appear by pure graphic method. A young woman who by her

41. **ACCIDENT IN A POWER PLANT**.
   1883. Oil on tin

42. **MIRACULOUS CURE OF SENORA CARMEN ESCOBAR**
   In Puebla de los Angeles, 1893. Oil on tin

43. A MIRACULOUS ESCAPE

From the Attack of a Wicked Man in the Street at Night.
Mexico City. Oil on tin

inscribed account "was cured of an obscure illness" is recognizable, without censure, socially, by her elaborately laced and ribboned bed, her bright and prosperous clothing, and her loneliness, except for the good madonna above.

In some pictures the subject shrinks to impotence before natural institutions. The earth is enormously the stronger, even a tree is more definitely at home on it than the man. Or the description can be more nearly symbolic. The storm is a single stroke of lightning, or an uprooted trunk, emotional perspective of catastrophic possibilities in the situation. Earthquake pictures are even more prophetically suggestive. They portray such material chaos as has never yet been seen, but as is surely felt impending in the first tremour.

A miracle artist sometimes develops a personal style, for the pure painter's fun of it. He has always, however, had the good faith and the good taste to accept forms which he cannot better. He may simplify, illustrate, give a new poignancy to that form. But poignancy the most intense, and grandeur, lies in the fact of a picture made by so many hands, to crystallization and synthesis; it cannot be dated; the year of it like the date of a birth, or a death, does not influence the fact.

Such a synthesis is the kneeling figure. On a national scale, there are others, which bridge epochs, as for instance the man-in-prison picture which punctuates familiarly every wall where ex-votos hang. He is always imprisoned "because of calumny". He cannot explain it otherwise. The catastrophe is a natural accident, like a fire or a railroad crash. He is always depicted alone. The walls are high, bare, usually gray, coldly lighted. Innumerable bricks in others, recede and progress to no end. Bricks are impressive to eyes accustomed to soft warm surfaces of earth and adobe. Kneeling or standing, the prisoner is static. He does not gnash his teeth or tear his hair to convey anguish and desolation. It is already given by colour, form, and design.

The drama painted in miracles is not a ballet Mexico, not the picturesque candy-coloured scene naïvely supposed to be Mexican. It is something real put together subtly, live blues cut by vermilion, lucent greens punctured with white, a gray light fused of the rainbow, occurring in a definite, inalternative relationship to the other elements of the event. By an attitude rationalistically absurd, the purest truth is sifted. It is defined in Rivera's philosophy of miracles, which is Rivera's because he is one of several hundred thousand Mexican painters.

"A miracle", he says, "is the thing seen as it is, that is, a true portrait. A true portrait, not a copy, nor an imitation, because, as much in the picture of a person, as in the representation of a miracle, what must dominate is the thing called super-realism, which might be named supernatural were it not that the spirit of Mexican painting is the sober, profound recognition of reality, of an intangible, yet nevertheless a universal and essential reality; a sensitiveness to truth that makes miracles of daily happenings and daily happenings miraculous—an intimacy with facts, even when those facts are miracles."

CHAPTER EIGHT

THE REFORM OF PROVIDENCE

The streets of Mexico are painted galleries. Cross in the capital outside the zone that fans from the central avenues of jewelry shops and restaurants, to a boulevard and bungalows; you walk between façades of artist's carnival. In every block there is at least one *pulqueria,* a plebeian drinking shop where only pulque is consumed. It is the focus of the block, focus to the eye, the ear, the nose, the memory. An insistent place, with an air of ritual about it, and a genial waywardness.

44.

Outside and in, the walls are broken into scenic panels and doors (startled, one sometimes in a glimpse mistakes which is the door) framed in scarlet, indigo, sulphur, cubes and spirals and blocks and scrolls which make the surfaces advance, retreat, bow; dance under lettered fantasy. The doors are curtained by tissue-paper fringes, chains, rosettes, little flags. The ceilings are hung so solidly in moving decoration, are further so broken and multiplied by mirrors and tinsel balls that they are limitless.

At the entrance women sell piquant rich meats and sauces appropriate to the milky, acrid, pungent intoxicant. Somebody plays the guitar. Sandaled feet grow heavy here; quick bodies drop in trance. Ribald and sorrowful, violent and whimsical, the drinkers sing. Sound, colour, and smell, a triple of warm life, are keyed in the after all indescribable tone of pulque.

A pulqueria is a post-Hispanic city institution. Pulque itself
is ancient. The Mexican pantheon had four hundred gods—
synonymous in Mexican for countless—tutelary of the drink.
Quetzalcoatl himself was overcome by its charm and wandered vaguely away to his legendary white-winged boat, insisting on his legendary return. The Tepozton in one of his
aspects is Ome Tochtli, a pulque god.

As an institution also, pulque is ancient. It was a valuable
channel to heightened sensation; a divine gift. Elaborate laws
regulated its use. None but the old and very honourable might
partake of it at pleasure. The *maguey* from which it is extracted was a sacred plant. Ritual governed the course of its
reservoir, from under the large, curled rosette to a destined
respectful gullet.

In the maguey fields and pulque brewery sheds, something
of the old religion holds. The drink is extracted as it always
has been, by a man whose profession it is, called a *tlachiquero*.
He carries a long gourd punctured at the narrow and full ends
and a bag made of the stomach of a pig, as apparatus. The
narrow end of the gourd is inserted into the maguey bowl,
which is first scraped raw and bleeding circularly, to admit
the tube. Then the sap is absorbed by suction from the other
end, started by the lips of the tlachiquero and continued on
the physical principle of the liquid seeking its own level. With
each successive gesture of his ceremony, the tlachiquero murmurs invocation and prayer. I do not know if all tlachiqueros
pray similarly, nor was I ever given the words intelligibly, but
most probably the prayer is frequently enough like older
poems for the same task, one of which, recorded long after
the conquest, goes as follows:

"Come now, enchanted stick, whose bliss is in the waters.
Now is the time you are ripened, woman of eight-in-a-row,
be aware that now to the hollow of your heart will enter the

charmed stick whose bliss is in the rains. . . Come, now, rasping-spoon, do your craft and clean your task, in the abiding place of the heart of the woman eight-in-a-row, whose skin you will leave clear and whom you shall make then to weep, and she will be saddened and shed many tears, and sweat, and a stream shall come from the woman eight-in-a-row."

The *tinacal* or brewery where the swelled quivering bags are emptied, is an oblong roofed structure, cool and dark, earthen floored. Here stand large vats of hide which hold earlier ferment. A shrine, usually of a saint or madonna, local patron of the drink, hangs or stands in the center of the end wall, as in a chapel. Lighted candles and flowers are kept below it. The image itself is adorned with paper blossoms and fringes, red and green; paper, because it is a traditional offering. No one enters this place except uncovering his head.

Pulque the religious institution and conscientiously administered native possession was affected by the conquest because it became a source of gold and a means of double-exploitation of the peasants. The symmetrical ranks of maguey grew in the hands of Spanish encomenderos. Fortunes out of pulque bought aristocracy for many immigrants. The drink was soon adulterated before, en route, and in *pulquerias;* was vulgarized. The quantity each man might drink was made unlimited, if his pocket and his stomach corresponded. "Peons are machines that run on pulque", hacendados have often said; contemptuously, but not regretfully. To the peons it is still a boon; at least the boon of escape in stupor, or as one old woman apologetically reflected: "Sometimes I cannot help drinking too much, for to tell the truth pulque soothes my sorrows and makes my insides dance".

To the busy, picturesque poor quarters of the cities, pulque flowed carrying still a religious sediment. Hence the paper fringes, the ritual air, and hence the murals, waif bastards of

raped temple decorations. Polychrome Aztec sculpture is translated literally in these solid walls of cubes, squares, scrolls,
moving by colour geometry around each other, into and out
of the wall, preserving unity. The fusion, the Spanish-Indian
image, is in the scenic panels which sometimes dethrone
abstract art and use it as a frame.

The Spanish-Indian image is also in the names of *pulquerias,*
literary complement of the painting, like the dedication to a
miracle-board. One really cannot speak of Indian or Spanish
here, only of Mexican. These names run in haphazard harmony a commentary on the national scene: "The Prowess
of Gaona", "The Glories of Obregon", "The Brave Charro
of the Sierras". They draw poetically on native and foreign
legend: "The Beautiful Helen of Troy", "The Loves of Cupid",
"The Lady Lion Tamer", "The Lovely Xochitl", "The Jewess",
"The Spirit of St. Louis". Deeper, aptly they make irony and
philosophical synthesis: "The Celebrating Monkeys", "Men
Wise Without Study", "My Consulting Room", "Why Do I
Laugh", "The Mysteries of Commerce". And, essence of Mexican mood, essence of national history, "Let's See What Happens", "Memories of the Future" and "The Reform of Provi-
dence".

Pulqueria murals are painted in cheap, brilliant oils which
quickly fade and peel. They are therefore constantly changing,
are always the national landscape in the present, which includes the beloved and amusing things of the past. The panels
are stratified sometimes like temple murals. But frequent artistic re-decoration is, while fundamentally the result of a living
art, also willingly part of the shop's budget. Attractive, novel
painting is a very real, financially reckonable asset to a
pulqueria.

Indeed, the metropolitan Department of Health at one time
for the sake of sanitation—or its imported masquerade—white-

washed many pulquerias, and required that bars, inside walls, ceilings, be gleaming and bare as an operating room. The pulquerias thus purified lost all their customers. Withal press censure of their artistic style as "degenerate, ridiculous, immoral, and absurd", and of the flaunted names as "ungrammatical and ignorant", (none of them being *casino,* like the bars of the more prosperous) the bloom of murals could not be stopped. The ban on them was eventually lifted because pulqueria owners marched in protest and presented numerical proof of damages. How can a government collect taxes if there is no revenue? And how pronounce dry a plant supremely fertile?

In pulqueria art painter and owner collaborate with their public to produce a national property. The public by selection, and by expressed admiration, by its personality and tastes, determines the subjects. Tradition, the painter's talent, and the owner's ideas, modify or heighten the subject and thus the artistic style, because the style is indivisibly part of subject and purpose, or eventual use. Pulqueria painting, since it has an economic status, is a profession. Seldom, however, is it an individual vehicle, because if the painter signs his name he does it as might a carpenter or a shoemaker, to establish his position in the trade. Economic reason and pulque traditions determine even the kind of paint employed, as one mural artist explained. Asked why he used such transient paints he answered: "Well, I like the quality of fresco better, and I know it lasts much longer, but that is just the point; neither the owner nor I could afford it, because if it lasts too long that spoils the business".

II.

As a place of emotional escape, a valve to the individual, the pulqueria is post-Spanish. It is needed in an alien régime.

As a place of catharsis, and solution of problems, of emotional and mental gymnastics, it is native. Fundamentally, as an institution, it is an artistic clearing-house. It corresponds in painting, to the ballad-publisher, who winds on the spool of his printing-press threads from all over the land. Paintings and ballads pass from city to country and ranch and village, and back again. The small-town pulqueria artist copies his metropolitan fellow-craftsman; but the metropolitan takes his theme and his imagery from the peasant.

So in ballads, which are the poetic parallel of pulqueria murals. *Corrido,* literally "event of the time" is the current name for ballad. Actual chronology in a ballad, however, as in the impermanent, newspaper-like mural, determines little, because there are always the same events, or new versions of familiar happenings. New heroes, new glories, new doubts, new ironies, are not because they are new other than heroes, nevertheless glories, doubts, jests, tragedies. Change the individual irrelevancies and the ballad or the mural serve the next man.

In a pulqueria the ballad-monger and troubadour finds his best audience. He stops in the plazas and market-places on his way, singing the news he carries in twopenny-halfpenny purple, pink, and yellow broadsides. New ballads and new melodies come out of the pulqueria with him. They are polished into quatrain, illustrated, and reprinted in the ballad-publisher's, who collaborates closely with his singing public.

Out of poverty, poetry; out of suffering, song. Hundreds and thousands of anonymous chants beat out a Mexican rhythm; couple the painted galleries with the same images in other terms. One form, the ballad, is the "romance" imported from Spain at the time of the conquest; and there are still current in Mexico Spanish ballads of more than four hundred years' residence. In quatrain heroes, crimes, fantastic accidents and

45. **THE LOVES OF CUPID**
    Detail of mural on pulqueria, Mexico City

miracles weave living woof into the warp of history. Structure
and concept of lyrics, hymns, lullabies, and serenades have been
cast into unique native form of rapid shift of rhythm and
melody, sustained plaint with a rattle and a suppressed, sudden
crashing laughter.

Aires de la tierra, musical breaths and groans and murmurs
and cries, blow through the fringed doorways of the temples
of pulque from over the land. The north sings restlessly, in
cattle ranches and wide plains, in harsh mountains. Sings
defiantly with rat-tat trot of horse's hoofs and a whirl at the
end like the lasso settling on a horned steer. It shears off into
savagery, into the Yaqui chant, made monotonously to hard
contrast with a fierce, rending, prolonged yelp. With a "guiri-
guiri-guiriiiiiii" and a "guiri-guiri-guiriaaaaaaa", the Yaqui
races:

> "Going to the mountains,
> I'm going after,
> My love I'm going
> Gone on a hunt for holy liberty!"

Then, from the far north, from beyond all borders, come profoundly sad numerous songs of exile:

> "How far I am from the soil where I was born
> Intensely nostalgia fills my soul
> Far and away, like a windblown leaf
> I would like to cry, I would like to die
> Because of grief.
>
> Oh land of the sun
> I sigh for your sight;
> Now that so distant
> I'm gone without love, without light,
> To see me so sad and alone, like a windblown leaf
> I would like to cry, I would like to die
> Because of grief."

Pounding fleshly songs, drawn from the sea, the throats of birds, the heavy flick of the monster lizard, and its desires, the far south brews earthy odours in the Mexican caldron. Michoacan, central south, sings thin, wistful bits, fragile as its spun glass. Guerrero, land of mangled hills and gashed fertile canyons sings of itself. The Guerrero lover is terribly familiar with his abyss:

> "High cliff, cliff of the mountain
> Beautiful cliff
> Tell me, where is my love.
> What have you done with my love.
>
> When I am sleeping
> Of her I'm dreaming
> If I am waking
> She walks before me—oh cliff!
> Cliff of the mountain,
> Why did you take my love!"

True romance, without the Indian's grimness, without the Indian irony, hardly blossoms in spirit as intensely wed to reality, to facts and accident and mystic order, as the Mexican, guitars and silver ornamented saddles notwithstanding. Nearest to Europe perhaps, nearest to New Spain, sings Jalisco, little *patria* of the reckless gallant *caballero* who nevertheless is no longer the caballero but the *charro tapatio* with this motto: "Jalisco never loses—and if it loses it grabs". The tapatio is the knight-errant, the bohemian, the lover and duellist. Soft vivid curses ripple through the red lips and mustaches that murmur love-words at the barred balconies of his pretty señorita, whose charms he chants as against those of any other señorita—her black eyes, her little feet, her shapely self. Nursery of poets and guerrilla heroes, is bonafide devil-may-care Jalisco.

In the valleys and plateaus that feed the metropolis, in the musical zone called *el bajio* the north is deepened and sorrowed, is slowed to the steady plod of traffic burros on small trails; the south is thinned of its overabundance, of its lust, becomes a pulse deep and tender. Here spring clear liquid serenades, questing, meditative, lyric, loving of small flowers, intimately speaking to birds, trees, rivers, madonnas. Mexico distilled and essential is the central and south plateau; potent, heady, fresh as dew, with the national bouquet of nostalgia for elysium.

The magic compact ring of voices spirals on sob and falsetto wail around the melody and tale Mexican mood. Mood of poetry in twilight, landscape, gray, grayer, purple and black, burnt at the edges; human with a small bell, and a swathed conic hatted bundle hedged against a black doorway, making a tiny musical lament. Mood of poetry in quiet dawn, when the sun stripes the sky and the bulls scratch their flanks on saplings and chew clover fodder. Mood of noon, a singing, screaming frying pan and a day of white light and keen black. Mood by the fire in a pilgrim camp, chattering and burning its fingers with pinwheels and rockets to entertain the madonna; of procession, torches burning and great projected shadow. Mood of bivouac on a night of stars; of wake; and of holiday . . . . *piñatas,* earthen-jars tissue-papered and gilded and bursting at the smart tap of a stick . . . . disguised, as silver sirens swaying their tails and gossiping; as fat charros bucking their legs pathetically for a horse; as Judases and generals; as ambassadors; and squat pierrots thumbing their noses at the sentimental sirens and the sentimental world. Peanuts, sugar-cane, chili, images of the Three Wise Men. . . . A blind beggar stumbling through the mob, piping on a tin whistle an *ora pro nobis,* over and over and again. All the world asking lodging at everybody else's door, and a child with a hungry face selling sparkler firecrackers, "a rain of stars". Then a whoop and a crack of laughter.

III.

That laughter is the *vacilada,* untranslatable word. It is caricature without a moral. *Vacilada* is argot for the hilarious trance caused by *marihuana,* the drug *canavis indica.* When a marihuana smoker has gulped to intoxication, he bursts into laughter; he dances; he makes nonsense rhymes. His mind spirals infinitely, with absurd clarity; his imagination turns lightning acrobat; he is happily mad.

This trance has served as simile for a strain, a tone, an attitude that runs through Mexican life and in life and art makes consciously, caricature. It is a talent possessed nationally and exercised frequently, in speech, in thought, in action, always in song. It is the oblique fantasy in pulqueria murals; the subtlety turned ridiculous in politics; in art, in love, a weird clairvoyance. So general and so contagious is this laughter that it causes great bewilderment to all the serious-minded visitors and critics; who, if they become resident, acquire the vice, and laugh thereafter though they speak in much solemnity.

The key of the *vacilada* is doubt. Doubt of everything, scientific facts and demonstrations included. Irreverent, preposterous, malicious, answer to all causes, even those with another part of the spirit espoused; espousal of all causes and no great seriousness in any, except suddenly for the most impossible; acceptance of anything as possible admitting rationally that it is not; readiness to attempt all, preferably the irrelevant.

Eliminate the *vacilada,* and the national scene is incomprehensible and shocking. Flight of fancy in reports of fact, and sudden thrust of brutal truth in fiction; a streak of farce in tragedy, and a grim vein in farce. The names of pulquerias are pure *vacilada,* a boiling-down of cosmic frustration: Memories of the Future. . . . Let's See What Happens. . . . The *vacilada* reverses values; as in a mural of a man simmering in a pot while a preoccupied hog stirs the stew. The *vacilada* paints a goat's head on a martyr. It juxtaposes, identifies, shuffles, jazzes: as Dead Men's Day in the city, which is half-denial, half-belief, moved unevenly and quickly to mockery. Marginal note, the word *vacilada,* to the baby with a cardboard skull tipped back on his head, chewing in great tranquillity a purple sugar funeral.

Events of the time are jerked out of time and place *vacilando,* are made grotesque; snickeringly macabre. When the quarrel between the presidency and the Church in 1926 sent many priests to exile and left their temples gaping; and when Indian villages bubbled sullenly at government inspectors who were taking inventory of their images, I saw, in a village festival, the people weep fervently in chapel and then laugh at the door of it with the clown of the day (whose function it is to keep the holiday moving), buffooning a priest. Instead of the customary motley and Spaniard or animal face, he wore a dry, brown, wooden clerical mask. A Satan's tail dragged under his cassock. Out of a prayer-book, held upside down, he read, whimpered, gurgled and sang his ribald pungencies.

In this same period an erring general was court-martialled and sentenced to be shot. He was escorted from prison to execution wall by the death-squad, and a brass band which played a jiggling nonsense ballad, the *Cucaracha,* once the marching song of Villa's opposition, but now again the *vacilada* it was when first composed. The rebel, arms folded, stood against the wall; the squad shouldered arms. Then the captain: "One, two—" turning to the press photographer, "is your camera ready? —Fire!"

Tragedies are introduced and closed with a *vacilada,* and then the drama itself is sculptured and quatrained in laughter; thereby is dismissed. The habitual unhappy ending of Mexican ballads, the habitual plaint, wrung out of real pain, is turned inside out and junked like an old stocking. Thus the following accident, a real catastrophe, in pulqueria version:

THE LOCOMOTIVE.

I have arrived here,
Because I just got here,
For anything I am ready;
I pass the time singing
And go along living
And that way my life is merry.

It happened in the year forty,
But nobody has forgotten
Hundreds of people were killed
Between Tula and Guanajuato.

A train that was racing
From station to station
Without any warning went crashing:
Against a plane that was passing
Too near the train flying
Got bumped; it was very surprising.

With his insides spilled out
Staring at the pilot
The engineer finished his run;
And the worthy air-man
Headless searched his helmet
To protect himself from the sun.

The survivors contemplated
And tears in their eyes were burning
While the locomotive whistled
With all of its wheels still turning.

The upstanding fireman
Was also a martyr
Buried in a sticky black tar;
And the faithful brakeman
Without body or face left
Was trying to stop the car.

For the candy butcher
With all his newspapers

They hunted and found him expiring;
The poor fellow asked them
If they wanted iced beer
And abandoned this world perspiring.

Nobody could ascertain
When or how this was occurring
But the locomotive whistled,
With all of its wheels still turning.

The Red Cross came hurrying
To do all the burying,
The White Cross to do first aid;
But the corpses in meeting
Feared medical treating,
Therefore in a body they fled.

When this they discovered,
They hardly recovered
From that disappointing day;
They even found bodies
Still dead when they got there
As far as four leagues away.

When they came to a ditch the dead men
Lay down in a row together,
And the locomotive whistled
With all of its wheels still turning.

Then in a tin Lizzie
Arrived Maximilian
Who was then the man at the top;
A worthless dead traffic cop,
Insisted on shouting,
And signalling "Go," and "Stop!"

The Pullman was open,
Maximilian was hungry,
He walked in and asked for dinner;
The cook in a hurry,
Prepared him some curry,
Made out of a dead man's liver.

Above them the buzzards were waiting,
And over the dead were yearning,
While the locomotive whistled
With all of its wheels still turning.

I don't want to bore you,
With all the catastrophe
Of so many people who perished;
I just want to beg you,
Now that you have heard it,
To pray for the souls they cherished.

Just to remember the tragedy
Makes anybody afraid of journeying,
For the locomotive still whistles
With all of its wheels still turning.

Vacilada is a mestizo mask, fusion of bland Indian irony
and Spanish picaresque baroqued by fantastic history to irresponsibility. The perfect faith of the Indian which admits
of miracles and paints gorgeous imagery as real, converges
to the Spanish doubt which torments into agonized mysticism.
The mask is double. One cannot tell the grin of joy on it
from the grimace of pain. Revolutions wear it; and artists like
José Clemente Orozco and the ballad-illustrator Guadalupe
Posada. Miguel Covarrubias reflects it amiably.

It is a complete gesture. To any Mexican it is conceivable
that an idea have several sides. You may take your choice.
If you are a virtuoso, you may play with your ideas, as he
with his images. You do not know when he turns his characteristic phrase whether he ridicules the subject, himself, or
you. He makes neat enigma, flexes his imagination to all
combinations of forms and ideas, and leaves still a double-
meaning and a valve, a tangent for the possibility he ignores.
By heroic abandon, this gesture reconciles accident with desire, in the man who no longer quite believes there is a God,
and cannot stomach pedantic substitute. By *vacilada* he may
undergo Job's torments and remain inviolate. Dismayed, despaired, he sobs and shrugs inhuman laughter; and gains a
unique glory.

46. SHEPHERDS
Decoration for Christmas celebration. Tempera on cardboard

47. **THE ROOSTERS' BANQUET**
Sign for lunchroom, Mexico City. Oil on wood

48. **EL CHARRITO**
Façade of pulqueria in Mexico City

49. ILLUSTRATION BY POSADA

Pleas of the lonely unmarried to Our Miraculous Saint Anthony of Padua, saint of lost objects and lovers

CHAPTER NINE

POSADA THE PROPHET

Guadalupe Posada the illustrator of ballads was the prophet of two revolutions, both of them violent. One was the armed mass uprising generally dated 1910-1921, from the fall of Diaz to the presidency of Obregón. When a Mexican speaks of "the revolution" he refers to this period, but more often, unless he is speaking of a particular event, to the ideology developed during and after this warring. Concretely, the revolution as yet has made no great changes in the social organization and the private welfares of most Mexican citizenry—largely still the contrary. It has, however, changed the public mind.

50.

Revolution in Mexico now means loyalty to native values;

185

means an attitude of facing mucky political and social messes
and cleaning them radically; means mental honesty; and the
highest respect for work. The cornerstone and yardstick of
national value is the native: the peasant, the laborer. Your true
revolutionary is likely to clasp more fervently than necessary,
the heretofore "degenerate and ridiculous" peasant to his heart;
and to kick spectacularly, foreign art, foreign systems, foreign
images, into the Gulf or the muddy Rio Grande. "Imposition"
—in the Mexican sense absentee landlordship of everything
including land—is the factual and ideological heart of the
heaped resentments which brought on revolution. The new
social religion is a burning anxiety in Mexico to be true to
herself.

The artistic expression of this national feeling ocurred before, after, and simultaneously with, the armed expression.
Guadalupe Posada foretold, in pictures, the ten years' travail
he did not witness; and the translation thereafter, in pure
artist's values; the travail which bore the new Mexican image
in painting, music, literature. Which bears a new philosophy,
a new aesthetic, a living and great national art.

Guadalupe Posada was born in Leon, Guanajuato, in 1864,
like most of the great men of Mexico from a middle-class, provincial family. Leon is a simple old town center of roads from
great mines; Guanajuato is a sage-green and gray-brown state
tufted and terraced and tunnelled, of surface usually sparse.
The landscape and the life of the people is biblical.

A flood famous in ballads in the year 1888 set young Posada
to thinking about other places than Leon, and he went to the
capital to seek his fortune, he said. Don Antonio Vanegas
Arroyo, founder of the best known publishing house in Mexico, employed him as illustrator. The house of Vanegas Arroyo was not a business organization. It was a family. The
children played with old clichés and learned to rhyme when

51. VERSES
Recited by a Water-carrier to a Servant Maid

52. DRAWING
Frightful fate of a soul snatched to hell because of a dog

they learned to read, and inherited the enterprise. Though revolutionary looters crashed most of the presses, and though vindictive bureaucrats later, accusing the house of pro-Church sentiments, committed therein vandalism, the children and grandchildren of the house of Vanegas Arroyo still edit its street-gazettes and print its hymns, plays, ballads and tales, tending its presses as if they were ancestral fields.

The eldest son of Don Antonio went mad when the presses were broken by government explosives. Don Blas, a middle son, is now the manager and editorial policy of the house. His mother the wife of the founder, tends the *expendio,* the retail shop. She sits crocheting among stacks of leaflets and leather-bound prayer books, and gossips of current and past events with the fruitmen, the flowerwomen, and the occasionally slightly drunk troubadours who drop in to tell or hear the usual latest, sometimes in verse. These latest are still illustrated by Posada, though he died nearly ten years ago. The cuts are sturdy enough for many reprintings, and as current events and personages resemble past, appropriate in subject.

Don Blas remembers Posada as an amiable man, already bald, with a fringe of white hair around his smooth dark skull. "He was very industrious. He began to work at eight o'clock in the morning and worked until seven at night. My father would enter the shop (we set up a shop for him after he had worked a while with us) with whatever he wanted to print, and say, 'Señor Posada, let's illustrate this', and Posada would read it and while he was reading would pick up his pen and say, 'What do you think about this little paragraph', and he would dip his pen into the special ink he used and then give the plate an acid bath and it was finished. He got three pesos a day whatever he did, and in that time it was a lot because whoever had as much as seventy-five pesos a month was at least a general. Posada was very good-humoured and peace-loving. He hated quarrels, and treated everybody well. He was no snob.

"One thing about him only, I suppose, could be considered a little out of the ordinary and this was that he liked to drink, but in a very special way. He saved all year, fifty cents a day, putting it in a little box. On the twentieth of December he broke the bank and sent the money to Leon, to his family, and they bought for him with it big barrels of *tequila,* high as your waist. Then on New Year's Eve he began to drink, alone, and drank and drank till he finished all the barrels, which took from a month to a month and a half. For a fortnight after he couldn't work, because his hands shook. He was slender as a young man but from drinking like that he grew very large in the stomach. . . And eight or a hundred litres of tequila a year finally killed him."

II.

In the house of Vanegas Arroyo the Spanish *romance* emerges as a Mexican *corrido,* and the woodcuts and prints which accompany it change from medieval, comparable to Spanish, French, German and British popular engraving, to modern Mexican. Manuel Manilla, Posada's predecessor, was an excellent craftsman who followed the colonial style developed directly from Spanish engravings. Manilla is romantic, has the simplicity of total acceptance, as well of text as of traditional attitude to the text, spiritual and artistic.

Posada created his own tradition, beginning with the mechanics of his art. He invented a technique of drawing in acid directly on zinc plates, departing thus from the older wood or zinc cut. His engravings are not examples of mass art. They establish him as a personal, highly competent, completely conscious and fully adequate master. There is the same distance

53. THE CHILD MARTYR
    Scandal occurred on the bridge El Blanquillo in the quarter
    of La Palma

between Manilla and Posada as between French popular engravings and Daumier.

One may call Posada a prophet because he breaks sharply
with the past, on the strength of the social philosophy and

54. ANTI-REELECTION RIOTS
Demonstrations dissolved by Diaz police. Mexico City, 1892

55. DRAWING BY POSADA
Solemn entrance of Francisco I. Madero into the capital, 1911

attitude which determined his position, his occupation, the choice of his subjects and the manner of portrayal; which links him with the revolution by mob, and the revolution on painted walls. Posada worked in the period just before the revolution; in the air of Mexico's age of gilt. Official Mexico was affectedly French, foreign. It had a strong hangover of bibelot from the time of Maximilian, a taste for landscape from rationalist France, and an idea four centuries old that, mentally and spiritually, the "decent" people, the upper minority, must belong to Europe. Mexico was loot. To Europe must be looked for culture.

This gilded age marks the ultimate divergence between native and white, between the culture of the people, in the medieval sense of that class, and the culture of the élite. The official artists of the period, who have sunk to the anonymity Posada espoused, were *fin de siècle*. Their patrons were formal bearded portly old gentlemen and large-volumed ladies bound in black (as if mourning in advance the bitter days to come) who lived among spindle-legged chairs, mirrors, and lace to grotesquerie. And who lived idly in euphemy.

To have taken much notice of ballads or their illustrations would in the gilded age have been considered a suspicious and at all events a ridiculous proceeding. These belonged in the servants' quarters. Posada chose, therefore, instead of immediate applause, to be unknown, widely distributed, and much enjoyed; to be also useful.

Perhaps in conversations with Don Antonio Vanegas Arroyo; perhaps only in his own mind, Posada drew significant and thoughtful commentary on the events of the time: protested, foreboded, and with a full heart scribbled on a corner of the national slate a *mene, mene, tekel upharsin*. He turns an obsidian mirror upon the land and makes a choice, deliberate image.

Manilla's illustrations for prayers, or for ballads such as
that of the unfortunate Juan who for stealing the jewel of a
saint was snatched to hell, show the artist's explicit and calm
belief in the form and manner of the saint, in the form and
nature of the demon, in the procedure of snatching. Posada's
fiends are extremely fiendish, caricatures, mockery. Manilla's
women are peasant women, arcadian, idyllic; Posada's are portraits, women of tragedy. Portrait of the national panorama
carries conviction enough, when it is conscious portrait, and
establishes the inevitable social outcome. A peasant family on
the march, to exile and in slavery; a patient crowd, restless
a little in time of hunger, women holding their empty baskets;
the plague, and people shoveled dead into carts, mounded. He
garbs the dictator and his cabinet in the skull and skeleton of
national carnival. He makes Federal policemen and soldiers
effeminate. Blandly he pictures an aristocrat's ball (an event
of the time), as a dance of perverts.

Chronologically last Posada chooses from Vanegas Arroyo's
"Street Gazette" (leaflets recording usually miracles and remarkable crimes) strikes, mobs, anti-Diaz meetings, dispersed
by the buckled and sworded police. Madero enters the capital
and Posada makes him bow and smile like a puppet. In the
earthquake which heralds his entrance at dawn on the day of
the parade, Posada symmetrically crashes the Mexican world
into shards. When the metropolitan press later describes Zapata
as a bloody, pernicious and monstrous "Attila of the South"
(about fifty miles south) and pictures Villa, echoing American reporters as a kind of genial Robin Hood, Posada
makes Villa plumply ambitious; of Zapata he builds somber
grandeur.

By implication not evident in the text he was illustrating; by
interpretation grown of conviction; because of his shafted
laughter; because of enormous pity and tranquil clairvoy-

ance, Posada is the prophet of that sudden shift in the national scene which comes with the revolution. There is a different reliance on miracles. Hope walks out of its mystic garments and girdles itself with bullets.

Guadalupe Posada the illustrator of ballads was smilingly aware of the genteel National Academy of Arts around the corner from his hole-in-the-wall workshop. Possibly he used its excellent library. Doubtless he occasionally nodded to a couple of restive youngsters who, on their way back from the pedagogues, elbowed each other in front of his window (as after on mural scaffolds), and cut off some of his light. Orozco and Rivera both were impressed by one thing in that window besides the artist himself. This was a very fine print of Michael Angelo's *Last Judgment*.

III.

The first revolutionary songs that Posada illustrated were ballads of love and exile, and prophetic lyrics like this:

> Suppose we were chaff, that was lying about
> When a very small whirlwind brushed us to the sky,
> And then at the moment when we sailed highest,
> A wind that was stronger blew us apart. . . .

Of ballads, Posada illustrated two classics, the prisoner and the soldier. These lovely things ache still in every singing voice of the land. They are very old. They span revolutionary history, and make it. The prisoner is "The Prisoner of San Juan de Ulua", a fortress built down into the waters of the Gulf of Mexico just off the coast of Veracruz. Here Diaz buried conscientious objectors. In a ballad-picture, one of them jumps off the parapet into the bellies of sharks below. The chant says in part:

I am imprisoned behind the bars
A prisoner I must remain;
I cannot weep, and from my heart
I sing my sadness and my pain.

In the morning I was taken
They sat me on a bench;
By the judge's verdict, deliberate
Guilty to prison I was sentenced.

It is no longer the boat or sail
That waits for me on the open waves,
In San Juan de Ulua, the terrible jail,
I'll end my sorrows and my days.

The ballad of the soldier is the story of a Federal, one of the
Diaz army. Any one.

At the age of fifteen,
Pressed into service
I was made a soldier
Of the fifteenth of Puebla.

I followed the profession
Happy and content
When some time had passed
They made me a sergeant.

Then I did not like
Fighting any more,
So I deserted
And went back home.

I was in my house,
With my poor mother,
When the patrol
Came sword in hand for me.

Señores, señores,
How do I harm you?
You rascal, you scoundrel
Deserted from the army.

Now they are taking him
To the colonel for trial
And his poor mother
Follows him crying.

Now they are dragging him
There by the hands,
And they burst fountains
Oh, blood of his veins!

Goodbye my old quarters
With its many doors,
Goodbye my lieutenant
And my corporal Dolores.

Be careful, be careful
Soldiers and drummers
He goes out tomorrow
To be shot with the others.

Goodbye little brothers,
Dear parents, farewell
Here my sins end,
I have no more to tell.

56. THE HANGED MAN
Scene of the Revolution

When the revolution was an act; when Madero, refused
sanctuary in the American Embassy, had been shot by people
who next Easter appeared in effigy on telephone posts; and
Villa filled the foreign press and his leather breeches with the
figure of the Mexican Bad Man, Posada died. He had caught
up the past and etched it to the future in hundreds of dramatic
little pictures permanent till dust and the ink of many reprintings erase them. He had sketched in two inches monumental
figures, national epics, that later grew to ten and fifteen feet
high on frescoed walls. His women are the rearguard of
gunned pilgrims thereafter; and the madonnas, the sweethearts, whose wooings became marching songs. Thus *Adelita,*
the Villa musical herald, sung always with spatter of bullets
and whoops at the end of each stanza:

> Adelita is the name of a maiden
> Whom I love though we be so far apart,
> She's a rose growing somewhere in a garden,
> That some day I will pin on my heart.
>
> If Adelita went off with another,
> Ceaseless her road I would gain,
> If by sea in a warship I'd follow,
> If by land in a military train.
>
> Adelita is a girl of the border,
> Green as the sea are her eyes,
> The soldiers all dream about her,
> Every one of them for Adelita cries.
>
> Oh, the bugle that calls us to battle,
> And the bugle that calls us to review
> In my soul echoes always your name only,
> Adelita my heart longs for you.
>
> If some day I am killed in a battle,
> If my body on the sierra is to lie,
> Adelita, if God will allow it,
> To the sierra you shall go and cry.

And thus *Valentina,* the Zapata shriek, sung by Indians disappeared under great sombreros or in the cracks of the hills, on horseback:

> Valentina, Valentina,
> Valentina I must say,
> I am driven by a passion,
> That is what brings me today.
>
> Because of this love, they have told me
> I'll suffer and pay, and pay
> Who cares, if it was the devil
> I'll be killed in my own way.
>
> If now I'm drinking tequila,
> Tomorrow I guzzle fine wine,
> Because today I'm a poor man,
> Tomorrow I shall be gone.
>
> Valentina, Valentina,
> Listen to what I shall say,
> If I'm to be dead tomorrow
> Let them kill me right away . . . !

57. THE PILGRIMS

CHAPTER TEN

T R A V A I L

The revolution in the south was Zapata, the story of a cause. The revolution in the north was Villa, and this was the legend of a man. Villa, the hero of women, poets, and the unredeemed poor, crystallized his philosophy in significant slang: *"Qué chico se me hace el mar para hacer un buche de agua. . .* I'll use the ocean to gargle!"

58.

Doroteo Arango, later Francisco Villa, was the son of a peasant stable-cleaner on a ranch in Chihuahua. Almost shorn of legend, he appears in boyhood a shock-headed, grubby-faced, morose youth, chopping wood in the forests, peddling buttons and trifles on a cinnamon coloured burro for maize to deceive the family hunger.

At the age of fourteen, say the ballads, with considerable scandal he removed the tyrannic foot from his neck. Villa had a beautiful sister. The son of the hacendado was lustful and greedy, in feudal tradition. One night he was seen in the shadow of the family hut. The boy bullied a confession out of his sister. Then he vowed furiously vengeance. First he went to the seducer and demanded that he marry the girl. The hacendado laughed at him. He went again, and this time he was the subject of a petulant order. "They just about broke my bones in the beating they gave me", said he always at this point of his story.

He began to save pennies most patiently, and after many

weeks he bought a very old, very rusty gun. In the bush of a trail through which his consecrate enemy sporadically rode, Villa watched nightly for six months. At last luck turned Don Juan his way. Villa, stepping out in his path, properly muttering bitterness and triumph, shot the young man (who had long forgotten the presumptuous peon and his raped sister) quite dead. Then he took himself and his not very trusty gun to the hills.

He was captured by government rangers and put in jail. An order came to convey him to another jail. This he knew for his death warrant, according to the infamous Diaz "fugitive law". An innocent removal from one jail to another jail, on horseback across open country, was almost infallibly the first step of its application. Next came a stop at a creek, where the prisoner was asked if he were thirsty, and was allowed to stoop down for a drink. The finale was an official note recording the death of an escaping criminal.

"My jailmates told me goodbye sadly", Villa would preface this chapter of his reminiscences. "At a beautiful little river, the captain said to me, 'Muchacho, aren't you thirsty?'

" 'Are you going to kill me already?' I asked him. He looked me up and down, and down and up, and then said, 'Drink, boy, no one will hurt you.' Afterwards he admitted that he really had orders to apply fugitive justice to me, but that I looked like such a fine youth, and promised so well, that he relented. Since then I've never doubted my luck."

He broke out of jail and again took to the hills, where, with his *compadre* or "pal" Urbina, he followed the only profession now open to him, that of banditry. Beginning with an occasional pack burro here, and a stray steer there, they managed within a comparatively short time to build up a thriving business. The gang stole cattle from rich ranches, dried the meat and sold it at a distance from its point of disappearance. The system was perfectly organized and Villa was a bold and capable chief. Supply therefore never failed the demand for their popular delicacy.

However probably the rangers grew troublesome, because Villa crossed the border and, he said, as one of Roosevelt's Rough Riders learned American army tactics and represented the stars and stripes in Cuba. With the first stir of the revolution of 1910 he was back in Mexico ambitiously. It was at this time he took the name of Villa, after a famous bandit of his native province. He succeeded Villa the First like a conscientious Elisha, staged sensational raids on haciendas with a flourish, gave to the poor money, food, and advice; showered manna and serenaded the yawning Lady Revolution chivalrously.

Personal attraction, skill as a leader, many promises, and some excellent oratory on his behalf, gathered to him as good a gang as any outlaw heart might desire. Villa, bandit, became then Villa crusading guerrilla. He preached revolt, paralleling Madero's fantastic soap-boxing in central Mexico, Carrillo Puerto's idealistic beginnings in Yucatan, the A.B.C. lessons in socialism of Plutarco Elias Calles the country schoolmaster. He was ardently Maderista, but he went very little into theory. He promised the only justice he conceived, which was a reversal of the good things from top to bottom, with prizes for the brave.

When Madero became president Villa was told by a political leader, who called himself a "red", that Madero was not a revolutionist, but merely a reformer, and pointed to his uncomfortable writhing in the face of the American Ambassador as proof of the saviour's unworthiness. Villa thereupon turned against him, but when Huerta, Madero's Minister of War, betrayed him with the compliance of the American representa-

59. THE FLAG
   Lithograph by Jose Clemente Orozco

tive, Villa remorsefully turned against Huerta too. Popular
sympathy turned with him.

To Villa came then poor devils of peasants, out for loot and
social vengeance; adolescent dreamers, disturbed by too obvious
misery too often; philosophers and poets, the intellectual martyrs of a suffering mass, hoping to bring Utopia, or at least
frijoles, to that mass; cut-throats and jailbirds, finding safety in
numbers, and other advantages; girls who had not yet learned
resignation to justice, and women who did not give a hang
about either justice or the proletariat. They all chased their
dreams on horseback and they did it Villa fashion.

"We learned", one of the men on his personal staff relates,
"berrenda tactics. The berrenda is a very swift deer that is
everywhere and nowhere, here today and yonder also today.
We learned real values, such as horseflesh and distance, with
our bodies. We learned to ride like hell, to eat when there was
food and to sing when there was none. When we had to move,

and move fast and silently, we shifted from horse's back to horse's back night into day at a gallop. He knew the roads, we thought, by smell. It was glorious, and heartbreaking. Men, good men, killed and more killed, and ten in the place of each come also to get killed. But how we loved him!"

Huerta's government pursued Villa listlessly. When Huerta fell Villa became an accepted fighting candidate, a champion of Mexican destinies. He swept the entire north in his train. The peasants who stayed at home, spied for him, fed him, and dreamed about what he was going to do for them. Once several of them were captured by Villa's opposition and tortured to tell his whereabouts.

"Where is Villa?"

"*Pues,* señor, who knows?"

"If you don't tell where he is you'll be shot."

"Yes, señor." And so on through the lot, each interview ending with the promised execution.

The guerrilla band was now become the famous "Invincible Division of the North". Villa and Carranza, both northern men, first allies against Huerta, split, each disclaiming they wanted the presidency, but each determined to be autonomous. Began the struggle that rocked Mexico, the great furnace that twisted and melted and smudged the accumulated building of four centuries. The land lay sacrificed, darkly patient. Villa, with the United States supposedly behind him; (because, it was whispered, he had been thought potentially malleable) with a well equipped and almost disciplined army, was hailed the Napoleon of Mexico. His name blossomed internationally, and hope and hurrahs made that image: horse, pistol, mustaches, amours,—the Mexican Bad Man. It was then Villa expressed a desire to gulp the ocean.

John Reed described the guerrilla at this time: "He is the most natural human being I ever saw. Natural in the sense of being nearest to a wild animal. He says almost nothing and seems so quiet as to be almost diffident. His mouth hangs open and if he isn't smiling he's looking gentle. All except his eyes, which are never still and full of energy and brutality. They are intelligent as hell and as merciless. The movements of his feet and legs are awkward—he always rode a horse—but those of his hands and arms are extraordinarily simple and direct. They're like a wolf's."

Austere physical discipline and pure hero-worship made many men fit seconds to their chief. Stories are multiple of their exploits, not a few like the tale of how Villa and his personal escort alone, won a renowned battle. They had gone out to reconnoiter, and stumbled into the pickets of a large detachment of Carranzistas. "There comes Pancho Villa with the whole Division of the North!" shouted one of the enemy scouts, terrified.

"Yes, you son of an unlucky mother, the whole Division of the North", Villa yelled back, "and if you don't surrender, we'll disembowel the lot of you!" They surrendered; and were forced to wait, disarmed, several mortifying hours until a few squads of the Division of the North came to march them into corral.

Villa breathed power. His lieutenants whitened if his dinner went wrong, for ill-temper made their chief's suspicions dynamic, and he was very suspicious. His one friend, he said, was his gun. Disloyalty maddened him. He would risk his life and the success of a big offensive to punish it, as he did in the case of his old friend "Butcher Urbina". "And though you hide under a pebble", Villa had said to him, "if you ever betray me, I'll dig you out and bury you again". Urbina despatched, Villa galloped home to his dinner, a frugal one as usual.

Two luxuries the Bad Man allowed himself. The first, which he did not consider a luxury at all, was women. The second was flattery. He was always deeply touched by loyalty; and he so craved friendship that he wooed even its monstrous caricatures. The merest court fool could "fondle his beard", as one says in Spanish. He had a poet laureate whose sole and important duty was to add to the many verses already sung about and to Don Pancho. When Villa listened it might be death to disturb him. The story is told of an orderly, driven frantic by an equally frantic officer in doubt about a clearly unnecessary execution, who entered in the middle of a stanza. Villa shot him over the neck of the guitar.

So long as the revolution in the north was guerrilla warfare, of the Mexican type, whose strength lies in elusiveness and sudden ubiquity, Villa could indeed be the Invincible Division of the North. Personal trusts and distrusts for army hierarchy, impulses for campaign plans, emotions for political consciousness, and long-sensitive instinct about when to swoop and when to run, were equipment for handling a genial gang, than which none could be fitter. His later big army, requiring some kind of military operative form, marching against troops under Obregon's literate strategy, defeated Villa.

The military genius on his staff was Felipe Angeles, a brilliant, cultured, tactful man, one of several who hoped Villa would be the physical lever of national rehabilitation. Better a primitive, they thought, comparing him with Carranza, than a schemer. Had Villa kept the wisdom, or the humbleness, that earlier made him listen to Angeles, Carranza's bright young generals might not have disproved the invincibility of the Division of the North. "But I committed the folly", Villa afterwards admitted, "of believing myself a military genius". The biggest frog-in-the-puddle urge that after all generated his power, made him shortsighted, hotheaded, and measured his downfall. Yet because of that urge, he jumped human hurdles lithely and picturesquely. It was very appealing.

II.

I was graduated from *Maderista* and the nursery to *Villista* when his heroes came to Aguascalientes retreating before the Carranza army under Obregon, and established their head-quarters for what proved to be Villa's biggest and last campaign. They came confident still, singing ballads of their triumphs, vowing in verse to make of Carranza's beard a cockade for their beloved Don Pancho. Convincing, this account of an early triumph:

> Allright, you old drunkard Huerta
> your bad heart will skip a beat
> when you learn, in Zacatecas
> your Barrón has met defeat.
>
> You may be thinking, said Villa
> there is a hard fight ahead
> but I've got my little roosters
> of those that to spurs are bred.
>
> All the streets of Zacatecas
> that day were paved with dead;
> and the hills around the city
> looked like a monstrous sheep-herd.
>
> The Federals were so frightened
> most of them ran away
> dressed like Indians and like women
> while their comrades round them lay.

The Division of the North traveled in the manner classic to Mexican revolutionaries. Troop trains scrambled and trudged in ceaselessly, bristling with soldiers, gorged to the windows with women and spoils that spilled out on the roof and the ground. Slung under the cars in blankets, men rode in asleep. One with the weariest, brownest face in the world, on the girder which held the wheel within six inches of his head, had lashed an important alarm clock.

They camped in front of our house, a soldier to a tree. His woman unrolled the blankets and spread a petate on the roots, drove nails into the trunk for hats and dug out a niche for an image. If you adventurously walked the avenue you had to be careful or you'd step on somebody's baby and dive into somebody's stew. Sometimes, when the women quarreled—one remembers about a revolutionary army, first the women—they rolled over and over in the dust, their hands buried in each other's hair, biting, scratching, dirty skirts flying and beads scattering, till the men, tired of this amusement (which didn't end, like a cock-fight) roughly pushed them apart.

There was always the noise of bugles and the shuffled march of sandaled feet; always the smell of scorching frijoles and prickling chile, always the rattle of gossip, always the patter of women's hands making tortillas and never a moment there was not the wail of a new child and the haunt of an old song.

60. DANCE OF THE TOP-HAT
Drawing by Jose Clemente Orozco

The churches were full. Young girls would come to the picket fence and beg for flowers to take to Our Lady. Once a soldier, who looked very small for a soldier, came too, asking for roses to offer Guadalupe; answering to the banter that only women take flowers to Our Lady, that he was a woman, and removing his hat from a newly cropped head to prove it.

A great tourist hotel across a field from our garden was turned into a hospital. One day we had the medical staff and some officers to lunch. The doctors, odorous of their make-shift calling, ate hardboiled eggs out of the shells with their knives, and told tales—a soldier who, dying, shouted Viva Carranza! in the teeth of the Villistas around him . . . tales of limbs gangrened and hacked off in the quick, without anes-thetics (there were none) with a flip of a *machete*. . . We were sent away from the table after this story. So we went to a window and watched the regiment take a bath in the irrigation canal that ran down the length of the avenue. There wasn't enough room for all the army in the water, so it prome-naded by turns nude along the thoroughfare, between washes.

Threading details of those days they are strange. Mobile youngsters with baskets, hanging to the shawls of their moth-ers, spiraling before the doors of the warehouse for the moment the dispensary of maize. Which were Villista people and which servants, or the wives of peons off trailing in one of the other armies, one could not tell. Their rebozos were all the same colour, dusty; they all turned their faces up to the big posters nearly every day new on a nearby wall, nearly all of them (for I went there and spelled them aloud to the crowd, which was very appreciative) promising liberties and other advantages in the name of the face on the poster, General Blank.

A colonel about to be married came to ask my mother for pretty ices, which were ordered made. At midnight on the night of his wedding a rhythmic crash with the butt of a gun on our front door set the nurses to singing hymns. It was his orderly bearing a tray of festal food, "with the colonel's compliments". The soldier women wistfully would knock on the high door of the cattle-corral and ask for milk. There was never enough for all of them, and on the ranch the soldiers were quartering the cattle. I'd see a circle of men around a plunging, bellowing calf, with ropes tied to its hoofs and a soldier hanging on each, in a tug-of-war to split a haunch first. Live meat ripped open glints rose and blue in the sun. . .

My father went once to "Butcher Urbina" to protest such waste. The general received him, he says, in a little room, sitting on bags of maize and coins. At first Urbina wanted to shoot him for an impudent foreigner, remarking that also, somebody in the army could wear to great comfort his to-be-discarded shoes. But neither Urbina nor my father were very ill-tempered that day, and the general graciously gave a sealed order to be presented to the lieutenants on the ranch. It read: "Don't kill Mr. Brenner's milch cows, but kill all the rest of them."

A former groom, tired of being Carranzista, came home with wornout sandals and many scraps of white damask from rifled churches, to make new baby-clothes for the Infant Christ, he said. He had tales of how the women danced to the *Cucaracha*, that mad chant, with their mouths open and their skirts pulled up on their legs, after a battle yelping:

> The little cockroach, the little cockroach
> Will not travel any more,
> Because it wants some, because it has no
> Marihuana smoke to blow!

They would carry gilded chairs and parrots plundered from mansions, on their horses, and tire of the chairs and use them for firewood, as if they had been pianos or big altar-pieces.

This man found a wallet of Villa money, worthless the moment the town changed generals, and spent it therefore breathlessly all in one day, with my delighted help. We bought several bushels of doughnuts and three crates of green figs, and five pairs of enormous shoes and several dozen bandannas. Then he tired of singing the *Cucaracha* and learned the *Adelita,* and went off with the piece of an army; came back talking about Chihuahua, where they were hanging so many people that the trees were black clusters of buzzards. The corpses made such curious gestures and faces after they'd hung a while, he said, that it was very interesting to observe them. The city came on Sundays, sight-seeing, and drank lemonade and ate peanuts on the site, to refresh itself.

One day Villa himself, a pair of mustaches on a round amiable face, two very taut short legs, a cloud of dust and a plunging horse, galloped suddenly past the front door, and this meant a battle almost in the backyard. He was reviewing some specially imported savages, fighters from the north. He disappeared at the end of the double-file of great bronze Indians, naked except for red loincloths, arrows fastened to their belts, beads dropping on bare chests and feathers twisted into heavy black hair that hung, tangled, over their eyes on a line with their necks; bulged forearms thrust through man-high bows, and profiles of unbearable sharpness—a carved immobile frieze.

Aeroplanes droned industriously on the other side of the irrigation ditch that day. That night, rumble of carts, spies to be shot or rich men who would not contribute to revolutions, to be threatened and possibly hanged. Bugles, endless shuffle of feet; and music from bivouac dancing, till dawn. Morning of shining sun and new-hatched ducks in the garden pool, and salmon pink carnations just burst into bloom. Behind the Hill of the Cross, where we usually went on picnics, a shaking, a

lazy grumbling, growing monotonously louder. . . With
noon, the house walls quivered sympathetically and women
began running in, dipping their shawls in the pool (disturbing
the pale green ducks) to freshen the mouths of their wounded
. . . Cows mooing, servants whimpering. . .

Then a line of stretchers, first slackly spaced, then linked like
a moving factory-belt, past the door, to the hospital. Blood
drops dimpling the dust, and feet making mud of it. Buckets
of filth showered heavily from the hospital windows, making
little hills of dark stained cotton below them. Voices following
the filth, calling to Jesus to let them die. From the hospital,
meeting the belt of stretchers, a shifting line of coffins, a black
ribbon hung on the day.

Villa had lost. That night he shuffled and bugled his army
away. Then the jigging sound of the Cucaracha, smells of burning, and shadows—hardly more sensed than shadows—of
bodies gibbeted on trees. . . New faces ringing the trees in
the avenues, more women cooking and quarreling, more naked
swollen-bellied children wedging their faces into the garden
to watch the baby ducks beginning to paddle. Again girls asking for flowers to take to the Virgin. New colour of official
money. Pink tickets this time.

Carranza became president. Villa was again in the hills. He
and the few hundred men he retained managed to keep Mexico
discomforted. He flared out against the United States, flamed
erratically from mountain to valley, crippled railroads, burned
ranches, frustrating even the gestures of reconstruction. Chihuahua he captured by smuggling into it soldiers who were
peasants disguised as peasants, in their civilian white, with
crates of vegetables and chickens to feed the hungry city.
Once in, they turned off the lights and opened a bombardment
on the garrison. What a *vacilada!*

Villa held Chihuahua for the sole purpose, he said, of "show-

ing the gringoes that Carranza is a poor devil and Villa a real
man". His last gesture was the Columbus raid. This invasion
of United States territory brought to his relish upon him the
same general who once had cordially, or diplomatically, embraced him. Villa with his seasoned rebels and his intimacy
with the hills, against Pershing with several thousand lumber-
ing, cannon-hampered, rule-encumbered recruits, played Mexican mountain cat to American domestic rat. The battles were
farce. Villa would squat in high caves and review the Pershing
army regularly. He got himself killed and resuscitated in
the American press, daily. He had a gorgeous time. Popular
sympathy was his again, and many new poems garlanded him.
This is one song of the moment:

> Mother mine of Guadalupe
> Bless this soldier of your nation,
> Tomorrow I march to the war,
> The war against intervention.
>
> Oh beautiful Guadalupe
> Sacred and beloved Virgin
> You must not let the gringoes
> Consume the blood of your children.
>
> Maybe they think that the Indians
> Have by now all disappeared,
> But there are plenty of us
> To whom liberty is still dear.
>
> Maybe they have guns and cannons,
> Maybe they are a lot stronger,
> We have only rocks and mountains
> But we know how to last longer.
>
> Go look somewhere else for riches
> Must you with greed be so blind
> That you can't see you have left us
> Nothing except the rind?

Came the overthrow of Carranza, Villa's personal target, by
Obregon. Overtures from the new president found the guer-

rilla wisely ready to settle. But he settled at his pleasure. At one swoop he lighted with his men on Mexico's biggest coal-mines. Right hand on the telegraph instrument and left on a dynamite bomb, Villa, renegade again and bandit, exacted from the president the privileges he was granted; or at least that is the tale. He was given an enormous hacienda, money and machinery enough for all of his "boys", and the consideration due a retiring gentleman. Simultaneously the sub, semi, and pseudo Villas also went back to the land, and with him changed their titles from General to Don. It was a neatly dramatic forging of machetes to tractors.

When Villa was peacefully assassinated in the fall of 1924, his epitaph was a universal sigh of regret and relief. He left behind him, stories to find in the bottles of old people whose guerrilla day is past, and stories that flow from the fountain pens of the poets who rather hoped but never quite believed Villa would save whatever it was they wanted saved; songs, many songs, and a scattering of wives who harvest the only material crops of that fame which is now legend.

III.

Call Villa a popular hero, but not Zapata. He is the traditional martyr to the land, the man who consciously dies as a symbol. The ballads that mourn for Zapata are like hymns. As this one:

> Señores, I bear a corrido
> That is silver to the ears,
> The death of Zapata I'm singing
> News that must bring many tears.
>
> There lived in Cuautla, Morelos
> A very singular man,
> All the people and their neighbors
> Followed under his command.

Beloved by all his people
He was considered the leader,
None of them want to forget him
They will remember his teaching.

His teaching was no new doctrine. It was the creed that "the land belongs to him who works it with his hands", melodramatized, made tragedy, by this man who contained in himself an old spirit, an old attitude, not by words, nor by personal idiosyncracy, but by the intensely native pattern of his life.

Emiliano Zapata was a *ranchero,* a small landowner, one of those who cultivate their own maize and give affectionate nicknames to their proud yoke of oxen. They are different from peons chiefly in that instead of white cotton they wear close-fitting tawny or gray leather, clamped to their persons with silver buttons. In appearance Zapata at first glance was typically the charro who valiantly straddles his horse and waves his goblet on nearly any pulqueria wall: the ideal, habitual ranch he-man. But really observed, Zapata was remarkable. Tall, lean, slid into dull close black; with a blood-red or a purple scarf about his throat; his face sheer bone, smoothly fleshed, built triangularly to his chin; his eyes gray, filmed, distant, pooled under the wall of his forehead; his mouth firm, silent, richly modelled; and over it two enormous mustachios, dropped like a Chinese priest's, accentuating the pull of his brooding jaws.

Zapatism, the thing that he meant to both city and peasantry, was a familiar and hopeful idea to his neighbours. They were perhaps the only rebels of the thousands who lustily, wearily, desperately, gleefully, or recklessly did with their lives violence, who could have described what they wanted. To the city, Zapatism was sinister, terrible. Indians in revolt! Human sacrifice would be their formula. To the soldiers who fought against it, Zapatism meant enormous upward-winged som-

breros jumping from rock to rock and disappearing, and reap-
pearing behind them; glimpsed around trees and still there,
comically still, riddled with bullets; when captured, only sombreros. For the heads that had filled them, recrowned, bore
other sombreros circling forever behind, over, suddenly in their
faces.

The Zapatista under his great petate sombrero was a slight,
taut person dressed in white cotton, girdled in crimson or
black, sandaled, and hung with enormous cartridge-belts;
astride a horse lean and agile, harmoniously flexible to himself. Horse and rider were a single vengeful being. It carried
sometimes a gun wrested from whoever had owned it, and
always a machete, the wide-bladed curved knife which had
served to harvest Morelos sugar-cane and now swept other
crops. When the Zapatista attacked, he invoked the Lady of
Guadalupe sewn to his hatband, expected the aid of his allied
Malintzins and Tepoztons and nevertheless chanted his "If I
am to die tomorrow, let them kill me right away . . ." When
a Zapatista fell his wife or his son or his uncle or his brother
donned his sombrero, and between gallops meditated:

> In the crown of a sombrero
> We bore the brains of his head;
> Let them serve henceforth to soften
> So many hearts made of lead.

Zapata became a rebel in his own mind much before the
missionaries of Madero supplied a social doctrine to uphold
him in their minds. A neighbouring hill village, bordering on
a huge estate, was flagrantly, suddenly violated, so flagrantly
that even the Diaz courts, subservient to hacendados, declared
that the 300 disputed hectares had been unlawfully taken, and
must be returned. Instead, the documents entitling the village
to its plot, disappeared. So Zapata led the townspeople to their

raped fields and forcibly restored them. He was arrested and put in the army.

It is said that in the capital he served as a groom to a rich general. The pampered horses, the gleaming stables, contrasted bitterly with the miserable huts and the atrociously starved and mistreated peons on the same rich man's—or his friends'— estates. In the whispering days toward the end of Diaz's nth presidential term Zapata had slipped back to his native Morelos and was earnestly converting grim picked men to Madero's standard. With him went metropolitan poets and patriots who supplied the words and did secretarial duty to their chief, and who afterwards forgot their theories and based a powerful political philosophy on the things they learned in the "Army of the South", which was then known as the "Horrendous Horde."

Zapata raided haciendas much in the manner of Villa, but he did not plunder, distribute, and consume as Villa. First, while doubtless his army looted boudoirs, he marched into the estate office and put a match to its documents and titles. Then he mapped out the surface and allotted even portions to the peons living upon it. He opened the jails, and the prisoners followed him like grateful starved dogs. Each village, every hut, was a garrison, storehouse, and courier; was eyes, ears, rampart and beanpot to him. When he rode down to them from his hills the path was scattered with flowers.

Madero, when Diaz was appropriately gnashing his teeth in the vessel that bore him to Paris, was taken out to Morelos to see the peasant leader, possibly to try to persuade him that his battles were all won. They met in the picturesque tourist town of Cuernavaca. There was a great crowd in the plaza. The band played, the palms flirted. The women swirled their skirts and twinkled their fans. Madero stood in the limelight and courageously held out his arms to the big mountain chief, and declaimed: "Now, my true-hearted and incorruptible General Zapata, let us unite in a single sentiment, and, bound together in brotherly embrace, let us shout before these nameless heroes: 'Long live Democracy!' Hurrah for Liberty!"

Embraced, Zapata looked off over the head of the virtuous president and said: "All right, Señor Madero. But, let me say, if you don't keep your promises", touching his gun demonstratively, "one bullet shall be for you, and the rest for the other traitors". Madero, being a cultured man and sincerely convinced that in his doctrines lay salvation, was, he said, a little surprised at the untactful simplicity of the peasant, but he smiled; and Señora Madero was heard remarking: "Was there ever such an impudent Indian!"

The ballad accounts of what happened after are perhaps a little unfair to Madero. He wears as a martyr rightfully (and more gracefully than ever he did alive) the title of Liberator. But the ballad accounts give the story.

Zapata fought for Madero, and helped his plans to succeed
So that then, little by little, they could fulfill his ideas;
They won a great victory after they had fought awhile
And all of their troops then marched into the capital.
Zapata was very glad to see that Madero won
For the workers of the land, now he said the land would own.
Those promises that he made, there in San Luís Potosí
In the plan that he proclaimed, Madero could not fulfill
Having arisen to power by means of what he proclaimed
Once that he had succeeded, he should have kept to his word.

Time passed, and Zapata waited for the promise that was made;
Of promise and promised lands, no longer a word was said.
Waiting for what never happened, seeing the last hope fail,
Zapata rose up in arms, at the Hill of the Nightingale.
If Madero has forgotten, and has furled the glorious banner
Though my life be the price of it, I'll make good my *Plan de Ayala*.
These were the words of Zapata: Land and Liberty for all;
And through the state of Morelos many men came to his call.

The Zapatista troop earned its name of Horrendous Horde. Orgies, outrageous and preposterous, celebrated the possession of each hacienda. Brutal tortures were inflicted on every man caught who was not wearing the religious costume of sandals, white cotton, and petate hat. As a disguise it did not serve, because corns are easily visible between the leather thongs of peasant footgear, and peasants don't have corns. They would dance, these shocked and delicate men, nude, crowned with a top hat; dance with the bullets spattering under their heels. The rebels stabled their horses in mirrored bedrooms and rubbed them down inside church doors. Smudges and blood mark nearly all the strong walls, nearly all ruined, in Morelos.

Said Zapata: "We must frighten them; we must terrify them; because if they do not fear us they will never listen to us. . ." And he added: "Let them curse me now. Afterwards they will lift me up as the martyr who sacrificed his own good name and happiness to the need of his people". A journalist familiar with the camp life of the agrarian chief relates the following story: "The general and his staff were supping, when a dispatch arrived, containing a newspaper account of an exploit of one of the Zapatista generals, the terrible Genovevo de la O. A train had been attacked, the passengers had been lined up and plundered, jewels were torn from the bleeding ears and fingers of the wearers. The rebels had their choice of the women. The men were mutilated indescribably and sent naked into the mountains. Zapata, hearing this, dictated a telegram to his subordinate: "My dear Genovevo: Fine work. Congratulations."

His family says that Zapata was a kind man. It would take courage even in an ungentle person, to perform systematically and deliberately as he did, human sacrifice. Abstractly too, because it seems probable he was not wilfully lustful and certainly he gleaned no fortune by it. In the end it was himself he sacrificed. He did it in the name of the land, as if he had been doing it in the name of Our Lady of Guadalupe, like Hidalgo. His upsetting reasoning, that this was the only way to achieve what seemed to him the only thing worth achieving by a revolution, has been proved correct reasoning. He did what he set out to do. He forced recognition of the problem he put first, as the first problem. Not, however, till he died.

The Zapatistas besieged Mexico City for several years. As they drew closer and closer around the city of palaces, the dwellers within felt sure they were being poisoned by that terrible vicinity. They would not drink the water that is piped to the capital from the suburbs, because how could it be possible that Zapata at the source had not envenomed it? They feared those Indians with the accumulated guilt and unease of their four vain centuries. When Zapata marched into the capital it might have been an American invasion that was expected, the way the shutters were locked and the children kept off the streets.

It was wonderful to see that quiet, secure procession of men coming in, not as armies stamp, because they wore no boots, but with the steady glide of their daily walk. They quartered themselves in the governmental palace on the main plaza, elbowing the great churrigueresque cathedral. They chose the smallest rooms, in the rear. These were not dwellings at all, but garages, dark storehouses, and stables. In the palace itself their tread was quiet. They stood thoughtfully before a picture, a carving, the splendid curve of a stair. Hat in hand, they went to the museum. It was expected that they would promptly rifle the place. But they behaved as if they had been in church. And instead of taking away the pretty things, they brought contributions, and laid them there with votive gesture. The rhymed account of this invasion is votive too:

The hero and spartan Zapata was the victim of much slander,
And many people had judged him as a man without a standard;
They said he would burn and plunder when he marched into the city
For they thought that he was evil, had no character nor pity.
But when he arrived in the city they found that all was a lie
As the troop in sober order, one by one in line filed by.

They gave their thanks to the people who with them had sympathized
But the credit and the honor to the leader of their cause.
If I molested my hearer while I was singing this song,
Let me beg to be forgiven, as I intended no wrong.
My only wish is to crown, with narcissus and sweet laurel
The great Emiliano Zapata, loved by the poor and humble.

Every Federal government after Madero fought Zapata. He
was killed by a spy in the employ of Pablo Gonzalez, a general
of the Carranza army and an official in the Carranza regime.
The murderer "joined" Zapata's troop, and betrayed him.
Legend says that the Zapatistas knew the plan beforehand, and
that the person who was killed was not Zapata at all, but a
man who impersonated him to save his life. The leader inhabits a cave, it is said, and waits for the proper moment to
return. He cannot rest until the peasants have all their land.
Either he or his ghost walks the fields of Morelos at night, dragging something that clanks, chains, perhaps, it is thought;
and he bleeds into the furrows. It is in Morelos than one is
told: "Do not eat the first fruits of the year; they are nourished
with blood."

IV.

After Zapata the people all hoped that they could believe
what they sang, which was this:

> Now it is all the same army
> No need to fight any more,
> Comrades, the war is over
> Let us go back to our homes.

The soldiers who fought so bravely
While there was fighting on hand,
Let them now go serve the country
By cultivating the land.

If the seeds begin to grow
Helped by the God in his heaven,
Green fields from what we sow
Is the reward we are given.

When the rain begins to fall
Who is there that is not glad?
It is a sign to us all
There will be food in the land.

Gold by itself has no value;
We must have health and nutrition,
Gold is only the mainspring
Of this time and generation.

Now the field begins to flower
The stalk is heavy with maize,
Bearing the life of mankind,
The holiest thing that there is.

How beautiful is a wheatfield,
Those plants with a lovely head;
This year, if God is willing
We shall have enough bread.

After Zapata too, came the articulate voicing of his yearning, in sociological terms. He was painted and sung about officially. In Yucatan Felipe Carrillo Puerto took up the native cycle, and recapitulated the native martyrdom. Felipe—seldom any but his enemies called him Carrillo Puerto—was a Maya Indian largely by blood and entirely by conviction. In the days when Yaqui Indians were still being stripped and beaten on Yucatan henequen plantations, and Maya Indians were being starved and exiled in the peon tradition, Felipe translated the Mexican Constitution into Maya and used it as a bible from which he preached organization, rebellion, reclamation. He was the type of a priest, not a warrior. He was imprisoned, suffered terribly duly, and when the dictator was virtually dead, was organizing *Ligas de Resistencia* as nuclei of the peaceful social revolution he visioned. He was borne from the country to the city, troubadours following after, and eventually was made governor of his state. His reforms infuriated the solid people. He built roads, established schools, changed Yucatecan laws chiefly to the advantage of Indians and women.

Came one of the several reactions that have plunged revolutionary Mexico like a bucking horse backward on its haunches. Felipe neither armed himself nor gathered armies about him, and it was easy for the solid people to capture him. He was killed. This is the lament:

THE DEATH OF FELIPE CARRILLO PUERTO, MARTYR GOVERNOR OF YUCATAN.

Who would be able to say,
That in Yucatan, her son
Who gave freedom to her people
Would be killed by the Reaction.

Mother mine, Guadalupana,
You who wept for poor Juan Diego
When you saw him with bare feet,
Half naked, hungry, and weak,

From your balcony in heaven
Had you seen the Indian betrayed
A knife sticking in his back,
Dying, what would you have said:

Where were all your angels gone,
Where are they now, that below
They did not see treason done
And Carrillo Puerto is dead.

With your priests you are in bondage;
Leave your gold frames and your altars,
A free people gives you homage
Come to the plains and the sierras.

Let us go to see Felipe,
Little virgin, little soldier,
His blood spilled upon the earth
From the earth you shall recover.

De la Huerta, Prieto Laurens,
They are to blame, my madonna
But he who really killed Felipe
Is one Juan Ricadez Broca.

Prisoner they took him in Mérida
Between the night and the morning,
Bound, in a coach they then hurried him
To traitors that waited his coming.

Obeying his secret orders,
Just when the sun began rising,
Just when the day was at dawning
Broca said to him smiling:

I give you freedom, my brother,
Though I am forbidden to do so;
Before this day is another
I am commanded to shoot you.

Just follow this little passage
The door at the end is not closed,
But De la Huerta will crack me,
If you ever tell what I told.

Felipe believed the traitor;
Felipe was caught in the trap;
He had gone only two paces
When he was shot in the back.

Shot in the back by a coward
Stabbed in the neck with a knife,
Staining with his blood the paving,
Felipe gave up his life.

Mother mine of Guadalupe,
The blood of that execution;
Colors for us to remember,
Red and Black of the revolution.

61. THE REARGUARD
   Lithograph by Jose Clemente Orozco

> Felipe Carrillo Puerto,
> Murdered for keeping the faith;
> Weeping these verses end telling,
> The tale of Felipe's death.

The *Ligas de Resistencia* survive, wreathed in red and black banners, in bare headquarters, on the doors of which is carved or painted Felipe's adopted symbol, the international sickle and hammer. I do not know whether it is Maya youngsters or Maya patriarchs who gather there daily. I looked for them both in church one Sunday in a Yucatecan village, but when I asked where the church was, I was taken to the *Liga*.

More recently I visited a large hacienda in plateau Mexico, an estate which seems one of the last strongholds of feudal

Mexico. Great thick walls, the walls of a fortress, enclose a manorial park, which leads gently to a palace. The typical estate buildings occupy an enormous space. Patios, arched and flowered, recede into other patios. The corridors shine invitingly, avenue to serene drawing rooms and formal dining halls. On the right, a chapel; on the left, the offices; beyond that, a pulque brewery, and beyond that a nuns' house; behind, stables, bakeries, gardens, orchards. Across, a flat roof large enough for even fatiguing evening promenades; at each corner, a turret, parapetted, and on one turret, the Spanish-smacking estate flag. Outside the walls, cubbies of lava rock tumbled among cacti, for the hundreds of half-nude, hardly articulate peons. Over it all the lavender shimmer of this land whose hills are gashed deep rose by opal mines.

The estate is owned by a man naïvely tearful because the peons who knew him when he was a little boy, and who still call him by his first name—adding a Niño or a Don before, and drooping humbly, hat in hand, as they speak—let themselves be talked into "unions" and "agrarian leagues", and even strike for their usual maize when it is evident that maize is unusually rare and unusually expensive this year, and the estate has not raised enough and can't conveniently buy it. This man has just installed too, a lifesize plaster saint, modern Parisian.

I was invited to the estate festival, devoted to the divine patron of the place. When the festival was held before, there was mass in the chapel, and the people prayed there, elbow to elbow all day. This year there was no mass, and the secular accompanying festivities were tinged ominously, because agrarian strangers known to be dangerously inclined, had mounted the estate horses and were behaving as if they had been the chief people of the place. The great house therefore hardly looked out of its windows. It went to chapel, however, and conducted services for a half dozen women. Then it went outside and watched a few men in half-hearted costume dance at the chapel door. Totally the worshippers in the chapel were a pitiful numerical representation of the peonage. At twilight, when the prayers became wails, weird, ecstatic wails unbearable with pain, I left the chapel. Outside I asked a man where all the peons were, and why they had not come to the fiesta. "Oh," he answered, "they've left religion at present. Now they are going into agrarianism".

PART THREE

CHAPTER ELEVEN

I N V E N T O R Y

Eyes must be washed by tears to see. When in bivouac, in studio and library across the Rio Grande and in Paris, Italy, and Spain, trios and solitary men took spiritual inventory of themselves and their country in revolution, they discovered that they possessed an Indian tradition, an American racial heritage of essential grandeur. Not too dramatically the emigrés marched home. Then in quiet conversations with their *tierra* they wooed that dark Cinderella. But they reformed the tale, and instead of clothing the princess in cloth of gold they found her ashen garments regal, and espoused her.

One of the great among the returned was the anthropologist Manuel Gamio, who put into scientific terms a spirit that was the only inexhaustible ammunition of the armies, and is the life source of the moving and powerful revolution in Mexican art. Welding a *patria,* Gamio remarked, must not now be like the previous pedantic and fruitless attempts to "civilize" the Indian, to "incorporate" him to modern progress. Rather it must be a re-education of the literate.

Governments must study their people and territory with devotion, he said; must understand both integrally as one. "Otherwise," he concluded, "they are doomed to failure, for they cannot logically rule people whose nature and way of living they ignore; and the people, unable to live under systems arbitrarily forced upon them, will vegetate degenerate and weak, or will explode their justified protest in revolutions." Are the laws incomprehensible to the natives? Let the laws be changed. Are the authorities and teachers hampered because the citizenry do not behave as other citizenry upon whose systems this has been modelled? Let the authorities be taught, and if they err let them be punished. Let the native be the basic unit of the economic and cultural ideal. Is this reverting to barbarism? If it is, better barbarism than sterility.

To demonstrate what he meant by the phrase, "welding a patria," Gamio, at the head of a "National Department of Anthropology" created by himself, plotted out a region embracing the Valley of San Juan Teotihuacan. Here went "missionaries" who spent their time not teaching nor reforming, but studying. As a by-product of their studies certain economic and legal improvements were made in the modern villages of the valley, and the magnificent archeological monuments which were excavated set a proud gem in the forehead of the land.

The idea creatively described in this undertaking cannot be completely measured in terms of physical and economic results, however, though development in these terms is part of it. Gamio asked on the basis of his findings in Teotihuacan a welfare not primarily expressed in terms of economic betterment, more schools and roads and more hygiene. The fields must be returned to the peasant, he said, because this investiture meant much more to the peasant than physical welfare. It meant recognition of his birthright, and this meant real citizens added by their own acceptance, to the nation. Furthermore all Mexico must for its own sake give the peasant much more than sympathy, much more than smiling interest in his bazaar. Every inhabitant must identify himself in spirit with the peasant if he would call himself a legitimate son of the land.

The achievement of welding a patria means to Gamio a

unification on the basis of race and tradition and the deepest
and oldest desires. It means founding or continuing a style,
in the sense that artists use the word. When his scientific researches and sociological projects from the Valley of Teotihuacan had piled ponderous data on his desk for a resumé of his
findings, Gamio pushed them aside and called in an artist
to crown the pyramid. "It was necessary," he wrote, "that a
painter, a true painter, of sound technique, broad vision, highly
sensitive and with a keen analytic point of view, be sent to live
in the valley; to . . . identify himself . . . with the brilliant
blue heaven, the hostile arid mountains, the eternally verdant
plains; with the aged colonial temples of stately legend, the
timeless ruins breathing mythologic drama, and with the stark
huts grasped in the claws of the magueys and the cacti. . . He
must live with and become the brother of the native of the
valley, accept for himself so long as he remained, the customs, the ideals, the pain, the pleasure, the beliefs and amusements of that man."

II.

63.

The return to native values, spiritual and artistic, which is a simplified description of modern Mexican art, in the case of the founders of
this new tradition often occurred by way of modern European art. The gesture is very close to
rejection of European values, very near to the
violence of junking absentee landlordship. Fundamentally, however, the feeling that the artist
be also a person with a definite social attitude,
a consciousness that must determine his choices
in daily life and in his work; and the search for
structural values, and simplification, might be seen as deriva-
tions in Mexico, as also in Europe, of a mood more than local.

Only in Mexico this mood is expressed in art with naturalness and purity.

Racially, few of the revolutionary Mexican artists are pure Indian. In colour they deepen from indoor white to the richest sunned tinge. Most of them have had years of study and observation in Europe, and some have also been guerrillas. Others are too young for either. Of geographic and social tradition they bear widely disparate contribution. They are typically a Mexican troop. Also, they are a brotherhood much like that of the Renaissance, which drew men and ideas from all of Europe and Asia quite as Mexico does now from all of America and the old western world.

The primitives of this renaissance are conscious innovators. Those who chronologically earliest expressed its mood, as for example Siqueiros and Carlos Merida, are the most abstract. They were the natural link to Mexico from contemporary Europe. In Mexico the idea and form acquired confidently real flesh and bone. Merida may have inherited the quality of abstraction, the taste for pure plastic symbol, of his Maya grandfathers, and the elegance and intensity that accompanies abstraction in Maya art. Or perhaps he absorbed these things from the monuments on which from babyhood to youth he must have notched his stature.

Carlos Merida was born in Xelahu, Quetzaltenango, of Maya stock grafted once from the Spanish priesthood. He went to Paris still almost in his boyhood. There he lived with Modigliani and worked with Picasso, nevertheless persistently on the track of something his own. At the moment when around him many artists were obsessed with the idea of portraying movement with violence, Merida kept to a static design, (to prove, perhaps, that not all things must move to live). When his friends were all engaged in disintegrating colour and form and adding extra dimensions and planes he was elimi-

64. WOMEN OF METEPEC
    Oil, by Carlos Merida

65. PEASANT BOY
    Oil by Carmen Fonserrada

nating extra dimensions and integrating form and line, to the simplest juxtapositions of colour. After all his ancestors evidently agreed with Cézanne that the line is most perfect when the colour is at its best.

The nearest Old World comparison to Merida would be Byzantine mosaics, which also create the optical form by the position and value of each colour in relation to the others. The mosaics are nearer to bas-relief Maya murals, in plastic idea, than to Merida, because his work is done on a flat surface. By sheer spectroscopic calculation, a kind of colour geometry, he makes a three-dimensional image of two-dimensional materials, avoiding the illusions of chiaroscuro and baroque. He begins with the ultimate of pure painting, colour, which he serves with religious devotion. His life pivots on painting and his painting pivots on colour.

His own good taste and the chiseled civilization of Paris turns him without philosophic preamble to the most beautiful models. He paints people of the fields: cane-cutters, fruit vendors, weavers, women in rich mantles. He does not overemphasize the picturesque or emotional surface of his models, because he is an Indian himself, feels that it is a fine thing to be, and can go deeper directly. Serene, like his ancestors, he renders the beauties he perceives in abstract and monumental plastic concept. By poise, balance, rhythm, accuracy, he re-creates their mood of contemplation.

When Merida returned to America there was no sign of that organic movement that has been called the artistic revolution. In 1921 he exhibited a series of paintings at the National Academy in Mexico City. This institution was still a myopic serf of Europe. A movement that had been called a revolution had been initiated in 1916 by the picturesque and eloquent critic, writer, painter, labour organizer, medicine-man and chef Dr. Atl. Impressionism was his chief innovation. It was a late

date for such a début, and anyhow Joaquin Clausell, who belongs in time and quality to the best moment of the French
school, was continuing to create the Mexican version of it more
than adequately. Dr. Atl left the Academy to go dispensing
brand new peso bills from the industrious Carranza printing
presses to the masses, which were yet hungry and fighting.
After the Carranza machines were disabled Dr. Atl was engaged city-planning, photographing popular art, and commun-
ing with the volcano Popocatepetl. The Academy therefore resumed the decorous repose from which he had
roused it. Its product hardened into apologetic and dogmatic
mould.

Merida's exhibit nevertheless aroused a good deal of interest
outside of the Academy. By his uniquely quiet personality, and
the security of his work, and by learned articles in simple
language, he sowed the breeze of the later tempest. At the
time, Diego Rivera was still in cubist labour in Paris; Orozco
was satirically destroying old artistic and social rubbish by
newspaper caricature, making political enemies and enjoying
the notoriety bestowed upon him by the pseudo-venom of
pseudo-critics' pens; Siqueiros was in Spain; Goitia was collaborating, as Merida afterwards occasionally did, with Gamio at
Teotihuacan; and Charlot had just bought his ticket for Vera
Cruz. Goitia was the artist whom Gamio sent to "synthesize"
Teotihuacan, to go through the process of mental and spiritual
identification with the native landscape that Gamio prescribed
to every citizen, for the rehabilitation of the *patria*.

From her hacienda in Michoacan, Carmen Fonserrada was
travelling the same road. She was rebuilding her *patria* slowly,
thinking hard, driven by that need for clarification, for facing
of issues, common to all her sincere post-revolutionary—or
revolutionary—colleagues. Her vehicle was portraiture, a careful, compact formulation of the visual image, embracing the

psychological and social implications. By this attitude she produced what might be called essential realism.

Her few pictures are traditional, almost ritual, moments and personages of the Mexican ranch. Her days have been spent seeing the crops grow and the cattle driven to branding by small-waisted, agile riders on nimbly dancing ponies. Her landscape has been the moundlike hills of Michoacan, the saucer lakes, the fences crocheted of plump adolescent saplings; the women like birds; the canoe paddles like spoons. Of these delicate materials the native commentators can make blown glass filigree; and she, suave grandeur, with a flower in a corner of the canvas.

Carmen Fonserrada went to Mexico City after the painters' revolution had been manifestoed. She joined the Syndicate of Painters and Sculptors which was its guerrilla troop, and also became a member of a radical party. Much of her time was spent organizing unions and doing other work for labour groups. She held her first exhibition in 1923, when it was discovered that she had been "painting wall-size" in small frames. By the accepted views of her colleagues, this quality and her other activities made her one of the vanguard.

III.

The armed revolution is generally dated ended in 1921. The latter part of this year marks the organized beginning of the revolution in art. José Vasconcelos, a philosopher who had a record of service under Villa, had been a friend of Zapata, and was called *maestro de la juventud,* was made Minister of Education by President Obregon. Vasconcelos' cultural régime began in a fever of building, publishing, painting, planning. The enthusiastic and dynamic little Minister kept open forum and budget to ideas. He subsidized all kinds of experiments and projects, suppressing many of his personal preferences and tastes to patriotic curiosity and faith. The result was a new educational orientation whose point of departure is the legitimate most numerous native. This viewpoint was almost forced upon him, and through the channel of art.

Whatever was undertaken in the Secretariat usually became a project headed by some energetic painter. When the teachers sought for new or more adequate pedagogy than the French humanism on which they and the Minister had been nurtured, they found themselves introducing systems of education founded on native art. And when the teachers of art looked for a new procedure they ended by forgetting to look for æsthetic formulæ because they became so interested in the painted lives of their small pupils. They rediscovered the secret of the colonial missionary friars, who taught with images, and the pre- and post-Hispanic pivot of emotion and tradition, which was images, made of the Secretariat the temple of a new faith.

Who walked into this headquarters, or the National Preparatory School, or any one of a number of other buildings under the jurisdiction of Vasconcelos in 1922, might have been even frightened by the monumental activity of the people inside, and by their extraordinary appearance. Overalled painters straddled high planks between and upon intricate beams and cross-beams of scaffolds patterning their own architecture upon unfinished fresco walls. Knots of confused or converted spectators in the patios made ardent comment pro and con. Spread across thresholds and pinned over doors, large sheets of paper with geometrically carved charcoal sketches pulled declamatory attention to themselves. The typewriters and desks in the offices thus ornamented seemed powdered red and green and sienna and blue from the grinding-stones which laboured to supply the longed-for national palette.

The explanation usually given to reporters and foreigners was that this was the revolution, and it was indeed. What happened in the schools was what had happened in the studios. Everybody had walked out and looked about, and enough of those who looked were urgently moved to say that they liked what they saw. Experiments on the children were almost a fortuitous by-product of experimenting on school walls. The work of the children under these forays astonished a great many people. It seemed the result of abnormal genius or pedagogical eureka. But the explanation is in the fact that art is a national habit in which they also indulge.

Adolfo Best-Maugard, the first pedagogical-artistic experimenter, went digging in archæological collections and bargaining at fairs, and burdened his elegant self with many pots and gourds which he deposited smartly on school desks. He explained that a few very simple lines and curves composed the apparently intricate native decoration, moreover according to certain principles the result of long development, good eyesight, love of surfaces and forms, and earthy craftsmanship. He discomposed this design into its lineal principles, seven primary elements all variations or derivatives of the spiral, which is the basic form in Mexican design. He noted the rhythms and the careful spacing. Lines and curves proceed and retrogress, make borders and forms, rarely cut into each other.

With this admirable description of native design, and models which the pupils were accustomed to seeing and using in their homes, the classrooms adopted the revolution. At the same time Carlos Orozco in Guadalajara set his pupils to making woodcuts, which they did, enthusiastically, and still do in craft centers and academy classes under Gabriel Fernandez Ledezma, himself a talented designer. Art for art's sake later slipped from the regular curriculum. Drawing and painting became the language adopted for the teaching of all other sub-

jects, from geography to hygiene. Nevertheless the fun of drawing and painting so overruns in time the regular courses, that
the National Academy founded many small art-schools, called
Escuelas al Aire Libre, and the deposits of children's work
stratify in the Secretariat faster than they are exported to galleries and school museums in Europe, the Orient, and the rest
of America.

The first stratum in the Secretariat archives is of decorative
designs, highly stylized, burning with colour, yet even precociously subtle. The next layer is suddenly changed. There is a
new panorama, a slice of life, like a churchful of ex-votos or a
street of pulquerias. This change occurred because Best-Maugard's successor, Manuel Rodriguez Lozano, was interested in
the *barrios,* where live the poorer *mestizo* classes from which
the public schools draw their attendance. The villages are
reflected in pottery, lacquer, and textiles; the *barrios* in miracle-
boards, popular murals, and ballads. The same children were
found to be on easy terms with both.

The astonished connoisseurs who in all sincerity flung their
palms heavenward and proclaimed ten children out of ten
wunderkinder were not merely patriotic enthusiasts; because
some youth, playing like his not very ancient elders with
brushes and paints, often enough became suddenly somebody
who must be considered at least a potential artistic personality. Fourteen-year-old Pacheco, mixing cement and grinding colours for Diego Rivera and Revueltas, found it amusing
after his day was over, to draw pictures which he explained
were memoirs. When he came legally of age he had been
given a whole schoolfull of walls to decorate. And while Best-
Maugard was puzzling over the desirable way to traduce
traditional decoration into modern painting, and Rodriguez
Lozano, between classes, was working with oil on cardboard to
get the ex-voto look, his young friend and housemate, Abra-

ham Angel, gaily did both, one morning when Lozano was fairly unkempt with the struggle.

Angel, fathered by the impetus of the moment, cleared the painful mental obstacles of older men; dipped into burning reds and lambent blues, fairly bit into his picture as if it had been a mango—a summer mango, flushed with the colour of blood. The women he portrayed are perennial sweethearts in calico. His landscapes are bathed in youthful love. "He responded to things so directly," says Lozano, "so keenly that they made him ill." And he died at the age of nineteen, as mysteriously and suddenly as he had painted; both, like a shot from a sling.

Angel, said Best-Maugard, "achieved in his extraordinary art a perfect expression of the popular spirit of Mexico, in its most complete form." Angel, said Diego Rivera, was the painter of Mexico City. Said Carlos Merida: "To us who have made a cult of reaching an artistic mode of our own, that is, an Indo-American art, the death of this young painter has been a tremendous blow . . . His first fruits—with faults if you like, influenced if one is exacting—display nevertheless what profound painter's temperament he possessed; what feeling for material, what gift of discovering the grave harmonies of colour and spirit in a line . ." ". . . He created new harmonies," said Lozano; "ignoring the recipes, the processes, the kitchen . . . unique colourist, recalling the tropical fruits of America, the colour of our potteries, the clay of our landscape." But none of the lyrics made for Angel equal his own, and the most touching plaint was the most universal: "Too bad he didn't get to do any walls."

IV.

The æsthetic ideal that made large surfaces the synonym of
painter's bliss was an organic development of the revolutionary
artists' reconstruction program. By their definition murals in
public buildings would return to art the social meaning and
function that it possessed in its great periods in Mexico and
elsewhere, and modern murals with a new social ideology
would dovetail into the Mexican tradition—would follow up,
or complete, the pre-Hispanic temple walls, the colonial church
frescoes, and the pulquerias. It was a most obviously legitimate
form of great native art. This view in turn grows of a deeper
purely æsthetic core, first expressed by David Alfaro Siqueiros
from Spain. In fact, he plotted the painters' revolution and
foretold its artistic results a year before it occurred, though he
did not give the date, nor the name of its governmental patron
because he did not know just who that patron would be.

Welding a *patria* was Siqueiros' idea too. His data was the
stock of scenes and desires accumulated through some years
of fighting and a lifetime of painting and thinking. His
method was careful observation and analysis of European art
at the beginning of its religious and æsthetic Renaissance, and
his yardstick was modern abstract art, most versions of which
he found, however, were a little too small to measure the walls
he and the other members of the Syndicate he organized were
going to paint.

David Alfaro Siqueiros when he ruminated in Spain startled
those of his friends who did not laugh with the doctrine
that has become prime credo in modern Mexico æsthetic. The
subject, he said, was as important as the style. The picture must
derive emotion, design, construction, and colour, from the
model. The model must not be chosen arbitrarily to demonstrate artistic gymnastics. This was the practice of most of his

66. YOUNG WOMAN
   Large oil by Abraham Angel

European contemporaries, he said, and this was the sterile behaviour of pedants, prima donnas and dilettantes. He used about the same words as Donatello reproaching Ucello (who at the moment was deeply immersed in mathematics) with "abandoning the substance for the shadow."

Siqueiros uttered many heresies to the prevailing European dogmas in the shocked privacy of continental studios, and then shouted them in the bold black type of *Vida Americana,* a magazine of which he published the first and only number in May, 1921. Apparently he could not breathe non-revolutionary atmosphere long enough to print a second. Mexicans, all Indo-Americans, he declared, must embrace their traditions—paint their own images; identify themselves in spirit with their remarkable artistic ancestry, and its descendance. When they did that they would create an art which would reclaim in modern terms the fundamental values of simplicity, architectonic construction, and literally, religious passion, laid down in pre-Hispanic, colonial, and contemporary native art, all of which is essentially monumental, whatever its physical dimensions.

"We must rebuild in painting and sculpture their lost values, and create at the same time new values," Siqueiros wrote. "Like the classic artists, we must achieve our purpose within the inviolable laws of æsthetic balance. We must like them, be good craftsmen; and like them too, we must have a constructive base and great sincerity. . . Now, we draw silhouettes with pretty colours; when we model we are interested in skin-deep arabesque, and we forget to conceive the great primal masses—cubes, cones, spheres, cylinders, pyramids, which should be the girders of all plastic architecture. Let us impose the constructive spirit upon the purely decorative. Colour and line are expressive elements of second rank; the fundamental, the base of a work of art, is the magnificent geometric structure of the form with the concept . . . Let us, according to our dynamic or static objectivity, be first constructors; let us love and plant solidly our personal emotional reaction to the world, adhering truthfully to the smallest real and significant detail . . . Let us describe organically and without vagueness the quality of the elements in our work, creating matter solid or fragile, harsh or suave, opaque or transparent, and let us consider and measure the weight of it . . . And on a stable frame, let us if necessary, caricature to humanize."

"Let us furthermore reject theories postulating a 'national art.' We can make ourselves universal. Our racial elements will appear inevitably . . . And let us close our ears to the criticism of our poets. They produce most beautiful literary articles completely separate from the true values we seek in our work . . . Let us observe the work of our ancient people, the Indian painters and sculptors (Mayas, Aztecs, Incas, etc.). Our nearness to them will enable us to assimilate the constructive vigour of their work, in which there is clear knowledge of the elements of nature, and these things can serve as the point of departure . . . We can possess their synthetic energy without falling into lamentable archæological reconstruction . . . Let us not flee to 'archaic' motifs. We must live our marvellous dynamic age. We must love modern machines, which give us new and unexpected plastic emotions, we must love the things of our daily lives, and the life in the cities that are now growing—soberly and practically engineered, stripped of architectural complexities—immense towers of cement jammed upon steel and nailed into the ground."

Loving his subject the revolutionary artist travelled a road analogous to that of the Indian who, understanding a human Christ, did not render him in the abstractions of his native deities, but made him realistic. Siqueiros, marching to his conclusions through purely æsthetic channels, carries æsthetics be-

yond painting, and from revolution in art passes without
noting a difference between a brush and a gun to organizing
his living materials into functioning bodies, much as he might
create a mural. Thus the Syndicate of Painters and Sculptors
bore also labour and peasant leaders.

Brush and gun are however not alternatives to any Mexican
artist. He bridges with either the beauties of mental inventions
to the living things about him. It is a need that perhaps most
modern artists do not have, but to the Mexican it is a priceless
juncture of passion and abstraction, his two native creative
sources; the two elements in pre-Hispanic art which again,
springing separately, make the complete arch.

CHAPTER TWELVE

THE SYNDICATE OF PAINTERS AND SCULPTORS

There is an epic quality about the Mexican artists that pulls at the imagination. They arise out of a long series of conflicts, testifying that nowhere as in Mexico has art so intimately been linked to the fate of its people. The fact that a group of personalities diverse as a metropolis became a unit that packed itself into the title of "Revolutionary Syndicate of Technical Workers, Painters, and Sculptors," spans the archaic periods of warfare and great art to theirs.

67.

Religion has always been the dynamo of Mexican art; idols on altars, crosses on mountains, idols behind crosses. The mountain has been the prized image of native beauty: solidity and grandeur the prime qualities. The same persistent, questing wants have built pyramids and modeled miniatures, cut tissue-paper fringes for *pulquerias,* and made in multiple masks and symbols the projection of a single beauty with many facets. The creeds reborn this century are not new creeds at all. The basic unit is again the man of the soil, and the craftsman's beatitude is the honesty and skilful toil of fruitful agrarian cultivation.

The expression of religious tradition in art is the living breath of the land, and it tastes of the soil, whatever the form that period and locality define. Thus there is a greater difference between Maya and Aztec than between Frenchman and Greek; but the modern Mexican is closer to his ancestors than to his European colleague. The architectural urge; the religious quality; the symbolic realism; the socially interpretative intention—these things of native spirit determine, more than the scientific researches of the old world, the modern form of Mexican art. The spirit does not dictate the plastic version; it is born of the image. Fra Angelico knelt to paint Christ, and Diego Rivera painted Zapata with a pistol in his belt.

"Bah!" snorts an associate of the revolutionary guild, criticizing a drawing of workers in the fields, "these men are not labouring. It is a pick and shovel ballet. And this team of oxen—why, in a real team, brutes, man, and yoke are all one thing, moving together and complete—and doesn't he know reality is a beautiful thing? Look at that yoke—it isn't even put on properly. A yoke is part of the head, not an ornament. A peon who looked at that would see at once that it isn't strapped right. Calls himself a Mexican painter, and can't even yoke a team of oxen!"

II.

"The Mexican agricultural labourer instead of being an isolated individual naturally belongs to a group and can with comparative ease act through a group," writes an American sociologist on the basis of a modern scientific survey. View in the light of this fact any Mexican craftsman; recall the organization of the old Mexican nation on the basis of occupational clans; and understand therefrom how naturally the Syndicate of Painters and Sculptors allied itself with the labourer, and sought to act as an organized group.

This group operated toward two ends which can be seen as one: the construction of a new art, redintegrated to a social function. "Art for art's sake," it proclaimed, "is an æsthetic fallacy; art for the people is a phrase of inconsistent and hypocritical sentimentalism. Art is necessarily a thing of the people, not an abstract concept, nor a vehicle for exploiting whims. The search for true expression of mass feeling is not to be confused with the doctrine that plastic art, to be reconstructive or revolutionary, must be subservient to the propagation of prescribed ideas. A panel sincerely and forcefully conceived from pure emotion, and portrayed according to the æsthetic laws of the craft, will generate its own *morale.*"

Siqueiros preached a core of their ideas, and painted nuclei of their ultimate æsthetic. Nevertheless theirs is a collective product, a group expression created and tempered in two years of close relationship and vigorous, thoughtful, devoted effort of several remarkable men. One formulated the technique of fresco adopted by all, another found the dense, fresh texture so different from Italian murals. The palette melted of the blues, carmines and browns of Siqueiros, the earthy grays, greens, and siennas of Orozco, the flat geometrical tones of Merida, the *pulqueria* relish of Revueltas. Rhythms of architectural composition, one might trace largely to Rivera; rhythms of monumental passion, to Orozco; many traditional abstractions, to Charlot's studious sketches; but to all of these things, each contributed. Where a single idea was born, when it was common to all, no one could have indisputably affirmed, and no one was especially concerned.

One knows without looking at the signature, which is not always there, however, who painted any panel. Rivera's mellow heaviness, Orozco's human grandeur, mark differences that cannot be defined in terms of school. Siqueiros, Charlot, Revueltas are each unmistakable, though all of them even literally painted each other's pictures. One night when Siqueiros had gone off to sleep, to deliver a speech, or to write an editorial for the painters' newspaper, *El Machete,* his colleague Guerrero put a head in Siqueiros' unfinished panel.

When Siqueiros discovered it he exclaimed: "Wonderful! Either I did it in my sleep or it is a miracle. Well, that's fine. I think I'll try it again tonight and see if it works." Orozco, overhearing, saw to it that the miracle was repeated, and the next day Siqueiros was more pleased than ever.

Ordinarily several men worked on each fresco: the master artist, his assistants, the master mason, and his apprentices. The artists sometimes mixed lime for each other's panels, and the masons took the brushes and put in a few strokes on their own account. Rivera boasted that one of his *peons* corrected the forms and angles of the pictured peasants' hats. Several masons in the course of the Syndicate's life became accepted painters. Social differences anyhow, were discarded, and physical dissimilarities became purely differences of bulk and stature. Gentlemen of former evening coat and top hat, bookish and monkish people, soldiers, erstwhile long-haired Bohemians, Indians from the villages, all sloughed their individualisms and clothed themselves in overalls. These garments became so fashionable that the sleekest of boudoir decorators ordered himself silk pajamas the colour and cut of unionalls and jumpers.

The work was done by contract based on the measurements of the walls and an eight-hour day, for which the master artist and master mason received an average of eight pesos. Some of the painters performed a nightly shift too, but this was an extra-official matter and wages were not provided. Once Rivera fell off a ten-foot scaffold from sheer exhaustion. His masons thought he was killed, and though the *maestro* arose from a twenty minute coma and lurched, the place where he fell was thereafter said to be haunted. It was generally remarked that he had not really fallen; the brawny colossus he had just equipped with hands, pushed him off!

In what was left of the twenty-four hour day, the guild

Aparece los Jueves   Periodico Semanario   Vale 5 centavos

EXTRA No. 1 | Responsable: XAVIER GUERRERO | México, D. F., cuarta semana de agosto de 1924 |

El machete sirve para cortar la caña,
para abrir las veredas en los bosques umbríos,

decapitar culebras, tronchar toda cizaña,
y humillar la-soberbia de los ricos impíos.

68. HEAD OF EL MACHETE. Painter's Newspaper

Sigue el Desarme de Campesinos

EL FUSIL EN MANOS PROLETARIAS
ES LA UNICA GARANTIA DE LIBERTAD

EL QUE NO SABE CONSERVAR EL RIFLE
NO MERECE CONSERVAR LA TIERRA

En el Orden Burgués Reinante hay que Buscar la Causa de la Decadencia Arquitectónica Contemporánea

Por D. ALFARO SIQUEIROS.

69. FACSIMILES FROM EL MACHETE
Sheets published by the Syndicate of Painters and Sculptors

associates studied Cennino Cennini's treatise on the technique of fresco, composition from Giotto, volume from Massaccio, and geometry from Ucello. They also drew pictures and wrote articles and poetry for *El Machete,* which was both a trade-paper and a political organ. Its strident red and black front page carried a large scythe across the top. This weapon stood for the name, policy, and artistic style of the sheet. Under it a lucid rhyme further explained that:

> The machete serves to harvest cane,
> To open paths through timbered wilds
> Behead vipers, mow out tares,
> And bow the merciless rich men.

Off the scaffold these painters also taught in the schools; explored the market-places, the villages and churches, and all the other national art museums; and were festive. Saturday night at Edward Weston's, the workers in paints drank tea and played the phonograph with union and non-union technical labour—scribes, musicians, architects, doctors, archæologists, cabinet-minsters, generals, stenographers, deputies, and occasional sombreroed peasants. One very gay week they attended the inauguration of the governor of Jalisco, himself a young cartoonist with a fearsome reputation. A virulent squad was lodged in storerooms of the Jalisco state museum; bedded in monastic cells among properties of the gilded age. The dined—and necessarily wined—painters one night cast their eyes upon all the gilt and plaster finery uneasily. Said they: "It is abominable that such things should survive; anybody would suppose that our host and his country had no taste. We must, therefore, in appreciation of his generosity, forfend his artistic honour." A carefully selected tribunal then examined each bibelot, debated its qualities, pronounced melancholy judgment, and gave it over to the "secular arm" for justice. Till an arduous dawn, the revolution waged against odious effigy, and triumphant retired to sleep with characteristic thoroughness and some professional pride.

III.

The first contracts for murals were signed at the end of 1922. In March, 1923, the following orange-colored broadside was sent to the Minister of Education:

INVITATION

To the fiesta which the
Syndicate of Technical Workers, Painters and Sculptors
Will hold on Tuesday 20 of this month in honor of

DIEGO RIVERA

Beloved comrade and master of the shop,

On the occasion of completing the work of decorating the Auditorium of the National Preparatory School, a work which resurrects monumental painting not only in Mexico, but in all the world, beginning thus in our country, a new flowering which will be comparable to those of ancient times, and the great qualities of which: good craftsmanship, wisdom in proportion and values, expressive clarity and emotional power, (all within a purely organic Mexicanism free of unhealthy and fatal picturesque) mark the work as insuperable, and lovers of the profession of painting can obtain from it the science and experience here cumulated.

(And in honor of:)

LICENCIADO DON JOSE VASCONCELOS

and

DON VICENTE LOMBARDO TOLEDANO

intelligent initiators and generous protectors of this work and of all the noble effort made toward the development of plastic art in Mexico. (And of:)

LUIS ESCOBAR, XAVIER GUERRERO, CARLOS MERIDA,
JUAN CHARLOT, AMADO DE LA CUEVA

expert assistants of the maestro Rivera.

All this to give thanks to the Lord who kept them from terrible and horrible fall from the scaffold in nearly a year of most painful labor at the height of almost ten meters.

12:30, at Mixcalco 12, Tres Guerras Co-operative Shop of Painting and Sculpture. Five pesos without fail in the pocket.

Very important note: So that the honorees be not accused of sponging, they also will pay for their meal.

This decoration portrays the creation of the world. The figures, about double life-size, ascend on either side of a pit which contains an organ encased in the back-wall of the stage. The deity rises head and torso, arms outstretched, within this cave-like place. Man and woman each form the base of half an architectural pyramid of figures representing arts, sciences, and virtues. The mural is a wax-painting, burned into the wall by a blowtorch applied almost simultaneously with the paint itself. The insistent colours, the monumental plane, the simplification necessary to work technically time-limited, the distortions dictated by the magnitude of the composition, architecture of the wall, and distance and angles from which it must be clear, and the scale, have shocked the dormant tastes of many people less provincial than Mexico City residents, and more acquainted with the early Italian frescoes and mosaics Rivera had kept in view. He was accused of painting "monstrous Indians with bull's-eyes." Offended gentlemen violently demanded satisfaction. If he considered such females beautiful, as he affirmed, would he marry one of them? The Minister was advised to send him and his colleagues to paint *pulquerias,* and when they heard of it they said that they would be very glad of any contract.

That same month Rivera moved his scaffolds from the

National Preparatory School to the Ministerial headquarters. Merida undertook the decoration of a juvenile library in the Secretariat, and Charlot and De la Cueva walls in an outside corridor. Revueltas, Ramon Alva, Amero, Fernando Leal, continued in the Preparatory School. Orozco was given three tiers of corridor walls and the remaining space on the main stairway of this building. Siqueiros chose a remote dark stairs leading from a small patio, also in the Preparatory School.

A visiting paterfamilias who lost his way stumbled into Siqueiros' den, which was at that time very red. The unfortunate parent crossed himself, approached the painter, demanded, "What are you making on these sacred walls—devils? And that monster—is that Goliath?"

"No, señor," Siqueiros amiably replied, "It is an angel." As an angel the figure was henceforth known.

An old doorkeeper at the *Preparatoria* remarked that many of the visitors who came to view the murals seemed much exercised. "They all say that a beautiful colonial building has been defiled by these paintings," he observed; "but it is this way: times change. It is true we never had any paintings like these in colonial buildings before, but we never had street cars either, and the streets are just as old. And we all ride in street cars."

Reporters made the rounds of the murals habitually as they visited the police courts. It became sport to bait the painters, but not very good sport because they were good-natured and clever, and their guns showed when they faced the wall. Usually they explained patiently their art and conduct. They wrote erudite pieces for the current magazines, on ancient and modern art. But they were picturesque and militant, and Rivera is mountainous. He was caricatured and parodied on the stage as well as in the press. If there were sight-seeing buses in Mexico they would have included him in their routes. He

70. MASONS AND PAINTERS AT WORK
    Chapingo

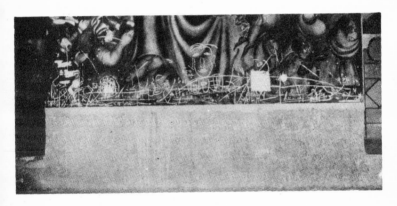

71. DETAIL OF MURAL BY OROZCO
    Showing attempted destruction of murals

went into kodak albums along with the beggars of the Cathedral and the pyramids of Teotihuacan.

Orozco had nearly covered a long wall the length of the patio corridor with huge frescoes that he called "tentative," most of which, furthermore, he later removed. A deity descending head down leapt clamorously in reds across the patio through intervening halls and arches to the first glance at the main entrance; a long-robed beardless dark Christ moved hugely on its left, bearing a great cross; golds and siennas vibrated with indigoes and deep glowing rose. In crypts on the stairway, St. Francis in grays and blacks kissed a leper and mercifully leant to the desolate.

An association of pious and socially supreme ladies required of the painter that he remove these frescos "temporarily." They were going to hold a charity bazaar in the courtyard and they could not bear, they declared, to set their tables against such a background. Orozco explained that fresco was not art that could be rolled up and taken away, and added that he did not think the painting would fade in time for the fête. The ladies assumed an authority called in Mexico "direct action", and nailed flags and evergreen boughs and garlands upon the walls.

Orozco perpetuated their triumphant profiles in his second series of murals. They march in grotesque procession on high-heeled shoes upon the meager bodies of the lowest social ranks, escorted by bloated gentlemen, to the feet of a theatrical "Father God" with a great hay-like beard—obviously, the rich in their heaven. The lovely blended soft tones of this procession, and the Isaiah spirit, is matched in other panels similarly "caricatured to humanize." Liberty, a drunken slut in a party cap, and justice, a leering lady embraced pornographically, holding scales crazily balanced, hang graced between red and gilt curtains. The false prophet leads the labourer into blindfold, and an unsavoury labour leader—(at the moment a be-diamonded bulwark of the government) picks his pocket and stabs him in the back.

These murals of course hit spots more vital than had even "monstrous Indians with bull's-eyes". Orozco is said to have helped overthrow two presidents by drawings in comic week-lies. In the *Preparatoria* he seemed to have painted with a thousand horse power piston dipped in vitriol. Souls creak and dominoes rip at every stroke. He was never asked to explain the "symbolism", but he was frequently told that he had dragged morals and beauty in the mud. The Syndicate slammed a bright pink broadside upon all the street-corners and telephone posts to which it would stick. The public was addressed therein as follows:

DECLARATION
Social, Political, and Aesthetic
of
The Syndicate of Technical Workers, Painters and Sculptors
to the native races humiliated through centuries; to the soldiers made executioners by their chiefs; to the workmen and peasants flogged by the rich; to the intellectuals not fawners of the bourgeoisie . . .

We are on the side of those who demand the disappearance of an aged and cruel system, within which you, worker of the fields, produce food for the gullets of overseers and politicians, while you starve; within which you, worker of the city, move the factories, weave the garments and make with your hands modern comforts for scoundrels and prostitutes, while your flesh crawls and freezes; within which you, Indian soldier, heroically abandon the earth you work and give your life endlessly to destroy the misery for centuries the portion of your race . .

Not only noble labor, but the smallest expression of the physical and spiritual life of our race springs from the native (and particularly the Indian). His admirable and extraordinarily peculiar gift of MAKING BEAUTY: THE ART OF THE MEXICAN PEOPLE IS THE GREATEST AND MOST HEALTHY SPIRITUAL EXPRESSION IN THE WORLD renders his tradition our greatest possession. It is great because, being of the people, it is collective, and that is why our fundamental aesthetic goal is to socialize artistic expression, and tend to obliterate totally, individualism, which is bourgeois.

We REPUDIATE the so-called easel painting and all the art of ultra-intellectual circles because it is aristocratic, and we glorify the expression of Monumental Art because it is a public possession.

We PROCLAIM that since this social moment is one of transition between a decrepit order and a new one, the creators of beauty must put forth their utmost efforts to make their production of ideological value to the people, and the ideal goal of art, which now is an expression of individualistic masturbation, should be one of beauty for all, of education and of battle."

Less formal declarations, printed like ballads, and in somewhat similar literary style, appeared from time to time. They bristled vigour, often in language aggressive and inelegant, but most expressive. Slogans and bywords trailed into it gorgeously. For example "The buzzards will eat those who are not with us," and "We paint only on walls and on toilet-paper." Rivera inscribed one fresco "Don't talk of what you do not understand." Over another he painted Netzahualcoyotl's agrarian policy, and into a scene of miners he wrote a poem by one of the "technical workers," Carlos Gutierrez Cruz. It reads:

> Comrade miner
> Bowed by the weight of the earth,
> When your hands take out the metals,
> Fashion daggers.
> Then you will know
> That all the metals are for you.

Every person who felt menaced or slandered murally, cried Oooooh, Bolshevik! and Shame! You're denigrating Mexico! (which means, Shhhhh! What will the neighbours think?) The Minister was accused of wasting the public moneys. Petitions rained on him and committees assaulted him. He must stop all this nonsense, in the name of culture and decorum!

The Syndicate printed a green manifesto, again for mural use
in the streets, as follows:

PROTEST

A campaign has been undertaken against the present movement of
painting in Mexico. This movement can be attacked only because of
ignorance or envy. And to make the badly calculated blow still more
infamous, the movement is deliberately confounded with personal politics. The stone of money is flung at us, stained with all that business of
GREAT SQUANDERING, FABULOUS PRICES, ENORMOUS
PROFITS, etc. The painter who earns most in the Secretariat receives
exactly the wages of an artesan who covers smooth walls by the square
meter. The public can satisfy itself by examining the contracts of the
painters with the National Secretariat of Education.

This protest is not an apology.

We are certain that the present movement of painting in Mexico is
the expression and the affirmation of our nationality. The enemies of
it do not attack because their good taste suffers, since the æsthetic of
this painting, holding itself Mexican, nevertheless is at one with the
taste of the civilized men of this country and of others: as is proved by
the opinions written of our work here in Mexico, in the United States,
and in Europe. Therefore our petty enemies, in the name of the development of our country, and of the good taste in all the world, should
be considered and treated as ignorant and backward, in the same sense
and with the same means as those who will not be vaccinated, bathed,
or taught the alphabet.

We protest with all the strength of our sincerity against that mob
which intrigues or clamors and places obstacles in the path of the march
onward of painting in Mexico, taking advantage of the lack of understanding in its public, the semi-educated and mediocre crowd: that same
bourgeois *vulgo* which tried to tear the pictures of Manet, protested
against the decorations of Puvis de Chavannes in the Pantheon, insulted
Delacroix and Ingres, stoned the David of Michael Angelo, hissed
Wagner; goaded by envious failures, by enemies of the artists who work
within the feeling of the people and the taste of the real élite without
regard for the uncomprehending bourgeois who wants to establish the
rights of art by the low standards of his own measure.

Political wheels moved; dissension grew bitter. "Direct
Action" was then taken by an adolescent rabble, children, it

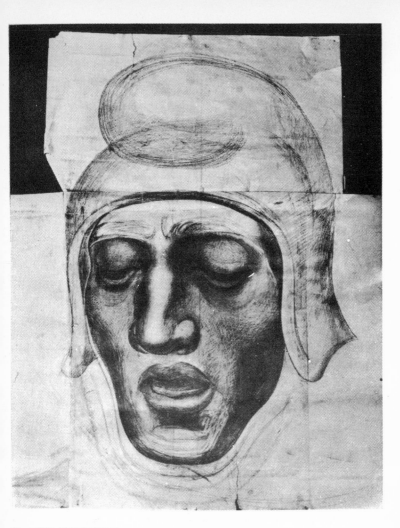

72. THE REVOLUTION
    Study for mural by Alfaro Siqueiros

73. BURIAL OF A WORKER

Stoned and unfinished fresco by Alfaro Siqueiros in National Preparatory School, Mexico City

was supposed, of the ladies pictorially annoyed. The murals in the Preparatory School were stoned, scratched, scraped, scrawled upon obscenely. Orozco's St. Francis was mutilated to the knee; the "caricatures" were defaced to the neck; Siqueiros' panels were hideously vandalized. Upon this outrage the self-appointed guardians of Diaz humanism built sermons, extolling the guilty raiders, saying that the students needed "peaceful and uplifting surroundings for spiritual contemplation," and if the Secretariat imposed distasteful interior decoration upon them they were fully privileged to protest in this manner. It was added that "art is an attribute of aristocracy; it cannot descend to the level of ignorance"—a thesis adequately proved by their own reaction. Even *littérateurs* supposedly friends of the painters whetted petty clevernesses upon their misfortune, and yawned prettily that really they were bored by it all.

Destruction continued to the almost complete obliteration of one of Siqueiros' panels. The director of the school was "unable to find the objecting students." The Minister was assailed. Orozco lost his job. The painters protested in accusing red type. At last a white petition signed by two hundred foreign residents, protesting IN THE NAME OF ART, WHICH IS NOT A NATIONAL BUT AN INTERNATIONAL PROPERTY, brought presidential orders that the murals were to be protected. The protection consisted in that the painters were asked to make no more targets for the "mischievous boys." All work in the building ceased.

Three months afterward a change of president brought change of cabinet, and Vasconcelos left. His unique enthusiasm was supplanted by the tepid indifference of a Minister more interested in the painting of prodigies than of adults. The new head of the Department of Fine Arts went on bombastic record with the remark that "The first thing I'll do is whitewash those horrible frescos." Two painters only were retained by the Secretariat. One was Roberto Montenegro, famous for his elegance, and the other was Diego Rivera.

Orozco retired to his studio beyond the city limits, and lived precariously by drawing for the press. Siqueiros fled to Jalisco,

74. EMILIANO ZAPATA
    Woodcut by Xavier Guerrero

declaring that if art was so little needed that a painter could not hold a job as well as might a plumber, he personally felt useless in that profession; and he would not be a "salon clown." In Jalisco he and De la Cueva were given walls and a welcome by the governor of the state, but Siqueiros was shaken. Thenceforth he devoted the greater part of his time and effort to labour organizations. *El Machete* became a communist organ, edited by Xavier Guerrero. Revueltas painted screaming eagles for American gasoline stations till the job gave out. He settled in the suburb of Guadalupe, taught desultorily in one of the National Academy's open air schools, mourned, and long afterwards resumed his palette. Charlot took to his easel for monumental painting, and to technical draughtsmanship for a living.

The Syndicate was disbanded. Yet the men who signed its manifestos had already established the new tradition and point of view described by them. They blazed a renaissance and made a great contribution to the art of the world. They formulated a living style, and a positive creed expressed profoundly. The qualities of their walls have been carried into their own and other aspirant canvases. These monuments make legion converts. Little by little they have become their own protectors.

75. CARTOON BY SIQUEIROS

CHAPTER THIRTEEN

DAVID ALFARO SIQUEIROS

DAVID ALFARO SIQUEIROS is as extraordinarily alive as a child. He was in many ways the romp and playboy of the Syndicate, but even when he works he paints, writes, speaks, with so much brilliant ease and gusto that work and play merge together; he seems continuously inventing games with himself. Innocent to the world, he will change the rules excitedly and the process looks much like irresponsibility. He is each time full of enthusiasm, full of energy, and fluid with ideas, which he never questions till they are carried out.

The revolution camped in his front yard during the Carranza-Villa agony, and he tramped away with it, a sixteen-year-old drummer boy cut off by a nondescript uniform from his wealthy, conservative and Catholic parents. Buoyantly he thumped his way to the rank of staff officer under one of the able Carranza leaders, General Dieguez. Bizarre tales come of these fighting days to match the genial grace of his toll in other battles. He would distract himself in Syndicate days by

76. DETAIL OF FIGURE 73

shooting monumental compositions into the ceiling of his room
as he lay abed, revolver cocked. But the seed of his person is
in the simpler fact that when he studied in the National
Academy he would consume with much appetite the edible
models for still-lifes, declaring that the real artist knew and
enjoyed the subjects of his paintings.

These two strands—Siqueiros the amorous and Siqueiros the
analytic—wind the cable of his work. The photograph of a
beauty generally in at least one of his pockets could never be
traced wholly to either his personal life or his pictures. Once
his wife, annoyed more than usual by the ubiquitous other
images, declared she would put a stop to it and stalked the
painter to his locked room with a knife, to cut his eyes out,
she said. Through the keyhole Siqueiros plead monotonously:
"My dear, I cannot come out if you are going to cut my eyes
out; you can cut anything else you like, but not my eyes,
because I need those the most. Please choose something else
to carve, will you?"

When the Carranza government was established it sent
Siqueiros to Europe to study, as Mexican governments generally do with their promising young men. In Spain, Italy,
France, he painted "realistic abstractions," essentially portraits
built upon a frame one might call cubistic, but which could
best be seen in the light of Siqueiros' ideas and the body of
his entire work, as architectonic. He returned to Mexico at the
end of 1921, with a stuffed portfolio of picture postcards,
chiefly Italian primitives and oil derricks.

Siqueiros the *machetero,* writing oratorical editorials in collaboration with his expressive wife, was preceded by an eager
young man on holiday, setting fuses to Judases, cracking
Christmas piñatas, quaffing deep of fair-day lemonades, sneez-
ing in the dust kicked up by ritual dancers; and by a contem-
plative person staring at the patterned walls of *pulquerias* and

77. THE PEASANT, THE SOLDIER, AND THE WORKER
Woodcut by David Alfaro Siqueiros

measuring the ancient sculptures in the National Museum. An
adult unfamiliar with even his conversation would have smiled
to see the apostolic editor of *El Machete* in his disheveled office,
new of pens and perhaps scissors too, blazingly recent as to
uniformed personnel (transient from studios, usually) encased
in overalls and jumpers still odorous of the factory and the

market-tables around the corner. For Siqueiros is guilelessly pretty, of baby-fine white skin, exaggerated Cupid's bow mouth, silky dark hair of archaic and infantile curl, and deeply fringed, fresh green eyes inherited possibly from a Roumanian Jewish grandmother. He would be smeared with ink and paint as if he had been in a jam-pot; and he would prattle episodes and ideas sulphurously radical, precociously naughty, naïvely truthful.

It would be difficult to suppose that Siqueiros found time to engineer amusements, political meetings, artistic expeditions, a paper, and paint so thoughtfully that none of his work is waste, unless one has heard him string glinting phrases through the night, seen him drop on a pile of large sketches with a coat rolled under his head for a pillow, and read of him scarcely three hours later sitting on a strike committee. Each of these things in its moment is to him more important than anything else. Yet in Siqueiros' view each of them definitely depends on the others, and he sits on strike committees, he will explain, because he is a conscious artist, and to be a conscious artist one must also be a workman, and workmen nowadays must sit on strike committees.

He brought two *pulqueria* painters to his first mural for collaboration. "Let's open a space here," he would say, and "let's make a mass there." They knew in these terms what he wanted, as they would not had he said "Let's make some Mexican decorations." The last portion of this work, a gigantic funeral procession, was done without collaboration. He was painting the coffin when Felipe Carrillo Puerto was killed in Yucatan. Siqueiros bored a hole in the wall and buried therein a bottle with Felipe's name on a paper inside. The painting itself was unaltered. It is the burial of an unnamed workman, painted apparently by an unknown hand. From this national portrait and memorial, to an ancient mural there is no great breach of viewpoint. The painting is a gesture at once symbolic, historic and racial.

II.

When the Syndicate disintegrated Siqueiros left Mexico City, or rather when Siqueiros left Mexico City the Syndicate ceased to exist. He left the Burial of a Workman unfinished, and in the process of disappearing, along with his other walls, from the stones and knives of the student vandals who also injured Orozco's murals. Amado de la Cueva had been given contracts for the decoration of the Jalisco state capitol and the university in Guadalajara. Siqueiros took with him one or two of the ring of younger artists ardently his followers. Guadalupe Zuno, the governor, commissioned also the building and decoration of his residence, in which work he himself took part.

A new phase of Mexican art might have been developed in Guadalajara had Siqueiros been in the mood to give much thought or time to painting. But he was mining deep into social structures and human configurations, and convinced by the crash in Mexico City that he must build an "organic" place for art, or abandon painting if he must for an art in closer contact with the life about him. He worked with De la Cueva on a hall in the university, however deliberately under De la Cueva and following the other man's ideas his regular eight hours a day, precisely as if he had been a *pulqueria* decorator. He joined the house-painters' and masons' unions, made designs for the craftsmen who were carving doors and furniture for the Zuno house and the university, and also laid out the plans of a market-house for which the masons' union had contracted.

Two days after the hall which Siqueiros and De la Cueva had painted was complete, De la Cueva was killed in a motor-cycle crash. This blow almost severed Siqueiros' connection

78. SAINT FRANCIS KISSING A LEPER

Mutilated fresco by José Clemente Orozco in National Preparatory School

79. ALVARADO THE CONQUEROR

Fresco by José Clemente Orozco, vaulted ceiling in National Preparatory School

with painting, and when some months later the Zuno house was finished and Zuno was overthrown, Siqueiros was out of a job as an artist but very much occupied as a leader and organizer of peasants and miners in the state of Jalisco.

There has been since, a good deal of trouble for the mining companies forced by Siqueiros' activities to better working conditions, eliminate death-traps, provide pensions for injured workmen. The peasant league in the state has grown ten thousand strong, and, affiliated with peasant, oil, and railroad labour in Tamaulipas, Veracruz, Tampico, and near Mexico City, has become a potent factor in national politics, possibly even the strongest, since the emotional root of this organization is the same agrarian impulse that defines the revolution, and is gradually pressing politics, government, education, all national activity, in the direction of its ancient desires.

Siqueiros the labour leader is the same indefatigable, turbulent, magnetic individual in overalls no longer a costume. A gift of speech and mental agility make him a political figure of consequence. Nevertheless his position is by conviction not political. His radicalism in labour thinking has been radicalism largely in opposition to the amalgamation of politics and social organization which was the policy of the C.R.O.M., a federation until its disintegration almost controlling recent Mexican governments. Furthermore as when he insisted on a group product and elimination of personal bent in plastic art and did not sign his murals, he now disregards the open ways to political prestige and position for himself. He races from meeting to mine on an old bicycle, jacketed in a drab sweater whose pockets are full of holes, but this is no inconvenience because he has nothing to put in them.

In the unsalaried art which now engages him, according to his own ideas he is still a craftsman out of a job. A salary, however, would by no means prove to him that a job was

"organic," because by that word he means production or creation necessary as bread to others as well as to himself. His way
here as in expressive art will have been that of a man who
chose to be great rather than famous.

III.

Three scarred walls, an almost hidden ceiling arch, a trunk-
ful of sketches and paintings largely unfinished, drawings and
woodcuts lost in old numbers of *El Machete,* are the identi-
fiable achievement of this man. The walls in the University of
Jalisco could hardly be considered more than half his own,
even the panels he painted himself, because the entire decoration is laid out according to a single design which he
attributes to De la Cueva. Carvings and paintings executed
by other men from his sketches, there are many, and many
more which he did not wittingly design bear nevertheless his
influence.

A certain sobriety and clarity of colour, a massive outline,
and great, perhaps shocking liberty of conception within austere design, are the qualities invariable in his originals which
generate similar traits in the work of other men. Beyond this
still visible influence his achievement is much greater, for the
entire mood of modern artistic Mexico is shot through with
the national wishes and abilities crystallized by him. The result
of the mural movement is the group product he wanted inspired. The æsthetic is monumental, is racial, is unified with
profound ideas, springs out of the subject.

In the Burial of a Workman surely first these qualities are
a unit. The men portrayed here are not known to be Mexican
because of a large hat or a wrapped blanket, a guitar, a horse, a
gun, or a sheaf of maize. Their bodies contain a racial outline,
a dark strength, the quintessence stripped of background. Any

one of their heads, conceived in terms of pure form, is brother to the ancient painted and carved heads which represent many deeply-feeling generations. The native painted by Siqueiros is the image or symbol toward which the work and thought of his colleagues converge, and his own achievement therefore is no less significant than that of other great forerunners.

CHAPTER FOURTEEN

JOSE CLEMENTE OROZCO

80.

Jose Clemente Orozco was born in a small town in the state of Jalisco of descent apparently pure Spanish, and perhaps for this reason he has been called the Mexican Goya. In loneliness and grandeur, in the taste for mockery, and because of a series of paintings and sketches of young women, and another of ink and pencil scenes of war, he is comparable to Goya, but his mockery is more painful, and the sense of drama that is the pitch of his work brings him closer to Posada than to either Goya or Daumier, with whom he is also sometimes matched.

The desperate laughter of the *vacilada,* familiar in Mexican art, subdominant in Orozco, is harsher than any humour of Europe, more violent and more compassionate; it is accompanied by a proportionate mercy. He is a master in contrasts. His emotions and realized expressions plunge in black to white antitheses, his vision is absolute tragedy or complete farce, and the whole pattern of his work is a pendulum of zigzag lightning. He asserts, denies, re-asserts, again denies, and thus makes truth and beauty out of constant torment, for he has a habit of pain.

One would believe that his political and social drawings for publication in dailies and magazines, had indeed, as the story goes, clubbed presidents and cabinets to oblivion, and one might also conclude. from his Revolution sketches that all

Mexico buried its guns because of Orozco. But if a truthful picture could annihilate this might have been his suicide long since. The fact is that by means of pictures he purposes to remove nothing except the pressure on his nerves, exposed in every tendril like vibrant and non-insulate electric wires to the human ugliness and beauty he loves. By sheer force he hurls his bitter and grief-stricken visions through the eyes into the seat of human emotions, making no detour to the brain, and thus it is that even his personal life is divided sharply into religiously subject friends and rank enemies.

Even if one has not seen the patio in the Preparatory School of Mexico City upon whose walls these things and many more are evident, one could look not superficially at Orozco and realize that he is tunneled by some infrequent fire. The face, a pleasant blur of a palish colour at bowing distance, raises with the most perfunctory smile a bulwark mustache on a rampart of teeth. Thick glasses cut between the world and his eyes a wall which glitters, one would swear, on either side. His left arm, a stump at the wrist since boyhood, jibs out the pocket of his coat like a revolver at the climax of the play.

Something more startling than menace is in his bearing, and his adobe studio, adjunct to a quiet suburban house, is a big place to tread in, with no object but a table in one corner to stumble against, and to meet the eye nothing but a wall of light. Orozco will wring the necks of the roosters that crow too loudly in his yard, but those that are left haven't enough sense to be quiet and so strangle eventually. The cook and the nurse are afraid of him because they find no shrines in the house, though once the nurse happened into the studio when a sketch for a fresco was pinned on the wall, and she said that this relieved her.

When the artists' talk about Mexico was become echo and garble in the press, overalls a fad, and the workman and the

Indian a slop-bowl phrase of oratory and papier-maché masquerade, Orozco strode in an American business suit and painted heroic symbols in parody—a pot and a crossed knife and fork instead of a star and a hammer and scythe, a flat-iron (which means in Mexican argot, "Like Hell") neatly pressed into a liberty cap. It is not clear which of his permanent fulminations turned laughter into the stones that mobbed him, or if these really were the cause. One can never tell about mobs, and perhaps the noble Saint Francis or the Indian Christ, beardless in a long robe, burdening his great cross, started violent contradictions muttering in the beholders.

Anyhow laughter and stones upon his frescos were the same as laughter and stones to himself, and he might have returned in kind but instead swung (when afterwards he was re-admitted) to scenes of the revolution which engulf the entire decoration in compassion and majesty. He would never explain what political or artistic doctrine he meant to expound by all this, and he titles his pictures if pressed, "Whatever You Like." You ought to know by looking at them what they are, and if you cannot think except in words Orozco, angrily at a loss, would eliminate insistency as he has done, with the remark, "Well, does a bridegroom on his wedding night discourse on the history of love?"

II.

Orozco is the only one of his great contemporaries who has not studied in Europe. Except for a disastrous visit to the United States and a sojourn in California tinting enlarged photographs shortly before he began the Preparatory School murals; and a flattering season in New York after he finished, he has not been outside of Mexico. In the National Academy he drew uncomplimentary portraits of the pedagogues who pulled the shades and pressed the buttons of complex lights

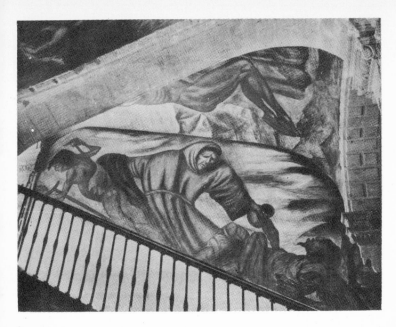

81. SAINT FRANCIS AND THE POOR
Fresco by José Clemente Orozco, National Preparatory School

82. THE REARGUARD
Fresco by José Clemente Orozco, National Preparatory School

and trailed flowing draperies to generate elegance for their not very numerous nor cultured patrons. They told him of course that he could not draw, and advised the starveling art departments of the press that Orozco was a caricaturist, so the press (but particularly that press which has no departments for art) promptly hired him.

Like all residents of Mexico born before 1930 Orozco was intimately affected by the revolution, and made to travel, as all the population did, either crusading, freebooting, pioneering, or in quest of sanctuary. Dr. Atl left the Academy after his venture in artistic revolution at the head of a "Red Battalion" which marched till it found a good place to camp, in the garrison and churches of Orizaba, which were emptied of images and stray enemy for the purpose. Orozco lodged with Atl, and, lacking a left hand, was not caparisoned but discharged instead of bullets instructive and destructive drawings published in the *Vanguardia,* a regimental sheet printed by Atl and Orozco first in a dismantled church and later in the box-car of an army train.

Carranza victorious, the Red Battalion strutted into the capital playing the fife and drum of an upper dog. Dr. Atl was supplied stacks of monetary tickets for the poor till the presses ran dry. An after the battle looseness reigned in the capital. Military Croesi drank themselves to hallucination across the table from ruined landholders now drugging for the last time, they hoped. Soldier-women paraded ostrich plumes and brocades stripped from mansions and chapels, and made chocolate in chasubles. Zapata on the edge of the city raised a fist significant as the proverbial cloud to the pedantic cabinet busily composing a Constitution full of inspired ideas but unseaworthy as to land, labour, oil, women, and other major problems.

The heavy odours emitted in fashionable and powerful

places sickened Orozco, so he starved in a cell possibly deliberately chosen on the most unfortunate street in the capital. He
exhibited the portraits of his neighbours in a pastel and water-
colour series of schoolgirls and slightly larger, less hopeful
young women. The shimmering, tender colour and the extraordinarily animate bodies limned scarcely, should have in-
sured him a respectful place in his country immediately, even
if as the Mexican Goya to whom these pictures were later
attributed, rather than in his own right. He was told in print
by the gentleman who afterwards at the head of the Fine Arts
Department hoped to whitewash the murals, that his painting
was sloppy, his technique mediocre, his soul debauched, and
that he could not draw.

"Orozco is a disillusioned youth with the soul of an old
man" brayed this critic; "of hybrid physical make-up and sar-
castic face in which spectacles deaden an intense gaze . . .
Lacking his left arm, with right hand he reflects the profound
failure of a premature defeat in the bouts of love . . . For
Orozco, the moment does not smile with the enchantment of
deceit . . he divines behind each smile calculation and under
the pressure of each embrace a cipher . . . Dead in sentiment,
to love, he can but use the satire of his brush to wound, ridi-
culing mercenary love in its lowest aspect . . Every vice is
suggested in his drawings, and the faithful worshipper of
Venus must pass with face averted buffeted by the tremendous
realism of his art. . ."

This foul moved Orozco to one of his rare published replies:
"I have supported patiently the flood of epithets which the
public has loosed upon my head on account of that unhappy
exhibit, but when in a newspaper which circulates widely I am
insulted in such fashion, I cannot remain quiet longer . . .
Perhaps the technique which the gentlemanly art critic calls
mediocre is not so mediocre if he feels himself 'wounded by

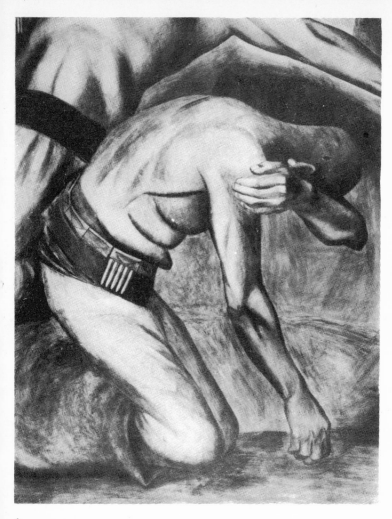

83. WOUNDED SOLDIER
   Detail from panel, The Trench. Fresco by José Clemente
   Orozco, National Preparatory School

such tremendous realism.' Perhaps his attitude is like that of
the country bumpkin who springs on the stage to defend the
heroine from the villain's dagger . . . But that is not lamentable as is the stupidity of confusing life itself with representations of it . . . I am made to appear degenerate physically and
morally . . . I am called 'a victim of premature defeat, in I
don't know what bouts. . .'

"What does the critic mean by all this? Was Francisco Goya
an imbecile like the Charles IV original and on canvas? . . .
I am far from believing myself a 'genius' . . . I am merely a
young man who observes . . . Very humbly and modestly I
present the small fruit of my study. I have no job and no in-
come. I live in misery. Each sheet of paper, each tube of paint,
is for me a sacrifice and a sadness, and it is unfair to subject
me to scorn and hostility and still further to insult me publicly.
The critic shall see soon, if he likes, a second exhibit, and he
may discover whether or no it is the 'Soul of an old prostitute'
determined to bring one grain of sand to the future monument
of Mexican art."

The second exhibit was held informally in the American
customs house at El Paso, whose officials decided like the critic
that Orozco was immoral, and though they permitted him to
cross the Rio Grande they destroyed over a hundred valuable
pictures, and that perhaps is why Orozco did not learn English
then and returned to Mexico shortly. He might have had to tint
photographs for a living anyhow, had he exhibited to the
larger public he sought in exile.

III.

The metropolitan weeklies of satire profited by his return,
and this and previous collaboration of Orozco have made the
extinct *El Ahuizote* and *Malora* famous in circles other than

the gaily plebeian public which supports their successors and the *Lirico* theater burlesques. Known to Vasconcelos vaguely as "a cartoonist of talent," Orozco received from the Secretariat surplus a commission making vignettes and tailpieces for Greek classics, and after work was begun in the Preparatory School by other men, he was signed on, perhaps to the later regret of the harassed Minister.

His first frescos were explosive, toned in reds, leaping in concept from Michael Angelo to the *vacilada*. One panel remains unchanged, a madonna and child among the complete series satisfactory to those nurtured in good European tradition, and of the magnificent Christ only the head has been left, inexplicably encased above a doorway in a strike scene, because a lady insisted. The satiric panels on the corridor above, which were the scapegoat of the misdevotees, are painted anathema in loving hue, rich soft greens and sienna and rose on a greyish golden patina.

El Machete received scant contribution from Orozco after his dispossession, and the scratched murals retained their wounds for nearly a year, during which interval a political weekly, L'A. B. C., derived point from savage drawings signed *Picoso* and other sonorous pseudonyms. A rare admirer who delved in Orozco's discarded studies for frescos proclaimed him Michael Angelo. Since this gentleman spent his life in Paris and was known as a connoisseur and patron of the arts, he sowed a little belated prestige in Orozco's troubled fields. Furthermore he commissioned the decoration of a great wall in the famous House of Tiles, once his personal residence and now a pharmacy and fashionable tearoom.

Francisco Iturbe had no interest in national or revolutionary art, and Orozco was desperately unhappy about the entire subject, so the choice of concept for the mural might have been made by either. The philosophic idea of creation, abstracted

84. SOLDIER'S WIFE

Detail from fresco, Deserted Field. José Clemente Orozco,
National Preparatory School

to the male and female principle, constructed like a grand
machine, by some lucid miracle is part of the colonial building and dignity inheres in both. The learned Charlot to his
distaste forbore the peacocks painted prettily above the cafe
tables to watch Orozco's composition grow. He sighed when it
was finished and blissfully wrote that here was the most beautiful wall ever painted in America.

Perhaps because of Iturbe's support Orozco was recalled by
the Secretariat and given the decoration of an industrial school
in the city of Orizaba, the new Minister's former home. The
fresco in Orizaba, the third tier in the Preparatory School and
the changed panels in the first; several oil paintings and about
fifty ink and pencil scenes of the revolution are all of a piece
in period, mood, control, and expressed passion. In the joy of
work the pendulum from denial swung to faith, more than as-
sertion, and the realistic themes rise above history and charac-
terization to racial symbol. Desolate the background, destruction the point of departure, and tragic the protagonists; but
strength and not chaos the chord.

In conflict the entire decoration is unified. The all-inclusive
subject is revolution, the plastic mechanism is destruction and
construction. The walls are broken and fitted together again
by planes. On a background of ultramarine rises high the rose
rectangle of a rural house. Blue and rose shift into steel and
the pink of Sunday skirts in the country, slide to gray and come
to a point in the white of ashes and bayonets in the sun. Ochres
with the blue, greens with reds, fuse static dense black, small
in quantity like its highest contrast white. Literally painted
with earths, tier to tier the ploughed tones make a field organic
gray-brown, heightened to focus bodies and faces prostrate or
driven within a great embrace.

The Preparatory School murals Orozco finished under the
patronage of the National University with the implicit under-

standing that he was to paint however he wished. Objection
had subsided, and if a student scratched a mural he did it
absentmindedly, like scribbling in telephone booths. Orozco
was even welcomed by a positive nucleus of admirers in the
student body, and indeed only the director, an elderly man,
remained hostile, to become distinguished for petty venom.
Occasionally Orozco is accused still of "denigrating" his country. How dare he present such frightful panorama to the gape
of cheerful civilization? It will think we are untutored savages!

That a people should have lived in such pain does seem incredible because it survives. If Orozco, like the mass of his countrymen, takes pain in marriage and presents to the world the
difficult fruit of that union, the world misinterprets if it supposes that he thinks the travail futile. And that one man has
carried in himself the cares of a whole people to transfusion in
glory noble souls like his own will believe.

85. WOMAN

Symbolic figure from The Creation. Encaustic mural, by
Diego Rivera. National Preparatory School

CHAPTER FIFTEEN

DIEGO RIVERA

The word masses is associated with Diego Rivera in many minds. It winds his conversation on nearly any theme, and the large smiling face, the girded bulk, the wide-winged hat, the tread deliberately ponderable cements the memory of his work, weighty and extensive. Four walls of two three-storied patios in the Secretariat of Education are lined, hundreds of yards, by strokes of his brush. That and the library of the Agricultural School of Chapingo, and the main buildings; the auditorium of the Preparatory School in Mexico City; paintings and drawings in great number scattered through the United States and Europe, and piled in his house; and the decoi tion of the National government palace in Mexico City, now under way, are the best biography of him, because this panorama is the toll of less than ten years' occupation.

The monster job outstrips the industry of any contemporary in any part of the world. One must imagine a ductless energy and patience to account for the working days of this unsabbatical artist. Eight hours at least, seven times a week he proves his belief that he is not an entertainer but a laborer in paints. One comes and goes, a month, a year, more years, and each time one returns to Mexico the permanent reassurance of the mountains, the pyramids, and Rivera declasses time. There he sits, curving the plank under him on a scaffold near some ceiling, huge Stetson jammed over his somnolent

86.

277

eyes and benevolent smile, heavy blunt cartridge belt fencing his expanse.

Why Rivera spends his life in khaki on a plank when he might easily acquire money and power in any of the under-takings that lead to those ends, is a worldly question which no worldly reason completely answers. He seems congenitally to need response from the human beings about him and it may be that this universal want in him is as remarkably large as his capacity to accomplish its perennial satisfaction. The Machiavellian prince who would conduct himself so as to gain renown by doing always the extraordinary is approximately duplicated in Rivera, but it would be unfair and inaccurate to say his success crowns only that activity.

Among baroque adventures in Paris (staged for the telling sometimes in Constantinople, Fiji, Oslo, and other improbable places of glamour) Don Diego retails that once on his door-step he was saluted by two reverent men in turbans who spoke French in deference they said, to his incognito. Later a sly in-fluential person tried to sell him warships and he concluded that he was the double of some oriental potentate. To be taken for an oriental occurs to most Mexicans travelling, but in old Florence Rivera would have been very much the native son, a kinsman perhaps of Castruccio Castracani the Lucchese. That gentleman's retort to the boaster who could drink barrels—"So does an ox"—came out of the same pot as Rivera's explanation of an epithet scratched on one of his murals: "Oh, somebody signed his name."

All the poise, the social agility, the plausible facade lacking which Orozco suffers, dwell with his supposed adversary Riv-era, whose every gesture is deliberate, every line calculated, to a target part of the pattern designed by his intellect. Discreetly too as the ideal Florentine prince Rivera directs his actions according to the spirit of his witnesses, and the awed court receives the impression he wishes to convey, which varies with its capacity except for the common zeal that his person is omniscient. The caricature of this virtuosity is a remark misquoted in legend:—"As a matter of fact Lenin and Trotzky disagreed first at a private conference on the fifth of October in Moscow. I was there!"

Wittily Rivera (Diego, Diegote, Dieguín, *El Gordo* and *Panzas* to his immediates) bares foils with all antagonists or sceptics, routs invoking the learning of the ages, and comforts the discomfited making pinwheels and rocking horses conversationally out of respectable abstractions, preferably mathematical or theologian. His mental prosperity brews out aromas civilized and mellow, spiced in irony, layered in epigram and paradox, doubtless unnecessarily consummate.

The Mexican press, which at least bi-weekly finds Rivera to be news, has the habit of prefacing his name with the word *discutido,* as if this were a title. Discussed and disputed he has been since his first mural, and he has by no means refused to aid the debates. Why he paints as he does was the noisiest query, but the enduring riddle is the social purpose he insists is the real point of his work. Radical describes his art and his ideas in the mouths of those who are not pleased by them, and charlatan more conscientious objectors sometimes miscall him. Those who find pleasure at his feet speak or think of him as the Master, but in all the spray of words few unassisted by himself have been able to ascribe a precise social or aesthetic affiliation to him.

One wonders that, knowing he cannot be except crudely classified, Rivera should attach himself so determinedly to this or that doctrine or party. He is nationalist, anti-imperialist, and communist, not less convinced because he is cosmopolite. He has been impressionist, pointillist, futurist, and is bracketed with Juan Gris. A quest is evident in his Mexican work, which is of the Syndicate School, monumental. Except perhaps Raphael and Picasso, few painters have been so much accused of plagiarism as Rivera, and the accusation is as justified in his case as in theirs, and as provable. But if his wisdom is conned by observation and not inspired in adversity he is still soundly the unflattered prince acquiring sagacity because he is already sage. He confesses that "Every painter is a field in which the seed of another painter germinates."

Rivera's self-portrait among the Builders at the head of the main stairway in the Secretariat is an architect. This autobiographic preference describes the qualities to be found in his work. His genius for organization, his taste for symmetry or rather for closed composition, the abstract exactness of relationships between forms and among colors, the lasting solidity and usability, the economical rhythms, postulate charts, blueprints, and tested materials. The care for spacing of an Aztec Rivera concludes is the definition of painting, saying that whereas the art of sculpture lies in the relationship of masses, that of painting is the play of their inverse.

No lyric, no dramatic urge informalizes this cerebral world. Rivera builds a house accessible to the mind. Upon the abstract structure conceived in aesthetic terms he pours a cast of philosophic ideas. The human beings and their courses that he represents are chosen for a symbolic purpose. He does not garble their textures but to sensual beauties he arrives last, curiously enough an exception to the native habit of seeing the physical object first.

The philosophic bent in Rivera is coupled to an impulse even more powerful than his need of response, and it may be that this need complements the greater drive for communication, for explaining. He is above all the *maestro,* ordering the universe according to principles, and pointing with careful wand to the word or the person on which he wishes to focus public

87. RESTORATION OF LAND
   Preliminary sketch for fresco in Secretariat of Education.
   Diego Rivera

88. SOLDIERS IN RAIN CAPES
   Detail from fresco by Diego Rivera. Secretariat of Education

89. WOMEN OF TEHUANTEPEC

Detail from fresco by Diego Rivera. Secretariat of Education

attention. The world is present to his Kantian outlook as an organism possessed of the logic, discipline and consistency regnant in himself. Thus Marx dovetails into his thinking, and Lenin into Marx. Through great concern for being comprehensible he pours his findings into folk-tale and parable, a method employed by a distinguished company in the history of humanity. Similarly he portrays heroes, typical ceremonies and diversions, folk-postures, to embody ideas so closely meshed with one another that they loom given meanings also upon subjects not before seen as symbolic. To clarify and instruct he will resort to knowledge ancestral and current as proverbs; to convince he will appeal to the A.B.C. emotions. Developing his aesthetic to his philosophy he has eliminated and purified. He arrives at an extreme of his logic on the third floor of the Secretariat with frescos pressing and lucid as posters.

II.

If temperament depends on corpuscles Rivera's gift for the abstract, his welding of art to doctrine, might be ascribed to the Indian shade of his pigment. His facility in traffic of pithy phrases, his love of symbol, his apostolic habits, could be traced also to American graves or to the Spanish Jews he says were forbears of a family safe from the Inquisition long before it brought him into the gray green mined world of Guanajuato. Its beliefs are now pruned but his sister is a clairvoyant and he believes in apparitions and ghosts.

Jewish flair more specifically is his rapid adjustment to the people whose horizon he happens to share. He won prizes in the National Academy painting landscapes under the master of that medium Velasco, that sent him to Europe much before the gilded age was ended. In Spain he painted picturesquely and gossiped in cafes; he intrigued in Italy and delicately traced

sweetly noble hills and bullocks till he fell on his knees at
Ravenna and drew hard and hieratic. He was genial in Paris
and a snob for simplicity. The Pennsylvania Station in New
York enchants him and he delivers orations on the beauty of
American plumbing. When a guest of the Soviet government
he split the aesthetic world of Moscow on the subject of pro-
letarian art.

Obviously he was moved to hang a Colt on his hip and
march in religious processions not less devout because the faith
was new and the temples auditoriums when he returned to
Mexico in 1921 after twelve years' absence. He hardly regretted
that he had not camped like most of his colleagues in desolate
churches because he felt more revolutionary than they. A year
or so later he listed service in Morelos under Zapata somewhere among the facts of his life such as being born and having learned much from Picasso. He married the most tempest-
uous beauty in Jalisco, and with this sea-eyed dark creature he
founded a house floored of *petates* and full of poets and popular
art. The first child lisps a vocabulary proper to a young lady
of energy and sophistication.

Rivera's artistic possession of the national scene in murals
dates from the spring of 1922, when he changed from encaus-
tique to fresco with pictures of soldiers and horses keyed in
gray on the first floor of the Secretariat. He proceeds to other
ideal occupations of peasant Mexico: dances, rituals, harvests, a
fair-day, sugar-making, mining, smelting, weaving, dyeing, pottery manufacture and receiving the promised lands. This catalogue is arranged also geographically, and is summed up in the
stairway, which begins with subterranean scenes, follows into
jungle and fertility cult, opens upon the ranching plateau, and,
growing more austere in tone, comes upon revolution, the burial
of a workman, a highland storm, to end with the Builders,
Rivera the architect, Pintao the sculptor, and the painter a

person in a peasant blouse whose face is turned from the public.

The lesson is simple. Here is at the same time a Mexico glorified and the enduring and familiar things which the cities glance upon shamefacedly. They are berated in scenes of city and suburban holiday where rural and urban make spiritual and aesthetic contact both occupied in the business of pleasure. Chiefly the difference is that the whites woefully lack grace. A certain attempt at their caricature betrays Rivera's catholic view. For all his conviction he cannot experience or give the gooseflesh in Orozco's portrayals of the same types.

A more definite social text is inscribed in the panels which Netzahualcoyotl's poem on agrarian policy and Gutierrez Cruz' injunction to the miners illuminate. The two magnificent scenes at the mouth of a mine in the Guanajuato hills by emotion tell the same tale. The miner contracts bowed into the earth; in the companion piece built on the lines of a cross, he ascends triple above the overseers who search him for stray bits of metal. On the stairway the hacienda scene where appears a villainous boss, thumbs and two guns in his belt, and the following panel of mourning diggers of the workman's grave, support the semi-prophetic Restoration of Lands on the first floor, viewed before, but painted after, and a Second of May across a wall of the inner patio in which peasant and labor masses deploy.

Agrarian themes are treated by similar allegory in the main building of the Agricultural School of Chapingo, which work was begun about contemporary to the stairway in the Secretariat. The Bad Government is presented in terms of sterility, the betrayal of the peasant by the politician, the false priest, the mercenary, and subsequent desolation, while the Good Government on the opposite wall is a scene of cultivation.

From the Creation in the Preparatory School to this phase,

Rivera is a modern who passed with Picasso into "realistic" monumental abstraction, remaining also a pupil of the early Italians, unbent by baroque or romanticism. Keep in mind the Sistine and Siqueiros' murals, and the changed manner in the library of Chapingo, once a chapel, will not seem too sudden a tangent. The subject is a Mexican analogy of Michael Angelo's. The largest figure in the decoration, a nude across the entire former crypt, is the fertilized earth. Man, woman, and the elements are the birth-watch. The counter panel and the counter idea is a sleeping nude, the virgin soil. Great nudes, male, sit, stand, bow, fully modeled in the vaults. The small salon would have been entirely crumbled by the ponderous volumes and the intense blues and siennas would have clamoured the decoration to chaos had not the painter opened the ceiling to the sky with a blue background upon which the figures are drawn in perspective, the soles of their feet seen first from below.

The Secretariat nevertheless is concluded in the flat unsculptural medium of its first portion. On the third floor the semi-realistic scenes serve an added symbolic purpose. Scenes of horses and men, scenes of harvest and cultivation, more genre than the landscaped similar subjects on the first floor, are meant because of the singers at the beginning of the series, and the written text of the songs—agrarian ballads—garlanded along the top, to signify the spiritual qualities of the nation. Verses from the tale of Zapata and the hero himself create the dominant mood. The opposite spirit is allegorized in panels portraying capitalists starving on gold, and poets, philosophers and prophets considered by Rivera false or bourgeois. Among them (surely ingratitude!) appears Vasconcelos.

The Secretariat of Education is built as simply as a skyscraper or a monastery. Its offices open upon corridors around two large unroofed patios, separated by a bridge which connects

90. RITUAL WAKE

Detail from fresco by Diego Rivera. Secretariat of Education

the two sides of the building. To make an inner architecture
of the decoration without violating the restful monotony of its
arches and office doors, yet filling the spaces between them not
boresomely, was the problem admirably solved by Rivera, than
whom temperamentally no painter was better endowed for
the task. Each painting lies partly in light, partly in shadow
daily. The top corridor is exposed to the sun at least by reflection all day.

These conditions have been carefully taken into account in
the colour of each portion, with even a flourish because the
lighter values on the third floor balance unexpectedly a majolica cupola which lies in the foreground of the neighbour-
hood skyline. Monochromes portraying the sciences and arts,
and single column-like figures of heroes (Zapata, Felipe Carrillo Puerto, Montaño) in absolute bright tones evacuate rather
than fill the space of the second floor, maintaining the grace of
the patios that might have been lost by unwise crowding. The
range of colour includes all the ingredients of white, the range
of value is limited. Uniformly the surface (all painted with
earths) glows intensely, heavier at the base and vivid toward
the crown, so that in colour as well as in architecture and philosophic plan, an earth-to-sky idea resides in the organism. It is
foreseen viewed from any point as a unit.

III.

Many battles other than aesthetic are fought in these corridors
daily, and many people look upon the frescos who did not
come there for that purpose. The public—largely bureaucrat—
which most immediately owns this national property has in
the main forgiven Rivera his "Indians with bull's-eyes" and
has become accustomed to the "deformities" which bury forever the Diaz days of illusion. When honours came to Rivera

from Russia and the Architects' League of New York that part of Mexico City which reads the newspapers was as amiably taken unawares as the peasant whose animal savings-bank some rare foreigner might covet, muttering incomprehensibly "Tang. ."

In spite of the *discutido* which will probably always be a part of his name, Rivera is respectfully treated in the same press which attacked him. The identical reporters who mocked now praise with the air of proud fathers *el arte de Diego Rivera*. Abetting with generous data and affable interviews the glory of one's own name is a North American custom which abashes a Mexican, but Rivera once explained that this habit and others less amusedly censured are a necessary part of his purpose. Doubtless the missionary technique he has in mind is that inclination of any public's ear to the opinions of well-known men.

The present Mexican government does not endorse communism, but the sermons in fresco fit just as well into the current thinking of "Revolutionaries," and no one in Mexico who has any pretense to office or intellect will be accepted as a legitimate pretender if he affiliates himself outside that exceedingly large and heterodox army. Furthermore one never hears of any conversions in social thinking because of Rivera's frescos, but the number is large of people injected with modern art because of their social thinking. One cannot consider separately the aesthetic and the ideas of Rivera's work, because in his own mind each determines the other; and so it is that even officials mishandled in his infrequent caricatures include in their revolutionary outlook respect for this painting become almost a dogma.

The younger painters of Mexico will in time surely revolt against the Rivera influence which at present lies on them all, and not to their disadvantage. Not only the painters, but the

91. REFINERY

Fresco Panel by Diego Rivera, Secretariat of Education

teachers, the poets, the actors, the musicians, the students, and above all the foreigners, succumb to his rhythmic and massive insistence. Central and South Americans uncomfortable under dictatorships and other archaic unfortunate institutions when they ponder the Mexican oil laws or prepare to emulate Zapata nearly always nail somewhere in their dwellings a photograph of one of his frescos. Too, many an American schoolteacher has been shocked and subsequently mellowed, departing to Kansas, Texas, California or New Jersey with a new and disturbing vision, and the phrase on her lips that "after all it is a matter of the point of view." That people who think last in terms of painting, and people whose most common language is plastic, may be brought thus to share a single affection by a man of genius is an achievement significant to all America. Art critics at least acknowledge the continental distinction.

CHAPTER SIXTEEN

FRANCISCO GOITIA

Mexican civilization expresses itself in no one man so completely as in the mystic Francisco Goitia. It so happens that this man has the attention to detail, the zeal for precision, the versatility in craftsmanship, and the passion for symbol of an ancient; the composure, the enormous patience, the intense humility, the sense of martyrdom, the unmeasured capacity to love, and the decorum which are the very heartbeat of his people.

92.

Now in Mexico one is tacit. Politics, the only loud phenomenon, runs in the headlines to the interest of a very small circle of individuals, who already know what those headlines were intended to report. Atrocities and heroisms occur in official circles daily; the first goes unpunished, the other unrewarded. Everybody knows this, few for their own satisfaction bestir their tongues about it. Venalities are left to disturb chiefly their perpetrators; opinions disturb no one. When punishment or limitation is exercised on an individual, a paper, or a theater, one speculates what feud or misdemeanour lies behind the given cause, which itself is usually dissimilar to things disapproved elsewhere, because the charge is generally that the offender was not a true revolutionary.

A tourist will struggle if he wants to be guided to the proper places of interest; there are none. His route will be interesting but original, whoever his guide. And what do

Mexicans think about this or that problem, he may guilelessly
ask if he is that kind of a tourist; the ubiquitous answer if
truthful will be "whom do you mean?" Long opinions and
great plans for Progress heralded in the press are received by
no one who has not his tongue in his cheek. And since the
real changes come like apparitions, what satisfaction is that
to the unfortunate guest whose kingdom is of this world?
He mourns in this tenor: "It is always the same thing. The
newspapers, year after year, have the same news. Always the
same factors in the national tragedy—or comedy, as you will.
The grafting general, the sly politician, the cunning clergy,
the Indian martyr, the dreamer exiled. It is very discouraging
if you believe in the country, as I do, because you cannot
justify it. You cannot point out definite progress. The land
apparently just stews along in its own juice."

Of course, there is the quality of that juice. Often missionaries have gone desperately hostile because of the cultured
amiability with which they are received, and unheard, by these
people already at peace with themselves. Often diplomatic en-
voys have bred a permanently vicious nature, because they cannot make themselves understood in terms of solid securities.
The solid securities presented to them have nothing to do with
banks or insurance, and anyhow other things come before
safety.

Still the press must contain what newspapers usually print,
just as the fruit on a vendor's tray must be arranged in heaps
of threes and fives. In the government files there certainly must
be statistics, because that is how the furniture is built. Nobody
uses this data except visiting investigators, and they generally
find it most curious. "For correctness" as one says in Mexico,
this will be suitably deplored. Once a distinguished American
thinker expounded his philosophy by invitation before the National University. The audience was very attentive and full of

compassionate murmurs, and shocked. *"Pobrecito!"* It said; "why does he complicate himself so much?"

A sheath of discretion, of courteous misstatement, preserves silence and privacy around each individual; that which moves him goes uncommented, like a rain. He means to live as the spiritual moment demands; so that "revolutionary" is not defined as a plan or philosophy to be fitted in every head like the cork of a bottle. It is in the end an innocent feeling that "revolutionary" are the things you prefer, and the opposite those you abhor.

Thus dogma and facts cannot contain him who is also deliberately impenetrable. The Indian who melts into the brown of the soil even when he stands highest upon it; the girl in the tropics who wears brilliant embroideries and in them cannot be seen in the jungle; the jaguar hunter clothed in a jaguar skin; the sun-dancer in the court of a church with a frontlet of mirrors over his eyes; and the official who deprecates—they are not four hundred years away from the Aztec merchant who travelled by night painted black, with a black staff in his hand, and a monotonous, low-voiced insistence that he was the humblest and poorest and most unimportant of mortals.

In those days the people manufactured their spiritual measuring-tapes out of the fiber of maguey. At close intervals these cords were knotted, and in each knot there was a thorn, also maguey. The man who could pass a large number of such knots through a hole in his tongue was convinced that he was a worthy being—*muy hombre* is the phrase nowadays, and others were aware of it also. He was rewarded by being allowed to devote himself to prayer and more penitence. This priest when he hung the mask of a god on his hat, and maybe another mask on top of that on another pyramidal hat, and feathers in the peak, enacted the part of the god in the rites; all religion was abstract drama which duplicated qualities of

93. PORTRAIT
    Oil by Francisco Goitia

spirit. It was a secret convention that all men live frugally and
quietly like him, and that like him all men were proxies of
divinity. He might beat on his chest in a sudden battle, or on
top of a pyramid roar with his face to the sky that he was
invincible; then he completed his rôle in the play by being
immolated.

II.

It seems that everyone who has heard of Diego Rivera knows
vaguely of Francisco Goitia. There is no reason for that
because only five men see him, about three times a year. One
of these men is the Subsecretary of Education, another is the
head of the National Department of Anthropology, the third
is a physician, the fourth an architect and the fifth Dr. Manuel
Gamio.

The Subsecretary sees him because a collection of Goitia's
paintings hang in his office, and Goitia is always changing one
picture for another, or adding a new one; that is, on each of
the three annual visits. His position in the Secretariat is not
explicit. He receives a small pension and returns it in as many
or as few pictures as he will. The collection looks as if some
viceroy had begun it, the curator of an art museum had mod-
ernized it, and the Subsecretary had added one or two paintings he thought suitably inoffensive in a public place. A buyer
would have no market proof that the series is all by one man,
because none of the pictures are signed.

Lengthy indecorous inquiry will disclose that Goitia came
from the state of Zacatecas, possibly from a ranch; that a famous
collector in Barcelona owns several studies by him; that he
was the artist Gamio sent to "identify himself" with Teotihuacan, and that in an Oaxaca forest somebody found him up
to the neck in the muddy water of a cave; that he lives on the
edge of a floating garden in the Indian village of Xochimilco,

and that although any Xochimilcan can direct you to his house, none of them do so. They take you canoe riding instead. He is said to be mad.

The house in Xochimilco is made of adobe tinted on the outside like all the other houses around it. You slap with the flat of your hand on a large wooden door built in an arch, it opens a crack, you inquire for *el Señor Francisco,* you wait, you raise your eyes to the hills, and you step down into a dark room smelling of earth, soaked maize, lime, woodfire, and chickens, like any Indian *jacal.* A woman patting tortillas gives you water to drink in a small brown mug inscribed *Un Recuerdo.* You sit on the three-legged stool of the house and tap the moist ground under you with your toe, in time one half-slower than the hands of the kneeling lady who tells you that there is much sun today.

Presently a cock crows behind you. He is perched on a great barracks of canvases, stretched and apparently painted because there are blue spots on the reverse, among other colours probably dropped by a fowl who wished to help his master. His clarion announces the young woman who opened the door. She ushers you to a white, dusty patio in the middle of which a very large tree blossoming yellow grows. A room built alone, square, with one door and one window, cuts across this space. Beyond there is maize and more space, bounded by cactus and a splendid youthful maguey, growing in a mound of sun-baked adobes, apparently left by whoever was building the hive of cells in a row against the wall which encloses the entire house and field.

The servant returns with your stool and a coat, which she takes to el *Señor Francisco* in the square room. Where else would he be? She pours soapy water into a puddle owned by a marriage of ducks, asks if your thirst is quenched, and tells you that your host is shaving. Of course! The unannounced

94. **VILLAGE ORCHESTRA**
Pastel by Francisco Goitia

95. **NEWS FROM THE BATTLEFIELD**
Charcoal study for etching. Francisco Goitia

visit of a lady! It is warm for a coat. Follows a measured and
formal exchange of greetings with a slight, compact man in his
thirties who looks like Saint Francis.

He presses his hands together, wringing them slowly as he
speaks in the voice of a child. The dark oval face and mobile
expression has something at once sweet and wild. The cropped
hair closes down on his skull in the soldierly way of a monk.
His deep large eyes gleam and turn in their sockets when he
hears that you have come because you are interested in his
painting; then are immediately dropped.

In the room which on rainy days is a studio, against white-
washed walls rests a book-case full of the names of artists on
the backs of fine bindings. The place also contains a colonial
chest, an etching press, a curtain, a wash-stand, and a table on
which lie two very long yellow tapers which the owner explains are intended for the model in a painting of a holiday he
has been thinking about, a shrine, and a very small mirror. A
goatskin spread in one corner, you suddenly realize, is his bed.

III.

The conversation of this anchorite inscribed itself for two
years into my mind. He troubled to explain himself with many
details about his work. On the way from his house I used notebook and pencil because he said so many things that had to be
thought out one at a time. The way from his house to the city
is long, and his sentences dropped deeper and deeper out of
disorder; composing his testament into that of his land. But I
was not aware of it then because he spoke so simply.

Francisco Goitia arrived in Mexico City from Zacatecas, he
says, "In the time of copying prints. For this reason I began to
realize that I could do nothing if I did not go to Europe to
study, and I pointed this out to my father, who was able to

send me. I stayed eight years. In Barcelona I was told that my studies of the landscape looked as if I were a native son. So I began to think that I would be doing my best work only if I returned to my country, for in that way I could express all I was. In Pompeii I observed the cactus and the volcanoes and the blue sky and thought it necessary that an architecture be developed in Mexico suitable to our volcanoes and cactus and sky."

The moonlight of an Italian village interested him, so he went out and painted in it. How else could one get its quality? He slipped out of his pension night after night carrying an easel and canvas, casting a great shadow in the road and breathing very lightly, but he discontinued this practice because the village rumored that a phantom walked from midnight to three carrying a gibbet. He was very unobtrusive. That village nevertheless considered him an extremely strange man dressed in gray, says his friend the architect who was there studying music.

"When the revolution came I returned to my country. As I belonged to the landowning classes I had not precisely a point of view, about the revolution, rather a prejudice, although I had never liked the attitude of order and obey between sons of *hacendados* and the peon boys with whom I played. I considered the matter from every angle. About the time when Villa was fighting the most, I was at last able to realize just what it meant, and so I set about planning my part of it. I went to General Angeles, who as a cultured man I judged would understand my position. After I had explained my ideas to him, and told him, I want to see this, he gave me the position of artist on his staff. I went everywhere with the army, observing. I did not carry weapons because I knew that the mission of killing was not mine, and also it was clear to me that if other lives were lost it would not be the same as if mine, which had already had so much preparation for its task, were among them.

"Villa was defeated, and so then I took my way and stayed on a small ranch in my state. Those were times of misery and disease, and I passed through the calvaries of the humble and for this reason I feel a kind of brotherhood between us, in spite of the difference of class, and the mutual respect. I wore the clothes of a muledriver, and went about as one, making the same journeys. Nights of frightful cold, days without water. . . . There was much robbery because the people were poor and there was sickness and hunger. I had a few cows on a little ranch and these were stolen, and I had therefore to take the side of him who defends his property, though I would have chosen otherwise. Another time that I was robbed ten armed men followed the bandits, and I hoped that they would not overtake them because I would not have lives lost on my account. Then I went to Mexico City and had many difficulties, looking for work to do. It was a long period in which, as during the revolution, I looked and observed and saw, but I did not do anything except make a few little notes, which I keep maturing for the right moment. Some arrangements were then made by means of which I was taken to Dr. Gamio, and through the position he gave me I was enabled to continue my task.

"The philosophy of my work is what interests me the most. To take each aspect of my land and of the race, and to make a whole so that it will be understood well . . in my way, and in my time, for since this is a true renascence each one works in a different direction. . . The ragged side is the first phase of the plan which I have drawn up. Although I have not been told so directly, I understand that they think my pictures discredit Mexico, because they reveal those things. Still, I take pleasure in battling in this sense, that is of imposing what I want. And I like it that a half nude skinny child should hang in the office of the Subsecretary, as if saying 'Look, don't get up too high, here I am.' The old man sitting on a garbage heap next to that child was the happiest man I ever saw. He owned not a thing in the world, not even a hat, and he sat there every day and enjoyed the blue sky. You see a kind of irony goes through my work. I think that old man would be well, hanging in the office of an American millionaire.

"However, I will also portray the second phase, which is that of the martyrdoms, a theme to which I am dedicated and which interests me deeply. An arm, a back. I have been working in the medical school dissecting room to see about a flagellated back, because there are certain welts that I know should be there. My model has a very beautiful brown skin and I take some blood that I get at the market and pour it upon him to get the spots as they ought to be.

"These martyrdoms will be of the revolution. For one of them I will be served by the story of General Lázaro Gomez, who went about in my state. He with his people were at a water-hole, partaking of a steer they had killed. He was advised that General Murgia was upon him, but he said unconcernedly, he won't come around here. Somebody told, and suddenly they fall upon Gomez and his people in that water-hole, which was almost a plain. The soldiers were able to mount and take to the field, but the horse of the general was fiery, it broke the rope and ran away, leaving him alone to face the enemy, which consisted of about twenty men. And he stayed fighting them. How skilful he must have been that he was untouched when the afternoon was ending. They could no longer see him, and they asked one another, where is he? And he, unwounded, could have been able to escape, would answer each time, here is your father. At last he shot very little, because he had no more ammunition, so the soldiers fell upon him and took him. He told them not to kill him. Take me to your camp, have them meet a man .. But one of them shot him in the back and for this reason the captain who came afterwards was very angry.

"The corpse they took on a donkey to a place nearby, and at a very strange tree, which is called the Sad Tree, they beheaded him, gave him a kick and hanged him by the wrists. The head of the steer from which he was partaking they put on his shoulders. In a few days, his clothes fell from him, and caught on his feet. That was a real phantom. Enormously long, with the head of the steer, nude, bled. . . There is my picture. Some time afterwards the same men of Gomez fought those of Murgia, behaving very valiantly. And he who had given the dead chief a kick fell in this contest . . . a coincidence rare and Mexican. I went there afterwards and was able to exhume the corpses, hanging them upon the tree, from which I made some drawings. Then I had to go to Mexico City and as the air is very dry the corpses don't rot, so I had a hut built around the tree and put a caretaker there and I have it for when I can return to continue my studies.

"You see it is natural that circumstances have made my temperament more inclined to the profound. There is a great deal of sadness in this country and I have tried to sum a certain phase of it in the Sad Indian. When I was in Teotihuacan I found a model who impressed me very much because of the way he sat. This was just like the way the idols sit. The man I was going to paint was a porter, and he would come in from his work of carrying large loads and sit with his head down. I made many different studies of him but somehow I never quite felt that thing which I wanted to paint. At last he got tired of posing, or else afraid. Anyhow he did not come any more. So I went to police headquarters and told them that he had robbed me, and they went out after him and brought him in. He dropped on a pile of sacks in my patio. What he was thinking about I do not know, but he was afraid, and very tired, and waiting. I felt it then, and in half an hour I had finished my picture.

"I also had to wait a very long time before the picture of two women weeping which is called Tata Jesucristo was accomplished. Dr. Gamio has done me the favour of telling me that it is one of the finest things I have done. I tried my models sitting this way and that, but no, I didn't feel it exactly right. At last I investigated everything I could about them. I then made them come and sit for me on the Day of the Dead, when of their own accord they would be dwelling on sorrow, and little by little I uncovered their sorrows and the revolution and their dead. And they writhed, and one turned her foot up in the pain. Then I knew I had it! Those hands and feet gave their grief the genuine form. I would never have thought of it myself, but of course that is the way grief is, and so I was satisfied at last. They weep tears of our race, pain and tears our own and different from others. All the sorrow in Mexico is there.

"On the other hand we have riches too, and I have expected to continue painting them. We have the beautiful women of the tropics with rosaries of beaten gold and amethysts around their necks, and a flower in their hair. In the Valley of Mexico there are the dancers with their animal masks, and in Teotihuacan I painted a band of musicians. I have been trying to make different studies of sunlight for a nude after a bath that I am beginning to think about. For how can any one understand the flesh of flowers and of the people, that is toasted and warm, unless he understands the sun?

"You shall come with me tomorrow afternoon at five o'clock to a house near the church of Our Lady of Soledad. It is a colonial building that has become a tenement. At five o'clock there is a certain warm smell in the air, and the murmur of doves. The women have finished washing their clothes and these are hung all across the patio to dry. There is a certain yellow coverlet that hangs there and catches the light. I am working on a study of this place, which will be the first of a series of four, each of them a house like this in a way, but different. Dr. Gamio was kind enough to like the pastel of the first. He wanted me to exhibit it and some other things, but I told him I was not quite ready to exhibit. There are certain things that must be finished and certain others that must be added. He finally asked me when I would be ready to exhibit, and I estimated that in about twenty or thirty years my task would be complete."

IV.

The long preparation of each picture is not evident in the amount of paint and the number of lines to be seen in the finished product, nor in the scarcity of these elements. One might say that they are not visible at all, in the sense that the clothing of a true elegant is harmoniously undistinctive. The paintings can be seen by the most learned or the most simple with appreciation. The technique—extraordinary if analyzed from the point of view of technique—does not shock, and the subjects, deliberately the most powerful focusses of human emotion, by sheer good taste and skill appear natural, unpicturesque.

The most remarkable thing to be seen in the paintings can be seen only by comparing the entire series. It becomes clear that each picture is completely dissimilar to the next. Composition, texture, design, colour, rhythm, even the rapidity of brush-strokes and the size of the canvas, seem to have been invented for the sole purpose of portraying one creature or one scene. The personality of the man, and his style, lies in that complete submergence of himself to the demands of his subject. The medium is so precisely not adjusted to, but the outgrowth of, the subject, that this miracle is visible only through critical dissection. The ragged child, for example, is a lucid study in contrasts. A portrait of a hill-woman is a ridged coarse-surfaced painting put together architecturally with large planes of colour, extremely limited, intense, and vibrant as if it had just been completed. The pastels of tenement houses are delicate, complex fusions of the rainbow. The "Women at the Battle of Ocotlan" is a carbon study, quivering, nervous, lighted by red and green flashes exactly complementary to each other and thus equal to the black and white of the drawing. Their faces are not visible. "Their pain," says Goitia, "can be felt in the lines of their garments."

Goitia believes that a perfect way, one only, exists of re-creating each already created thing. This is a combination of circumstances such as the hour of the day, the quality of the light, the brand and weight of the paint used, the history and state of mind of the subject—or state of being, if it is inanimate—its physical nature—volume, texture, temperature, function. One is reminded that for each building, no matter how strong, a musical note exists which can bring it down. His religious attention to minutiæ is comprehensible too, in the nature of those Catholic saints who scrutinized with love every scrap of matter or of life that their eyes, their hands, their feet, touched upon.

Goitia's point of departure is the physical aspect, and he must in the end reduce all the concomitant aspects to this, or rather, find them in it, and transpose them into corresponding, not identical, artistic existence, and if he breaks any conventions to do it he takes it for granted that he must. He takes also for granted the mastery that permits him to do so. Before the living subject, he is humble and in a torture of the senses

96. TATA JESUCRISTO
Oil by Francisco Goitia

to grasp and enclose its inherent qualities unviolated. Before the easel, he is absolute sovereign. The artist abstracting the significant structure of his subject, thus creating symbol, is at one in Goitia with the mystic to whom every structure is significant. To Cézanne's observation that the line is most perfect when the colour is at its best, he would add that both are exact when the spirit is comprehended, or the inverse.

The modernistic painter absorbed in the invention of systems of expression into which any subject can be interpreted disproportionately submerges the subject, and he knows it, but he is less the scientist he believes himself to be, because of it. To take liberties with the eyes, divorcing an art from emotion to pattern, with the mind, is an amusement distasteful to the man who inherits a traditional respect for material, a craftsman's seriousness, and senses that will not permit themselves to be taught systematic reactions. The momentary discrepancy thus between Goitia and the æsthetic now regnant in the western world, even in Mexico makes him unremarked as he wishes to be; though in Mexico spectators trained to æsthetic prejudice are not frequent enough to offend or distort diverse efforts, nor to call except affectionately mad that man who for the sake of a pure work of art tenders his people the sacrifice of an unworldly life.

V.

Across the way from Goitia's adobe house there is a tiny colonial chapel with a charming majolica cupola. This chapel, and the house which will be built around Goitia's room and upon the field next door he has been acquiring by small mortgages, will be a national property "that will bring visitors as does El Greco's residence," says Goitia. The house will be built on a plan "suited to the volcanoes, the sky, and the cactus, which look upon it." The decoration of the house will be fresco, and it will include "the flora and fauna of the land, and also the revolution."

As to the chapel, "The spaces of the vaults must be suitably filled, as might Benozzo Gozzoli. It would seem that the place requires a theme of religion. To that theme I shall give a direction, although they say that this is encouraging fanaticism; a point which seems hardly accurate to me, as this people has always been religious and will continue so. Yesterday it was the idols and today it is the saints, and if they take those images there would be others. I have a model for my Saint Peter. He is a fisherman who lives here in Xochimilco. What more appropriate and exact for a representation of Saint Peter than one of these poor and humble persons, particularly as this man is also a fisherman? Furthermore, there is an analogy which I would make and which is not generally now understood in the same sense as I see it. Purgatory and hell, resurrection and the apocalypse, are perfectly things of this race. You will have thought of purgatory in the Secretariat. The apocalypse arises out of those elements which can be seen as ugly, but which are really beautiful and above all, must be accepted because they are ours."

97. MOURNERS

Battle of Ocotlan. Charcoal drawing, Francisco Goitia

CHAPTER SEVENTEEN

JEAN CHARLOT

Desirée Charnay, that charming Frenchman who hunted Atlantis and Egypt in the Maya jungles, and made casts of magnificent stelæ with wet newspapers, presented Jean Charlot on the occasion of his first communion with some ancient American grave-pottery, remarking that it seemed an appropriate gift 98. because he had found it in the grave of a child. This was not, however, Charlot's introduction to American art. At that age he probably already regarded himself as a colleague. He had begun to draw at the age of three and to examine critically Mexican picture manuscripts in the collection of his family, which had branched to Mexico represented by an adventuresome great-great-great-grandfather somewhere around 1820. One of the offspring married an Indian woman the colour of whose skin is still commented on the Parisian side; another married a Jewess of Spanish descent in Mexico City and with Maximilian's best wishes returned to Paris. Their daughter married a Frenchman from Russia sympathetic to the then persecuted Bolshevists. He was Jean Charlot's father.

By the time Charlot was born his immediate family was again Parisian. He early asserted this fact by studying minutely Greek vases; by composing rigidly classic quatrains; and by adopting the almost discarded traditional night-cap. He spent his time in art galleries and strained his eyes on medieval

303

books, he worked for Poiret, won prizes for abstract sculpture and a Via Crucis series of woodcuts. When the war came along to teach Europe something about death, Charlot's university class volunteered and he marched, a gamin artillery lieutenant with the face of a novice and the cocked eyebrow of an engineering surveyor. The end of the war found him in Germany with the Army of Occupation, absorbed in Mathias Grünewald. Perhaps this was the reason he lagged behind his own battery, recovering crisply issuing orders to another several miles behind. He received insignia of honour, most likely not for that feat.

Charlot arrived in Mexico (one might almost say he returned) in 1921, to live with an uncle whose collection of antiquities did not yet repose in the French National Library and the Trocadero, like most of the rest of the family possessions. He revived woodcut; illustrated the poems of a leading *Estridentista* (literally strident) poet; wrote neatly scholastic reports of Mexican popular and modern art for Parisian revues, and for Mexican; fell in love with a gorgeous friend of the Syndicate; discovered an Indian model who largely because of his paintings became a "classic" native female in modern Mexican painting; and painted the first mural in the Preparatory School, which was also the first fresco.

With Rivera and De la Cueva, Charlot moved to the Secretariat, where he instructed the *maestro's* masons on the preparation of walls for true fresco, painted backgrounds and details in these walls, and three panels of his own, one of which was later moved and re-painted by Rivera to make room for a large composition. Charlot went on painting "monumentally" on canvas after walls were no longer available, at the same time recording in a series of very small, very dark, very simple pictures the results of his unfatigued explorations and carefully limited æsthetic experiments. The *Mexican Folkways,* a maga-

99. LANDSCAPE MORELOS
   Oil by Jean Charlot

100. NATIVE SCULPTOR
   Tlaquepaque. Water color by Jean Charlot

zine devoted to Mexican art and custom informally, was born with Charlot officiating as art editor, serious and preoccupied as a very bright modest child.

In 1926 the Carnegie Institution archæological staff at Chichen-Itzá, Yucatan, engaged him to copy Maya frescos and bas-reliefs which could not be satisfactorily photographed. He was found to know much about Maya art that could enlighten archæologists as to the Mayas; was sent hunting stelæ, and found a prize one; and worked so skillfully and uniquely under the blinding Yucatan sun that the head of the expedition pronounced him the discovery of the season, and retained him. Sundays and holidays he painted the Yucatan pristine to modern art, reflecting much upon it.

II.

"When I came to Mexico," Charlot wrote, "I had a stage country in my head; many feathers, blue, green, and tropical pantomime. I was shown the most popular actress, the National Theater, and also many too-white young girls with enormously high heels; themselves wound round with ruffles of organdie. And they showed me gentlemen with false collars. One of these, very much a millionaire and even more a valetudinarian, said to me: "Here, there are the savages, and ourselves. How can one speak of equality?

"Very soon I knew that indeed there was no equality. One day I went out upon the streets at six o'clock in the morning. At six o'clock in the morning the fair ladies are in garage and their automobiles are still asleep. For that reason I could look upon the true countenance of this city so covered with ornament throughout the day that one can hardly recognize her. Deserted, the residence sections look like a music-hall after the performance, but in any other part, among the low, cubic, painted houses, beautiful beings people the streets, there are numberless Ladies of Guadalupe. They follow one foot with the other noiselessly, and ancient beauty is reborn.

"Put a *chic* woman beside one of the virgins of the Parthenon, and that will be a sight to burst with laughter or weep with shame; any one of these Indians is a sister of that ancient. It is the same posture, the same gesture, the trace of the foot on the ground is the same, as is the manner of walking, the foot always horizontal and adhering to the earth like a hand. And when they come out of early mass! Wide skirts, folds of drapery, is not this the very rhythm of the Panathenæ? At first sight they are entirely colour of the dust; it seems as if flesh and worn clothing had fused in this gray which is extreme poverty and humility. When the eye becomes accustomed and the soul also, this rebel race discovers to loving observation the beauty of its weaves, and of its flesh.

"Their *rebozos*—wrapped in a thousand ways, always with nobility, never keep a fold not essential to the body and its movement, the reverse of those fashionable cloths which crinkle like poodle dogs. Apparently alike, they are really composites of fine taste and artistic self-restraint; gray upon gray, black and light brown, rose and tenuous violet, blue, from midnight to pastel, pigeon's throat, mauve, but fused so wisely that a scarcely attentive glance confuses them. The fringes affirm the texture as a musical motif begun over again with more accentuation; from the back, the braided hair with its red cord rounding the shoulder implies the flesh; face to face, the ovoid or spherical ocher-pigmented countenance transfers into the basic tone of the warp, while the white of teeth and eyes match the surface finish. By itself the rebozo is like a broken wing; it needs the tension and the living folds which model the face, though the face be hidden.

"Blessed too the cold days when the man wraps himself in a

101. MOTHER AND CHILD
    Yucatan. Lithograph by Jean Charlot

sarape: he looks then like the tribune clothed in the waves of the sea. A piece of green wool here is worth the toga in marble. The sarapes: of multiple colours which come together in a white-gray-black and certainly the most beautiful of them are those without design, whose surface and texture is like the thin skin of a hard-beaten little burro, with white threads interwoven like the scars of the blows. This garment away from its wearer is no more than the shirt of a dead man, still retaining the form of his torso. The decoration is always simple, taken from familiar things of nature and craft; beauty of hard earth and birds, better than Solomon in all his glory; and put together with an abstract geometry such as only this people after the Greeks of Crete have possessed."

Obviously Charlot's first Mexican sketches were of women in *rebozos,* carrying baskets, babies, flowers, kneeling covered from tip of the head to just over the heel; and of men in sarapes, hunched, rounded, pyramidal, ending in the woven sculptured *petate* hat. Their contrasts the *chic* engaged his attention to the extent of a few drawings compounded of artistic disdain toward the subject, an exquisitely controlled pen, and a large shadow of ethical censure. *The Rich in Hell,* for example. This drawing belongs almost to folk-art. It was followed long after by the portrait of a lady in purple with a red wig and a preposterous hat, wearing the medal of a religious organization large and golden upon her bosom. She was the only comment on the troubles of Mother Church that a devout son permitted himself; and his indignation is tempered by a pleased interest in the ornate hat. Anyhow, says Charlot, you can pretty well tell what things are good and what are bad, but as to people you never know who they are. To be sure he examines lengthily every scrap of "bad art" that comes his way; whereas good pictures receive a friendly and satisfied glance.

The first fresco in the National Preparatory School is a

102. WORKMAN

Chichen-Itza, Oil, Jean Charlot

battle scene (The Fall of Tenochtitlan) based frankly on
Ucello. The colour key in fine grays, and the transparency of
the figures, compared with other Mexican murals is clearly
European. It is encrusted with brasses to break the fine surface
and to catch the light, which, he was reproached, are not
archæological. Of course not. They are curtain rings. Char-
acteristically Charlot confined himself here to one problem,
that of composition on a large scale, and to one technical
result, a successful true fresco. These two contributions were
of great value to later mural work, both his own and that of
other men. In the Secretariat his two panels which remain are
not distinguishable at once from the surrounding Riveras. The
tones compounded of earths, and the subjects, washerwomen
and porters, interpolate no parenthesis in the series that encases
them, but the arrangement is more formal, the rhythms simpler and evident, and the more angular geometry implies the
young man who taught mathematics to artillery officers in
training.

Paradoxically Charlot, who stylizes to abstraction his subjects, is a realist, in the sense that his subjects are the frequent
and familiar things that one sees: the woman with a child at
her breast or slung on her back, the woman at a river washing
her clothes nude from the waist up, or with her hands full of
suds in the head of her son; grinding maize for tortillas knelt
before her metate, dropped in a very low chair with her face in
her hands, folded from head to bare sole in her rebozo; the
man on his haunches with his head almost between his knees;
with his knees slipped under him and his hands in the clay of
his pottery; and bent to an arc under his burden, and standing,
sombrero limp in his hand, mantle dropped like resting wings
from his shoulders. These gestures and postures one does not
turn the head to observe. They are all that one knows is the
presence of a native. One cannot turn a page of an old picture

manuscript without finding each time the complete repertoire, through generations become formal as a ritual ballet; one cannot walk through an archæological museum or stop at the smallest ceramics booth except almost unaware that sizes, ages, colours, materials (from rock to flesh), are a change only of intonation, and any other would be unthinkable.

Each figure is then a symbol for a thousand others. And one is so accustomed to the rectangular and pyramidal, monumental, squat, dark, native's vision of himself articulated of a limited number of volumes, that one discounts, to Charlot's gratification, the startling sum of studious analysis and amorous observation that his work represents. Many a distinguished lady, enchanted with the feather-tongued young man she supposes an ambassadorial attaché, except for the fact that he opens all the books in her library and carries most of her pictures to the window, ultimately feels injured by the crudeness she perforce discovers in his. And one romantic admirer who anticipated a burly illiterate peasant sneered at the schoolboy upon whom he had wasted ardent letters, and would probably have broken his collegiate goggles if he had not been taught in his childhood that little gentlemen never do such things.

Tenacious to physical aspects Charlot developed in the course of his work an intimate vision of plateau Mexico, the place of religion and revolution; grinding and polishing his own technique by undertaking pictorial problems consecutively more complex, consistently less than his complete capacity. In the elusive charm of his less watchful water colours; the precisely cutting, raced line of notebook sketches; the elaborate simplicity of certain pastel-toned paintings of Yucatecan women, might be surprised the Frenchman whose achievement lies in what was omitted. With a secret kind of amusement at his own intellectual complexities Charlot packs all his thought and a large portion of skill into compositions naïve, apparently, as

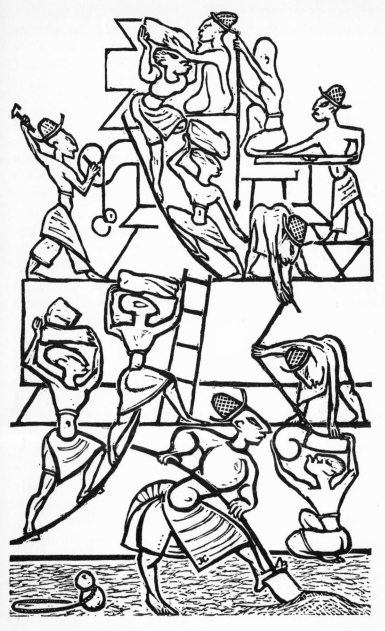

103. PYRAMID BUILDERS
   Yucatan. Woodcut, Jean Charlot

skyscrapers or houses of cards; which on the other hand satisfy his zeal for clarity and deep æsthetic and spiritual need
of order.

III.

An apprentice archæologist reading Charlot's conclusions
about the Mayas whose art he records and describes, will be
discomforted; because these conclusions, which tally with data
found by respectable archæological method of pick and shovel,
are based on the unasserted calm view that all artists think
alike. The glamour of antiquity and the mysteries of racial
origin he regards as much less relevant to the Mayas than, for
example, their habit of composing closed, complete, symmetrical, and extremely complex bas-reliefs which cover exactly the surface on which they are carved. Thus when he
observes younger Mayas with their striped mason's aprons
looped like Egyptians', and their arms thrust up, climbing
pyramid stairs with the broken heads of plumed serpents, to
replace them on columns which bear sculptures of Mayas with
aprons looped like Egyptians' and their arms thrust up, he
portrays them in complex, mathematical, closed, and abstract
compositions.

It does not seem curious in the face of these pictures that a
twentieth century Parisian should have corroborated in Mexico
a suspicion that centuries are conventions, particularly a twentieth century Parisian who was bred in the twelfth, and who
is inclined to write letters numbering the paragraphs and
heading them with a textual description of the contents, but
not in Latin, because that would be too bizarre. The twelfth
century in France and the twentieth in Mexico have certainly
more in common than the twelfth in Mexico and the twelfth
in France, or the corresponding twenties. In the case of Charlot
one must speculate which of the two, twelfth or twentieth,

104. FRESCO
By Amado de la Cueva in University of Jalisco, Guadalajara

105.   CHILDREN OF REVOLUTION

Bas-relief in wood. By Juan Hernandez, from design of
Xavier Guerrero

106.   ROAD TO THE FAIR

Bas-relief in clay. Mural, museum, San Juan Teothuacan,
by Yela Gunther

France or Mexico predominates; one cannot be sure because he is too consistent a unit.

Perhaps a shade of that vague feeling among young Europeans that Europe is dying; perhaps an irritated repudiation, after the war, of trivial and smart gymnastics; and certainly an expressed conviction that Mexico has a new value to contribute to the artistic and spiritual world, made of Charlot an American. He is pleased in New York to look "like a toothpaste salesman" and to amuse himself with five cent magazines, tabloids, crime-tales, and movies; and assumes that if Russians and Spaniards and New Yorkers go to Paris for the sake of their souls, as Germans and Frenchmen and Greeks went to Florence and Rome, he belongs legitimately to the place and the art in whose new life he feels at home.

CHAPTER EIGHTEEN

REVOLUTION AND RENASCENCE

In the span of one generation Mexico has come to herself. Her first and definitive gesture is artistic. While the government shifts and guerrillas still battle for *Cristo Rey* and other interests, the builders, necessary as the destroyers, refound the nation. It is a nation which establishes a school for sculpture before thinking of a Juvenile Court, and which paints the walls of its buildings much sooner than it organizes a Federal Bank. Sanitation, jobs, and reliably workable laws are attended to literally as a by-product of art; for the revolution is a change of régime, because of a change in artistic style, or, if one wishes a more usual description, of spirit.

107.

In goods of this world the nation is poor. It is uncomfortable, exposed to many diseases, hungry, and generous to death. Its scenic and racial beauties and dangers are largely unmapped, unexploited, unlinked to western civilization except by an occasional aeroplane. On the east coast adventurers, gunmen, oilmen and natives clutch at each other's throats; farther south in the forests many Indians die of overwork for chicle and lumber and fruit interests, or die underfed, or retreat still farther; in the plateau often mines once rich are deserted, and others are flooded or boycotted by restless peons demanding a higher wage and less disastrous conditions than those traditional since the conquest; in the cities the governments wrestle with all these evils, and with the murder and lust in their own personnel.

Ancient Greece at grips with the barbarians and before that torn in class conflict and family disputes, the Italian city-states rising and breaking by battle and treachery, had no more desolate and painful a social panorama than this. But one cannot admire Greek thought and maintain a relationship with the Renaissance at all cordially intimate if one prudishly requires of each, Protestant virtues. The greatness of these civilizations lies in achievements that were the results of all their conditions and aptitudes. They were organic, consistent with themselves. The beauty of Mexico lies in precisely the same quality of unified culture; in the flowering of culture at the crossing of many threads, with great pain. And what else than consistency is beauty? Insistently Mexico has died and killed for a phrase: Land and liberty. Never does it open interested eyes to the slogan Prosperity. The cult of health, wealth, and happiness is meager for people who practice the three heroisms that they preach: of emotion, and thought, and expression.

Zapata was murdered, and the lands are not yet completely restored to his people, as he visioned; Carrillo Puerto was betrayed, and his Mayas are not much better in health or in wealth since his death; Orozco's critiques of social disasters have had no measurable practical result; the Syndicate disappeared without having created an economic niche for the artist. But in all of these things are embodied the three heroisms, and that is enough. Yet these ideas and images with a life of their own reproduce others similar. They travel to other arts, to music, literature, government; and to other places. Their seepage to practical matters eventually bursts old dams. Thus material changes come sudden and enormous as floods.

II.

When the Syndicate disappeared several men had already made permanent influential records in murals: Siqueiros, Orozco, Rivera, Charlot. Fermin Revueltas had decorated a hall in which machines were to be kept, in an abstract manner appropriate to machines and reminiscent of pulquerias. This was an original and personal contribution to the art of pure decoration. Merida had adorned a children's library in a charming and simple style, which was followed by other painters on the walls of primary-school classrooms. Many painters who sighed for walls and never received them, were on canvas increasing the volume of "revolutionary art" which has changed metropolitan taste.

Recently a building (Headquarters of the Police and Fire Department) went up which is neither European nor colonial. It is re-enforced concrete with an angularly tiered cornice, broad arched patios, and for single decoration a large carving of the native god of fire in lava rock. This building was much admired. The architect was asked what style he had followed. He said that it was smelted of native pre-Spanish and native post-Spanish lines, and designed in the modern spirit which the material implies, and therefore it could be called modern Mexican.

The open-air schools of painting, multiplying to date, have been followed by craft centers, groups of woodcut students, tapestry and embroidery classes, a sculpture workshop where the carving is done by young boys directly on hard rock from living animal models, and groups of mural students in the primary schools, who decorate the walls of their classrooms. Dolores Cueto embroiders on fine tapestries motifs borrowed from children's work, from popular art, and from the work of the modern painters. Potters and weavers from nearby vil-

108. CUPOLA

From Fire and Police Headquarters, Mexico City. Re-enforced concrete and tile. Architectural design by Guillermo Zárraga

109. MURAL DECORATION

Of hall for machines, Mexico City. Fresco. By Fermin Revueltas

lages "take samples" from their friends among the painters to copy in their own materials. They lend these patterns to other villages, or send them already woven or worked in clay, assimilated to popular tradition. On the sixteenth of September, the Day of the Dead, Christmas or Easter week, when the villages bring their wares to the capital, one may discover, in one of the many booths filled with "Aztecistic" ceramics, lacquers, and textiles designed for the foreigners who buy them, patterns of modern metropolitan origin. However their modernity is no more strikingly evident than is the antiquity of certain forms and designs whose counterparts are found under lava.

Folk-art influence is in turn now common in the work of metropolitan artists, sometimes because these artists came to the city from towns and villages whose art, they discovered, was much admired in the capital, and sometimes, as in the case of Manuel Roderiguez Lozano, deliberately courted. Rodriguez Lozano was bred in Paris. When he returned to Mexico he was made head of the department of drawing in the Secretariat, under Vasconcelos. He changed the Best-Maugard tradition because he was interested in the folk-art of the city. The results in the classrooms, pulqueria art, and miracle-boards, together with the work of Abraham Angel which was likened to these arts, helped to determine the course of Lozano's own style. Steadily it has become simpler, more solid, less apparently sophisticated. Younger men learning from him develop under his influence painting which is at once learned and naïve. One of the more interesting among them is Julio Castellanos.

Of other painters in Mexico City who consider themselves the next generation, and who have worked in the wake of the Syndicate, Rufino Tamayo and Agustin Lazo are to be watched with critical interest. Lazo, influenced by Rivera, later in Paris developed his original tendency toward the abstract and the intellectual, not without affectation. Tamayo has been original and industrious. His rich and delicate water colours imply at once the tropics from which he came, the fruits odorous in his house. Tamayo least the cerebral, most the intuitive whose improvisations fall sensual and skilful as the ballads he sings with his famous guitar. After Covarrubias, Tamayo captivated blasé New York, but he returned to Mexico.

The success of Rivera and of the school children in foreign countries re-converted the Secretariat to the idea of murals, and this was of benefit to Maximo Pacheco, who had been associated with both Rivera and the much commented schools. Maximo Pacheco is a shy and very dark Indian youth from a village in the state of Hidalgo. He mixed lime for Rivera's and Revueltas' masons unaware that he also was a painter until Charlot and Siqueiros told him so. For some time after, until he was eighteen, he worked as Rivera's assistant and drew at night. Then he went to work in a factory, half-time, which gave him the afternoon and night to paint in. He exhibited with extraordinary success in Mexico City, becoming the only painter who lived on the financial results of his work, but he lives with Indian frugality. Later a painting sent to the Pan-American Exposition in San Francisco excited much comment.

The Minister of Education was moved by the fantastic charm of his work (which he says is all autobiographical) and the wild untouched childishness of his person to give him a commission decorating a very new, very small, extremely pretty school in one of the poor quarters of Mexico City. Here among children shy and dark like him, he found models which pleased him as much as his own self. His frescos are scenes of children at play, at work, in the fields, in the woods, eating fruits the texture and colour of their brown and apricot faces. "I want to paint revolutionary things," he says, "and I

110. STREET SINGERS
      Drawing by Paul Higgins

can put toy guns in the hands of the boys, but that isn't exactly revolution. So I am working out the ideas of a children's revolution. For example in that scene in the woods, there is one boy who is very greedy and takes all the fruit. This is so heavy that he stumbles and falls, and at that moment an overripe *zapote* drops on his head. The only thing that bothers me is that I've already used up the best walls, and I have much more to paint. Also I can't work very much at night because there are too many mosquitoes." And he sighs.

Pacheco's successor as assistant to Rivera was Paul Higgins, the son of a California judge. Higgins was known in California as a pianist, having at the age of ten given his first virtuoso concert. He abandoned music for painting and the United States for Mexico because, he says, he could not compose music, and he had seen modern Mexican art which attracted him. Within several years he has also changed shoes for sandals and an overcoat for a sarape. He lives on a roof which is a kind of clubhouse for Indian craftsmen, and when his family's friends come to Mexico City Higgins takes his dark companions to have tea with them. If he were not very blond one would be surprised to hear that his name is Higgins and not Gonzalez, especially because of his work. Purity of line and clarity of

vision record a sincere and extremely sensitive and gifted Irishman "gone Mexican."

Several other Americans and Europeans have "gone Mexican" not so successfully, because not so completely. Higgins' only approximate emulator is Lowell Houser, who went for the day to Lake Chapala while vacationing in Guadalajara, and stayed three years. Subsequently he was engaged by the Carnegie Institution to

III. TORTILLERAS
Yucatan. Woodcut by Lowell Houser assist Charlot in Chichen-Itza. Houser's fine talent for design and original bent in colour had been expended on intricate magazine covers and illustrations. The difference between this work and that done after his stay in Mexico is great, but no doubt, because of his youth, his style though already formalized, would have changed anyhow. The richness of his colour feeds on Mexican scene and popular design, and the new simplicity and charm of his lines are qualities inherent in the scene which inspired them. However only an artist wise and responsive finds them.

112. STREET SINGERS
Oil on cardboard. By Manuel Rodriguez Lozano

113. CHILDREN
Water color by Rufino Tamayo

That part of the Syndicate which went to Guadalajara became a group headed by Amado De la Cueva, nicknamed,
because of a taste for frightful drives on his motorcycle, the
Black Devil. De la Cueva had spent some time in Europe, wor-
shiping Massaccio. The work done under him in the University of Guadalajara nevertheless is of a nature directly the
opposite of Massaccio, for De la Cueva was determined to
develop a style of decoration that would be architectural but
not modelled nor chiaroscuro. The salon divided between himself and Siqueiros is decorated as if one man had done
the entire work. Its colour key is extremely simple: reds
and blacks on a background of cream. The designs are
stylized motifs abstracted from the subject matter which
engaged the Syndicate's interest: men with machines and
simpler implements of labour, such as plows and machetes.

The Zuno house, designed by Zuno and De la Cueva with
occasional suggestions from Siqueiros, was decorated largely
by Xavier Guerrero. Guerrero had painted rooms in the residence of the director in the agrarian school at Chapingo, in a
conventional manner more strident than that he adopted for
the Zuno house, and with different subject matter. The earlier
frescos are in subject and colour key, of the most exuberant
Syndicate moment, while those of the Zuno house are birds,
animals and flowers in cool tones. From their charm one supposes that in the pretty house the painter must have forgotten
for a moment the social-revolution fire which burns him, and
which has stamped on his face a moody, determined expression impressive because Guerrero is a Tarahumara Indian, and
looks it. These frescos and a sculptured stone tiger in the
Zuno patio are a very small portion of Guerrero's work, much
of which is scattered through the Syndicate and the later Communist *Machete*. Guerrero is very active in agrarian and labour

organization. He annotates these occupations with drawings and woodcuts that serve propaganda purposes.

Siqueiros, De la Cueva, Guerrero and Roberto Reyes Perez, who had been an assistant to some of the mural painters in the Preparatory School, with Zuno's support implanted in Guadalajara the Syndicate artistic tradition. Guerrero and Siqueiros supplied the craftsmen who manufactured the Zuno furniture and who carved doors for public buildings, with designs—revolutionary of course. One craftsman, Juan Hernandez, was discovered to be a sculptor who gave to the drawings he copied a personal treatment and interpretation. Juan Hernandez was not a carver by trade, he was a mechanic who fell ill and had to spend some weeks in a hospital. To amuse himself he whittled, by the time he was convalescent he carved, and when his doctor saw him for the last time he bought Hernandez' first sculpture. For the Zuno house too, the best potters of Tonala' invented flat soft ceramic tiles, decorated like vases, occasionally also with more modern designs. Hernandez carved panels derived from these tiles, and in the end it was impossible to attribute any one work to any one person.

The capital of the radical state of Veracruz during the term of one governor also fomented artistic revolution. A group was formed here which drew from painters who had worked in the Preparatory School. The most distinctive among them, Ramon Alva de la Canal, had been an assistant of Rivera in the Preparatory School and in Chapingo, and had done mural work of his own. Younger painters in Veracruz followed him to a certain extent, in the spirit of subject matter and general æsthetic orientation. The group in Veracruz was led by the poet Manuel Maples Arce, and the interchange between writers and painters is to be seen in the style of some of the literature that can be traced to this workshop.

III.

Modern Mexican literature is as yet largely printed on broadsides to be sung. It is true that "you can't throw a stone here without hitting a poet," but unless the stone is aimed it will hit a littérateur of ballads and current rhymes, household and pulqueria tales. The number and quality of the gentlemen to be found between pasteboard covers is by no means comparable to the number and quality of their contemporaries in the silent arts. Disparate sporadic efforts to link colonial and popular tradition in literature to modern, unhappily seldom find a suitable point of departure in European forms which to be intelligible, and because the language is Spanish, they require. Most of the writers in the public eye are journalists or sophisticates who by miracles of wit and ingenuity wring a pardon for their affectation, necessarily the result of attempting to wedge Mexico into Cocteau.

Nevertheless occasional fresh and vigorous voices such as those of Gutierrez Cruz, Maples Arce, Xavier Icaza, Martin Luis Guzman deserve the honour to which they aspire of being called revolutionary. They mean by that term exactly that spirit of being with pleasure and talent Mexican, defined already in murals, and achieved fully by only one man as great as the greater of the painters. This writer is Mariano Azuela, by profession a doctor. In one of his novels Azuela pictures a taciturn, gruff and unkempt person unbeloved in a small town thickly tarnished with the shellac of Diaz days, because of his social skepticism and in spite of (or also because of) a tremendous kindliness. This man is a self-portrait in whom for the sake of art Azuela's silence becomes taciturnity, and kindliness serves in the place of his great understanding and mercy.

When scattered and whooping guerrillas announced to that

town that a revolution had come, (much as drops of rain in the face insist on a breaking storm) Azuela, perhaps gruffly, tethered his horse in a mountain camp. His experiences with a band transformed in the course of Villa's career from twenty sweating and singing men into a flamboyant army banqueting on frijoles and champagne in looted cities, became a masterpiece, *Los de Abajo*. The last scene of this tale was written in a cave overlooking the catastrophic end of the band, and the rest in exile over the Rio Grande.

Los de Abajo is the literary counterpart of Orozco's black-and-whites of the revolution. Dramatic, terse, compact, the story races in rich native idiom from canyon to canyon. Each picturesque brutal scene flashes hundreds of similar scenes in the minds of Mexican readers, for of all these extraordinary pictures there is not one that is extraordinary to any Mexican at home during the revolution, nor is any one in the vivid range of common experience omitted. Too rapid a foreign reader however will mistake fatigue for futility, and his shocked nerves may not permit him to sense below the carnage an inarticulate text that these men who were killed to no immediate practical purpose and who died in charred crops without realizing that they were part of a great spiritual change were not less heroic because they were not underwritten with idealistic post-revolutionary social dogma.

Azuela's earlier books build like the period in which they are laid to this conclusion. *Los Caciques*, a tragedy in a village preyed upon by profiteers dealing in rotten maize and real-estate values; *Mala Yerba*, a pitiful account of complaisant natives outraged by a family of parasites immigrant from Spain; *Sin Amor*, the story of a plebeian girl who marries a rich *hacendado* and benefits by this loveless union, in growing monstrously fat, have each the definite social implication which made the author an armed revolutionary also.

114. ADOLESCENT HEAD

Pencil study by Maximo Pacheco

As a craftsman Azuela's glory lies in the close relationship of the style of each piece of work, with its subject matter. *Los de Abajo* needs footnotes in Spain, as its heroes would need interpreters. Its companion piece, subtitled "The Tribulations of a Decent Family in the Revolution," is written in *bourgeois,* and the first part in effeminate bourgeois which mirrors its pomaded speaker. *Los Caciques* is written in provincial odorous of nineteenth century notaries and household remedies, affectionately because Azuela, like most of Mexico's great men, is not a metropolitan. In Mexico City he inhabits a small house in one of the poor quarters where his patients live. His patio is full of low pots flowering sturdy familiar blooms, and his children disorder his literary notes because they do not mind if their father is illustrious.

The orchestration of national elements which in a sense Azuela and the painters represent, is literally the achievement of the musician Carlos Chavez. Radically abstract modern Europe and the scraped bones, thronged drums, clay bells and razor-toned flutes of native America juxtapose and become identified in his cerebral, unsweet, deeply felt compositions, which from the first insistent chord carve rhythmically a structure that levies desperate attention. Because of their symmetry and lucidity, probably, Paul Rosenfeldt calls Chavez the classic of moderns, but the shock to New York audiences is generally not much alleviated by that recommendation.

Chavez was born in the small capital of the central state of Aguascalientes, of ancestry familiar in Mexican history for martial and philosophic achievements in times of revolution and lapses of peace. He may have inherited from that grandfather whose statue in a military posture stands in one of the town plazas, his genius for organization, but except with the baton of the National Symphony Orchestra in his fist, Chavez does not resemble him. For his scientific tastes and skill on the piano he was sent to Europe to study; likely he discoursed entertainingly even then on the physics of music and the history of notation. When he returned to Mexico he wrote two ballets on mythologic themes, collaborating with modern Mexican poets and painters, and with Rivera on another called H.P.

Walter Pater prefigured the personal character of Chavez in that essay on the one type of person so infrequent that the world does not recognize it as a type. "It is the spirit that sees external circumstances as they are, and realizes the given conditions of its life, not disquieted by the desire for change, or the preference of one part of life rather than another, or passion, or opinion. The character we mean to indicate achieves this perfect life by a happy gift of nature, without any struggle at all . . . That truthfulness of temper, that receptivity, which professors often strive in vain to form, is engendered here less by wisdom than by innocence. Such a character . . has something of the clear ring, the eternal outline of the antique. Perhaps it is nearly always found with a corresponding outward semblance . . . It is just this sort of entire transparency of nature that lets through unconsciously all that is really lifegiving in the established order of things; it detects without difficulty all sorts of affinities between its own elements, and the nobler elements in that order. But then its wistfulness and a confidence in perfection it has makes it love the lords of change. What makes revolutionists is either self-pity, or indignation for the sake of others, or a sympathetic perception of the dominant undercurrent of progress in things. The nature before us is revolutionist from the direct sense of personal worth, that pride of life, which to the Greek was a heavenly grace. . . . Over and over again the world has been surprised by the heroism, the insight, the passion, of this clear crystal nature."

IV.

In the eight years since the revolution in the Secretariat, its influence has spread to other buildings, other cities, other arts, over the Rio Grande and beyond the Panama Canal. The Rio Grande basin and the isthmus region have been cultural junctures of the continent since undated peoples first travelled these routes. The Rio Grande basin is an archæological zone affiliated with Mexico, but differentiated from it, and affiliated too with the Pueblos on the other side of the river. Possible differences of race and difference of culture contributed to, rather than hindered, the civilization which grew in this zone. What fusion occurred came about partly by trade, and surely in the only way that cultural fusion and new development is certain, and that is by intermarriage.

Nowadays there is trade of material implements and objects of art as formerly; also intercourse of ideas. But Mexicans migrating to the United States settle unhappily in solid blocks, and stay dark and are reprehensible, and eventually return, while Americans to the other side of the river are mysterious objectionable creatures. The Texan stands with his legs wide apart and mutters across the puddle, "Dirty Greaser," and the Mexican sits with his head in his hands wrapped in his blanket and sighs "Gringo Dumbell."

Nevertheless automobiles, tractors and factories make of northern Mexico an industrialized region not absolutely a break with the other side of the border. The migrants forced out by the Diaz program of real-estate and industrial integration which benefited native and foreign owners, returning dropped in the north first, radical American ideas of comfort for the plebeians, a voice in government, organized labour. These ideas became swords in the sides of those investors and industrials who had profited by Diaz' gratis concessions and the abominable state of the people which providing the cheapest of labour, made profits more luring than any to be gained in the United States. There is a saying in Mexico that revolutions are made in the United States. This is based on the fact that ammunition for revolutions comes over the Rio Grande, smuggled or approved; and on the diplomatic custom of threatening notes to those governments disapproved in Washington.

Because of its geographic position Mexico was the first of the Latin American countries to flare into nationalism directly resentful of the United States. Its revolution began with strikes, and ended with revision of weak-titled concessions and a government bulwarked by labour. The same course is foreshadowed more and more imminently to the south. Strike butcheries and guerrillas of the Mexican school threaten not less volcanically because disorganized, unreported, and crushed, the triple alliance of venal clergy, colonial feudalism, and foreign industry based on cheap and atrociously treated labour in those countries whose social régime is exactly comparable to pre-revolution Mexico.

Precisely as Mexican plotters against Diaz fled to the United States to escape "fugitive justice" and life sentences in undersea dungeons, Venezuelans who breathe against Gomez and are injected with arsenic, Peruvians who organize labour or write of its benefits and are jailed, Nicaraguans, Hondurans, Guatemalans, race if in political danger to the Mexican Embassy and from thence exile themselves to Mexico City. These revolutionaries for any of the four reasons Pater recognizes, find an ideological form already cast for their sentiments, and for their energies. They find it because they speak the same language in Mexican literature, and because they are similarly minded and moved, in Mexican pictures. Then they write and they whisper lyrically: "My dreams, brewed in your soil, my

America, race of my grandfathers; my dreams, brewed in your soil, perfumed and steaming as barbecues, I place in the prow, in the hands of your Mexico, which protects my country with its body; I leave them in those paws, dark and robust, learned in caresses, brushes and guns."

Except to believers in miracles, pictures and verses are no shield against bullets. As shields and as symbols however they are taken by persons who hope to re-duplicate the Mexican miracle, and the Mexican heroisms. The assistance that Mexico gives them is moral: Vasconcelos protests against Gomez' murder of students, and Mexico breaks diplomatic relations with the country he rules; labor unions in Mexico send votes of adherence to strikers in Cuba, Peru, and Colombia; Mexican papers and magazines reflect sympathetically on Sandino. But the greatest protection that Mexico means farther south, is a matter of spirit. So long as that country paints and sings because it has fought, continues consistently itself, its unhappy neighbors can also sing and hope to fight.

The drama unfolds in the grace that ennobles the Mexican day. It is a conflict of unmaterial values, of attitude, in the end, and the concrete determinants which on the one hand push for more goods of this world, and on the other struggle for grace, are attributes of two disparate viewpoints. Geographical factors distribute these viewpoints racially; economic factors also; but each of the racial groups numbers allies to the predominant spirit in the other. It is drama because it is conflict of two incompatible powers. In its course it unfolds the rise of America.

FINIS

APPENDICES

115. DESCENT OF CHRIST TO LIMBO

NOTES ON ILLUSTRATIONS

By far the majority of the illustrations in *Idols Behind Altars* are published here for the first time. They were selected from material collected by the author, the photographers, and collaborating artists, in many months of careful and loving research. Most of the photographs were taken in villages and buildings not usually included even in artist's itineraries. Photographs and other illustrations were chosen in all cases for their artistic value, bearing in mind the typical, and the best expressions of Mexican art. The pleasant amazement which no doubt they will cause to artists and collectors will be amazement only because the ancient and modern art of this continent, as strong and as unique as that of any people in the history of humanity, has been so little examined.

I. FRONTISPIECE.

Amado Galván, whose hand appears in the frontispiece, is one of the most gifted of contemporary Mexican craftsmen. Pottery decoration is a tradition in his family which dates to untraceable beginnings, as is the case in the families of most of his neighbours in the potters' village of Tonalá, in the state of Jalisco.

2. UNFINISHED SKETCH. Vignette.

From a post-Spanish native picture manuscript, the *Codex Dehessa*. Few of the ancient pictographic records escaped destruction by the Spaniards. However by request and under the direction of several wise missionaries, among whom the most famous is Father Bernardino Sahagun, native artists portrayed the life and beliefs of the people in a manner somewhat similar to the customary style of Mexican scribes. These records have been examined heretofore chiefly for information, although they are a rich source for the student of pre-Spanish Mexican art. In manuscripts such as the *Lienzo de Tlaxcala* and the codices collected by Sahagun, the hierarchic and abstract symbolism prevalent in native draughtsmanship, of which a typical example is the *Codex De Zouche,* is evidently already influenced by Spanish realism. The sketch from the *Codex Dehessa* reproduced here is an example of realistic description with line.

4. LEAD SOLDIERS FROM GUADALAJARA.

Modern toys, height 1½ inches. Polychrome in red and green.

6. THE SAD INDIAN.

A famous pre-Spanish sculpture discovered in Mexico City is known by the name of "The Sad Indian." It was found on a street that has been called "Street of the Sad Indian," although the story of the Indian who pined away because of grief after the conquest also is given as the origin of that name. This pastel has the same pose as that of the sculpture, which sits in the characteristic Indian manner. It is intended by the painter as a modern interpretation of the pre-Spanish artistic version of the same subject. Property of the National Secretariat of Education. Replica exists in the Suttor collection, Paris.

7. A PAINTER.

From Sahagem MSS. Note the Chinese manner of holding the brush.

8. ARCHAIC TERRA COTTA.

Height, four inches. Uncovered at Chupícuaro, Guanajuato. Note the slanting eyes. Though realistic in appearance, it has almost certainly a religious connotation. Female representation in ancient

Mexican art is usually linked with the idea of fertility, a dominating theme.

9. POLYCHROME MAYA SCULPTURE.

This is a fragment broken off a life-size reclining portrait-figure in a subterranean chamber of the House of the Governor, Uxmal, Yucatan. Such sculptures were hollow to receive the ashes of the dead. This example belongs to the Maya New Empire period, to be dated approximately around the twelfth century, A.D. Head at present in the Museum of the American Indian, Heye Foundation, New York City. It is reproduced by courtesy of that institution.

10. PYRAMID OF THE SUN, SAN JUAN TEOTIHUACAN.

Until recently this pyramid was covered by earth and stubble and presented the appearance of a volcanic mound. This is the case with many other as yet unexcavated monuments. The Pyramid of the Sun was uncovered, along with several other important monuments, by the National Department of Archeology. The base measures 46,225 square meters. The height is 64.46 meters. This remarkable proportion is typical of Mexican architecture, in which the base is the most important element, and is accentuated. The fact that the pyramids were truncated is significant of the lack of interest in height. Such a structure is the antithesis of a Gothic cathedral. These pyramids were generally covered with a smooth stucco surface, and, most probably, fresco paintings.

11. SMILING HEAD.

Height, six inches. These masks have occasionally been found with bodies. They are generally cast. The simple and pleasant quality, which by no means lessens their strength, should be of interest particularly to students of art who labour under the impression that pre-Spanish Mexican sculpture is all highly complex and of a "bloody and fearful" nature.

12. DETAIL OF PAINTING.

In the Temple of the Tigers, Chichen-Itzá, Yucatan. This famous Maya mural of a battle scene is not wholly preserved. The line drawing reproduced here appears in light red in the original, and was a free sketch to be covered later with heavier pigments. Corrections are sometimes visible in these drawings. Due to weathering much of the coating has disappeared, thus making the preparatory outlines visible. The background of the mural is *terre verte,* suggesting a field; the skins of the figures, various shades of brown; garments and implements vividly coloured in carmine, blue, and emerald green.

13. SERPENT HEAD.

Colossal detail of monument in the National Museum, Mexico City. In such theogonic sculptures far removed from objective or optical appearances the Aztec sculptors were free to create what is probably the most abstract representation attempted by man. Compare with modern works of same tendency. The much weathered surface of this sculpture was probably, like other Aztec sculptures, smoothed with stucco and polychromed.

14. DRAWING.

From *Lienzo de Tlaxcala,* a post-Spanish picture manuscript recording the feats of Cortez and other events of the conquest contemporary to the making of the record. This manuscript is the best example of native art influenced by Spanish realism.

15. SAINT JAMES.

Wood sculpture, polychromed. Statue is dressed as Spanish *caballero.* St. James was the official patron of the conquerors and for this reason, plus the impression made on the natives by horses, the cult of St. James is extremely widespread. This representation cannot be dated, as similar ones have been made throughout to date, since the conquest.

16. SCENE OF THE CONQUEST.

From Sahagun manuscript. Scrolls under the eyes of the women are symbolical representations of tears.

18. HEAD OF CHRIST.

From sculpture representing Christ after the flagellation. Total height of statuette, 15 inches. For realistic emphasis, the back of this statue is flayed, bits of real leather adhering to it. The spine and ribs are partially uncovered, and are made of real bone, as well as the teeth. The eyes are inlaid glass. It is most probable that a wig of real hair completed the illusion. In the collection of Jean Proal, Mexico City.

19. Vignette, chapter four. Anonymous woodcut, *Ecce Homo*. Used by the firm of Antonio Vanegas Arroyo for illustrating popular leaflets of hymns, and other religious subjects. Dates probably from first half of nineteenth century.

20. THE LAST JUDGMENT.

Mural painting in the Monastery of San Agustín Acolman. General tonality of painting, sienna earth. Artist unknown. Murals in this and other convents were usually painted by native artists directed by Spaniards, though in some cases Spanish artists also executed part of the work. However since foreign artists were in charge of the work it is difficult to be certain whether the painter of a given panel was a native or a foreigner. These and many other murals were covered with a thick coating of lime by later occupants of the monasteries. The frescos of Acolman were brought to light recently by the Department of Artistic Monuments of the National Museum, under the direction of Sr. Jorge Encizo.

21. ARCHITECTURAL DETAIL, SAN FRANCISCO ECATEPEC.

The small church of San Francisco Ecatepec is a vivid example of Mexican baroque in its most exuberant form. The outside of this building is entirely covered with polychrome tile in brilliant blue and yellow, and the interior is decorated in a manner similar to the detail reproduced. The process is stone and wood sculpture and stucco modeling, polychromed and gilded.

23. MAIN PLAZA, MEXICO CITY, IN COLONIAL PERIOD.

On the right, the outer gates of the cathedral, still standing. On the left, booths of the market-place, and sunshades of fruit, vegetable and other produce merchants. The old market, which was the trading place of the Aztecs, continued in the same site after the conquest. Later it was moved away a short distance from this plaza, known today as the *Zócalo*. Immediately adjoining the *Zócalo*, nowadays, the market-zone begins with the *Volador,* and continues into the market of *La Merced* and smaller trading places. The painting is reproduced by courtesy of the National Museum of Mexico.

24. CHRIST IN THE GARDEN OF OLIVES.

This woodcarving by Manuel Martinez Pintao was exhibited with the Mexican group at the Independents', New York City, 1924.

26. GLYPH.

From *Codex Mendocino,* part of the Sahagun mss. Conical shape is that of a mountain, and the human head represents the in-dwelling spirit. Entire composition is strongly reminiscent of the characteristic Indian pose. The glyph in this case is a place-name.

27. DETAIL POLYCHROME STATUETTE.

Height of detail, four inches. Representations of animals such as this serve as toys and savingsbanks, and are sold in great quan-tities to the peasants and poorer classes. They are manufactured in craft-centers which supply surrounding zones. Tlaquepaque, ad-joining Tonalá, in the state of Jalisco, is well known for these sculptures. Small figures of human beings and animals have also been commonly used, as in China, for burials, and as proxies for absent persons or for deities, in rites. Colours of this example: Spots, black on cream background; mane and nose, bright red.

28. WOMAN COMBING HER HAIR.

Calabash from Guatemala, representative of southern work. Background yellow, painting black and brown. Diameter, eight inches.

29. TORTILLERA. (Woman making *tortillas,* that is, maize-bread.)

Though a very small object, pervaded with monumental feel-ing. Not a current market-piece, but probably portrait, made in the family. Unpainted, except for black in the eyes. Realistic portraits, brightly polychromed, are to be found on sale very commonly at fairs, in ceramic shops, and in native ceramic-booths. They gen-erally represent occupations. Most of those in the market now are modelled, or modelled and cast, by a dynasty of artists in Tlaque-paque, the Panduro family. The Panduros are also famous for por-traits of well-known Mexicans. Portraiture in clay is not a Spanish innovation, as similar sculptures have been made by Mexican artists since long before the conquest.

30. DETAIL FROM VASE.

By Amado Galván. Pottery decoration, though dating from pre-Spanish days, and remaining homogeneous in style and technique, nevertheless adapts readily new forms. This was the case in every period of its manufacture. For example, the horse is a new form dating from the conquest, and in decoration proper many floral designs are evidently of Spanish origin, even though they often become stylized into characteristic Mexican patterns in which the scroll occurs frequently. Pottery manufacture and decoration is in Tonalá and in many other craft-centers still distributed according to families. For example Galván's characteristic style is soft-textured, toned in grays, blue, and earths, whereas that of the Lucano family, also in Tonalá, is utterly dissimilar in pattern and colour and is, unlike Galván's, highly glazed. Galván and other potters have been remarkably uninfluenced in technique, and this is to be expected since even when in the colonial period Mexican potters worked for Spaniards and from Spanish models, they retained their own processes. Galván holds his brush in the ancient native manner, which is surprisingly like the Chinese way. The vase from which the reproduced detail was taken is unusually large, being approximately three feet high. It is decorated in blue, black and white on a gray background. Owned by the State Museum of Jalisco, in Guadalajara.

31. DANCER'S MASK.

From the state of Guerrero, modern. The keen observation shown in this mask, which is of a more realistic type than usual, could be due in part to Chinese influence dating from the colonial period. It is an interesting fact that comic masks generally represent Spanish countenances. This mask is re-published by courtesy of Sr. Roberto Montenegro, author of the monograph, *Máscaras Mexicanas. Talleres Gráficos de la Nación*, Mexico City, 1926.

32. INTERIOR OF NATIVE HOUSE.

Excellent illustration of the versatile *petate*. Family altar where perpetual light burns, can be seen to the left of the hearth.

33. FIGURE.

From *Codex Dehessa*, representing a folk-loric being, probably a magician in the form of a bird, i.e., a *nahual*.

34. RITUAL DANCER FROM OAXACA.

Height, six inches. Costume similar to this customary in religious dances called *Apaches* in the Valley of Mexico. Short fringed skirt, high feather head-dress, rattles, etc. This figure probably represents a wizard. Note the eagle in head-dress.

35. OUR LADY OF SOLEDAD.

This madonna is dressed in mourning for Passion Week. It is generally the case that images each possess a wardrobe of their own.

36. OUR LORD OF THE TREE.

The Christ of the Tree reproduced here was famous as a miraculous image, having emerged unscathed from a fire which consumed the church in which it was enshrined. The image is now preserved in the State Museum of Michoacan, Morelia. Confrontation of the two images reveals strikingly the primary geometric construction to be found also in pre-Spanish works.

37. This engraving by Guadalupe Posada illustrates an account of a miraculous apparition in the heart of a maguey. It is titled: "Second Apparition of Our Lady of Guadalupe on the Hacienda de la Lechería. Complete Success, which leaves no further doubt of this amazing miracle."

38. SILVER EX-VOTO.

Representing an eye. Such miniature sculptures can be found in any shrine and are offered to most images in Mexico, in great numbers. An ex-voto of an eye would be offered most likely for the cure of that diseased organ. The manufacture of sculptured ex-votos is a small industry, much more limited to certain individuals than painted ex-votos, and this is explicable in view of the mechanical difficulties involved. Miniature sculpture in metal is an ancient craft and it is by no means discontinued, as is sometimes supposed.

40. DETAIL FROM EX-VOTO.

The ex-voto consists of the part reproduced here, and an image of Our Lady of Soledad. It is an example of simplified symbolic representation, the subject matter being limited to the two factors of miracles, the agent and the receiver. The text reads: "This is dedicated to Our Lady of Soledad of the Holy Cross."

42. MIRACULOUS CURE OF SEÑORA CARMEN ESCOBAR.

Complete text: *En Puebla de los Angeles, 18 de Setiembre de 1893. Allandose gravemente enferma del Estomago la Sra. Carmen Escobar y encomendadose al Sr. Ecce Homo y al Santisimo Sacramento quedo sana a Dios gracias.*

43. A MIRACULOUS ESCAPE.

Text: *Este retablo se lo dedico a la Virgen de la Soledad y demás imágenes que estan por ser ellas que me salvaron de las heridas que recibí el 21 de Junio de 1896 . . . Isidro Rios . . . Juana Olivera.*

44. EL TLACHIQUERO.

Man taking unfermented sap from the bowl of the maguey. Zinc cut by Manuel Manilla, predecessor of Posada in the publishing house of Antonio Vanegas Arroyo. For work of Manuel Manilla see article by Jean Charlot in *Forma*, No. 2.

45. Detail of *pulqueria* mural. Note sign giving price of liter of *pulque*. Such signs as this, and others giving name of the plantation which supplies the shop, are often incorporated into the painting and are made part of the decoration.

46. FROM CHURCH IN MEXICO CITY. LIFE-SIZE.

49. ILLUSTRATION BY POSADA.

The Spanish text is headed:

> Tiernas Súplicas
> Conque invocan las jóvenes de cuarenta años
> Al milagrosisimo San Antonio de Padua
> Pidiendole su consuelo.
>
> San Antonio milagroso
> yo te suplico llorando
> que me des un buen esposo
> porque ya me estoy pasando.

A copy of the ballad is in the collection of the National Museum of Mexico.

50. ZINC CUT BY GUADALUPE POSADA.

Represents a *calavera;* used for illustrating Dead Men's Day text. Uniform of Diaz period.

54. ANTI-REELECTION RIOTS.

Illustration in *Gaceta Callejera* No. 2. Published by Antonio Vanegas Arroyo.

55. DRAWING ON ZINC BY GUADALUPE POSADA.

Illustration of ballad of entrance of Francisco I. Madero into Mexico City. As in Italian primitives and in some native murals and manuscripts, the importance of the personage is given by scale, i.e., the most important the largest, etc. This and the illustrations following belong to the last period of Posada's work, and differ from earlier technically, and to some extent in style. Here the subject was drawn directly on the plate and the relief was obtained with an acid bath. Further reference to work of Posada can be found in *Revista de Revistas*, Aug. 30, 1925, *Un Precursor del Movimiento de Arte Mexicano*, by Jean Charlot, *The Arts*, 1929, *A Mexican Prophet*, by Anita Brenner. The *Mexican Folkways* devoted a special number to this artist in 1929.

58. WOODCUT.

Maize and guns, by Xavier Guerrero. Used as typographic ornament in *El Machete*.

59. THE FLAG.

This lithograph by José Clemente Orozco is made from a drawing which is part of a series of scenes of the Mexican revolution, to which figure 60 also belongs.

61. THE REARGUARD.

Lithograph by José Clemente Orozco, made from drawing included in the series of scenes of the revolution. This series was exhibited at the Marie Sterner Galleries, New York City, in 1929; in the same year also at the Galerie Fermé la Nuit, Paris, and at the Art Students' League, New York City. Both in New York and in Paris they attracted much attention. One lithograph made from a drawing in the series, *The Requiem*, was included among the best fifty American prints of the year, 1929, and was shown at the Metropolitan Museum, 1929, in an exhibit of prints owned by that institution. The scenes of the revolution series is occasionally erroneously said to discredit Mexico, but this opinion comes as a rule from Mexicans disqualified as art critics and mistaken as to the implications in the foreign mind of the passion and tragedy revealed by the artist.

62. WOODCUT BY FRANCISCO MARIN.

Pupil of Carlos Orozco. Privately published in *Los Pequeños Grabadores en Madera* in Guadalajara, 1925. It is reprinted by courtesy of Sres. Carlos Orozco and José Guadalupe Zuno, the publishers.

63. LINE DRAWING BY CARLOS MERIDA.

Woman of Teotihuacan.

64. WOMEN OF METEPEC.

It is perhaps necessary to repeat that the work of Carlos Merida can hardly be even approximately appreciated in photographic reproduction, because of the delicate and important relation of colour to line. This painting was exhibited at the Independents', New York, 1924. On his return to Mexico from France Merida painted a first series of oils and water colours of Guatemalan subjects. These were exhibited at the National Academy in Mexico City in the early part of 1921 and can be said to be the root of what was to become a Mexican renaissance. Merida painted a second series on Mexican subjects of which *Women of Metepec* is an example. They were shown at the Dudensing Galleries, New York City, in 1926, and later in Paris at the *Galerie de Quatre Chemins* where they aroused great interest. André Salmon, the noted French critic, wrote an enthusiastic introduction to the catalogue of this exhibition, and the preface of a portfolio of colour-reproductions published in 1928 under the title *Images de Guatemala* by the *Galerie de Quatre Chemins*.

Bibliography: *A Painter from the Land of the Mayas*, Anita Brenner, *International Studio*, 1926.
The Art of a Guatemalan Painter, Carleton Beals, *Arts and Decoration*, 1927.
Carlos Merida: by Jean Charlot, *Contemporaneos*, (Mexico City) no. 6. November, 1928.
Carlos Merida: By Luis Cardoza y Aragón. Monograph, *Ediciones Gaceta Literaria*, Madrid, 1927.

66. YOUNG WOMAN.

More than life-size. A monograph on the work of Abraham Angel was published at the time of his death in 1924. It was compiled by his dear friend Manuel Rodriguez Lozano, and contains reproductions of practically all of Angel's work. Reference: *Abraham Angel.* (Talleres Gráficos de la Nación, Mexico City, 1924.)

67. WOODCUT BY DAVID ALFARO SIQUEIROS.

Used graphically to represent the editorial staff of *El Machete*.

68, 69. WOODCUTS AND LAYOUT BY DAVID ALFARO SIQUEIROS.

70. MASONS AND PAINTERS AT WORK.

This photograph is taken from an approximate height of sixteen feet. Three master-masons are preparing the wall for the day's work, while two painters, Maximo Pacheco and Ramon Alva Guadarrama, complete the decorative elements of the vaults. Diego Rivera, who was in charge of this piece of work, does not appear in the photograph.

71. DETAIL OF MURAL BY OROZCO.

Orozco's mural composition, "The Rich in Heaven," on the second flood in the main patio of the National Preparatory School, as it remained for several months after the vandalism. Repair work was entrusted by the artist to the master-masons.

73. BURIAL OF A WORKER.

The gigantic mural was intended as a tribute to Felipe Carrillo Puerto, the murdered governor of Yucatan. The frescos were grievously mutilated before completion, and were abandoned by the artist.

Bibliography: *Vida Americana,* May, 1920. Vol. I, no. 1. Madrid. *Alfaro Siqueiros, un Verdadero Rebelde.* Anita Brenner, *Forma* no. 3, Mexico City, 1927.

74. EMILIANO ZAPATA.

This portrait by Xavier Guerrero appeared in a special number of *El Machete* commemorating the death of Zapata.

75. CARTOON BY SIQUEIROS.

One of Siqueiros' cartoons for wood sculpture. Designed for Juan Hernandez. Subject, "The Revolutionary School."

77. THE PEASANT, THE SOLDIER AND THE WORKER.

Second state of woodcut by Siqueiros used repeatedly in *El Machete.*

80. MAGUEY.

Detail of sketch for mural, by Orozco, inner vault of arch over entrance of main stairway, National Preparatory School.

The development of José Clemente Orozco's mural work has been traced by Jean Charlot in *Forma* as follows:

Surrender of the Spaniards at San Juan de Ulúa (1913). Though an oil, this is monumental painting and its style announces the frescos. (Painting hangs in the reception salon, fortress of San Juan de Ulúa.)

First Frescos in the Preparatory School: below:
The Sun, Schoolgirls, Spring, Tzontemoc. Painted and removed, on the panel now occupied by the *Wounded Soldier.*
The Christ. (Destroyed.) Head remains in the panel. *The Strike.*
Struggle of Man with a Gorilla. The Mason. (Destroyed.)
Rich Dining and Workers Fighting. Motherhood. (Still in existence.)
Revolutionary Trinity. (Changed subsequently.)

On the stairway:
Three, *Saint Francis.*
Frescos of the corridor of the first floor. (Changed subsequently.)
On second floor: *Troops Defending a Bank Against Strikers.* (Unfinished, destroyed.)

Fresco in "House of Tiles":
Introspection, Power, and Beauty.
Fresco in Orizaba: *Scene of the Revolution.*
Last frescos in Preparatory School:
Below: *The Strike, Destruction of the Old Order.*
Two panels, on either side of doorway to stairs.
On the stairway itself: *Cortez and Malintzin.*
Boy Running. The Indian. The Conqueror. Indians and Bloody Teocalli.

On the second floor:

Two Groups with Plows. The Grave-digger. Labour. Justice. Peace. The Camp-Followers.

Because of subjects and style similar to those of the frescos, oil paintings executed at the time the artist was completing his murals should be added to his monumental work. Two of these paintings are to be found in the collections of Lic. Genaro Estrada and Dr. M. Puig Casauranc."

Exhibitions: Series of water-colours, subjects, women of the city. Mexico City, 1916. The water-colours destroyed by American customs officials belonged to this series. A collection remains in possession of Sr. José Juan Tablada, Forest Hills, New York.

Exhibition of studies for frescos, *Bernheim Jeune,* Paris, 1927.

Series of wash drawings, *Mexico in Revolution.* Marie Sterner Galleries, New York; Art Students' League, New York; *Galerie Fermé la Nuit,* Paris; and in Philadelphia, all 1929. The exhibition at *Galerie Fermé la Nuit* included drawings, studies for frescos, and the exhibition at Art Students' League was a retrospective comprehensive show of the artist's mural period, including the oil paintings mentioned by Charlot in *Forma,* and also New York paintings. The exhibition in Philadelphia included the artist's Mexican oils and wash drawings.

New York paintings, *Downtown Gallery,* New York, 1929.

Bibliography:

José Clemente Orozco, the Mexican Goya. José Juan Tablada, *International Studio,* 1924.

Decoración Mural de José Clemente Orozco en la Casa de Azulejos. Carlos Merida, *Revista de Revistas,* Mexico City, 1925.

A Mexican Rebel. Anita Brenner, *The Arts,* 1926.

José Clemente Orozco, Su Obra Monumental. Jean Charlot, *Forma,* Mexico City, 1928.

New World, New Races and New Art. By José Clemente Orozco, *Creative Art,* 1929. In same number: *Notes on Orozco's Murals,* Emily S. Hamblen.

Emotional Attitude versus Pictorial Aptitude. Dorothy Grafly. *Philadelphia Public Ledger,* Feb. 17, 1929.

A book on the significance of José Clemente Orozco's work is in preparation by Miss Emily S. Hamblen.

85. WOMAN.

Photograph taken before figure was defaced by a splash of vitriol, thrown by an unknown illiterate.

86. CHILD.

Detail of illustration for *Cuauhtemoc: Tragedia.* Joaquin Mendez Rivas, Mexico, 1925.

87. RESTORATION OF LAND.

This drawing is reprinted by courtesy of *El Arquitecto,* Mexico City.

The artistic autobiography of Diego Rivera was published in *El Arquitecto,* April, 1926. Mexico City. It reads:

1886.—Born in the City of Guanajuato.

1891.—Went to Mexico City with parents.

1897.—Began to attend evening classes in drawing at the National Academy of Art, received lessons from Don Andrés Ríos.

1899-1901.—Lessons from Don Santiago Rebull, Don José María Velasco and Don Felix Parra.

1902.—Began to work independently, disgusted with the orientation of the school under the Catalan Fabrés.

1907.—To Spain where the clash between Mexican tradition, old painting, and the atmosphere and production in Spain at the moment, affected the artist's timidity, trained toward Europe, and misguided him, making him produce detestable pictures much inferior to those already painted by him in Mexico before leaving; worked this year in the *atelier* of Don Eduardo Chicharro.

1908-1910.—Travels through France, Belgium, Holland and England; little work, neuter canvasses, some of which are possessed by the National Academy. (Mexico City.)

October, 1910.—Returns to Mexico where remains until June, 1911. Witnesses the beginning of the Mexican Revolution in the states of Morelos and Mexico, and the Zapatista movement, paints nothing but in his spirit the values which will direct his working life to date, are defined.

July, 1911.—Returns to Paris and begins orderly work.

1911.—Neo-impressionist influences. (Seurat.) 1912. Greco-cézanesque influences. 1913. Picassian influences; friendship with Pisarro.

1914.—The indications of his Mexican personality appear in his Cubist pictures.

1915.—His Cubist colleagues decry his exoticism,—Paris.

1916.—Development of this exoticism (Mexican co-efficient), —Paris.

1917.—The results of his labour upon structure in a work of art, begin to be seen in his paintings, and these diverge from Cubism.

1918.—New influences of Cézanne and Renoir. Friendship with Elie Faure.

1920-21.—Trip through Italy. 350 drawings according to the Byzantine Primitive Christians, pre-renaissance, and from models.

September, 1921.—Returns to Mexico. Oils in Yucatan and Puebla; drawings of the encounter with Mexican beauty. The personality of the painter appears at last.

1922.—Decoration of the Auditorium in the National Preparatory School. Does not succeed in making an autonomous work of art and Italian influences are extremely visible.

1923-26.—Murals in the Secretariat of Education and the National School of Agriculture in Chapingo. This work numbers one hundred sixty-eight frescos in which little by little the artist emerges from influences and extends his personality which, he and some critics believe, always tended toward mural painting.

Diego Rivera was awarded first prize at the Pan-American exhibit in San Francisco, 1926, and a medal for outstanding achievement by the American Institute of Architects, New York, 1929.

Bibliography: (Includes only Mexican period.)

Diego Rivera, Mexican Painter. José Juan Tablada, *The Arts,* 1923.

Rivera's Mural Paintings. Frederic Leighton. *International Studio,* 1924.

From a Mexican Painter's Notebook. By Diego Rivera, translated by Katherine A. Porter, *The Arts,* 1925.

La Obra de Diego Rivera. Manuel Amábilis. Monograph of *El Arquitecto,* Mexico City, 1925. Followed by volume two of monograph, same publication, 1926.

If I Should Go Back to Mexico. Ernestine Evans, *Century,* 1926.

Rivera, Socialist Painter of Mexico. H. W. Laidler, *Mentor,* 1926.

Diego Rivera. Ernestine Evans, *Art Work,* London, 1927.

Diego Rivera, by Xavier Villaurrutia. *Forma* no. 5, 1927.

The Work of Diego Rivera. Howard Putzel, *American Magazine of Art,* 1928.

La Obra de Diego Rivera. G. G. Maroto, *Contemporaneos,* Mexico City, 1928.

The Revolution in Painting; the Evolution of Diego Rivera. Walter Pach, *Creative Art,* 1929. In same number, article by the painter, and thorough analysis by Lee Simonson.

A monograph on Diego Rivera was published in 1928 by A. Mizrachi, Mexico City, and another appears in the fall of 1929: *Diego Rivera,* by Ernestine Evans. New York. See *Mexican Folkways* for years 1927-28-29 for reproductions of Rivera's work.

92. MAN WITH CANDLE.

Quick sketch for painting, a religious procession.

93. OIL BY GOITIA.

Hangs in the office of the Subsecretary, National Secretariat of Education, Mexico City.

94. VILLAGE ORCHESTRA.

Original in collection of Dr. Manuel Gamio, Mexico City.

95. NEWS FROM THE BATTLEFIELDS.

Original drawing in office of Subsecretary, National Secretariat of Education; trial proofs of an etching exist, but the final version is not to date complete.

96. TATA JESUCRISTO.

This is the picture to which Goitia refers in his accounts of how his models were made to grieve. See Chapter Sixteen.

98. WOMAN AND CHILD.

Woodcut; originally illustration for *Irradiador,* vehicle of the *estridentista* literary movement in Mexico. 1923.

In France, Charlot executed a prize-winning woodcut *Via Crucis,* 1917. Also polychrome wood sculptures; paintings; and projects for murals. First work in Mexico, drawings, woodcuts, lithographs; mural, *The Battle;* National Preparatory School; in same place, two panels, *Cuauhtemoc,* and *Saint Christopher.* In Secretariat of Education building: murals, *Burden-Bearers,* and *Washer-Women.* A third panel, *Dance of the Ribbons,* was destroyed to make space for Rivera's triple panel composition, the

Market-Place. Series of dark, small oils, Valley of Mexico. Exhibited at *Art Center,* New York, 1926, prologue of catalogue by Walter Pach. Series of paintings from Yucatan, and parallel lithographs and woodcuts. Series of water colours, *Dancers.* See *Mexican Folkways* until 1926 for work as art editor of that publication. See *Zeitbilder,* Berlin, 1927: *Der Maler des Indios,* by Alphonse Goldschmidt. In *Forma* No. 5, Mexico City, 1927, woodcuts. One lithograph, (Yucatan, *The Tiger Hunter*), and two woodcuts, in Metropolitan Museum collection of prints.

98. MOURNERS.

In possession of the National Secretariat of Education, Mexico City.

106. ROAD TO THE FAIR.

Bas-relief in clay, is one of three panels depicting the three epochs of civilization in San Juan Teotihuacan, i.e., pre-Spanish, colonial, and modern. Executed by Yela Gunther for the museum at San Juan Teotihuacan, by commission of National Department of Anthropology under Dr. Manuel Gamio.

107. CARTOON BY XAVIER GUERRERO.

For wood-sculpture by Juan Hernandez. Panel for a door in house of José G. Zuno, Guadalajara, Jalisco. For reproductions and note on the work of Juan Hernandez, see *Forma,* No. 1, Mexico City, 1926.

108. CUPOLA.

Interesting amalgamation of modern concrete with traditional majolica to be seen in this detail of the edifice.

109. MURAL DECORATION.

This decoration is characteristic of the forceful and original artistic personality of Fermín Revueltas. While it is in line with the tendencies of modern decoration, it is also intimately linked to popular murals, that is, *pulqueria* paintings, which in turn are at one with the abstract and geometric decoration of pre-Spanish walls.

111. TORTILLERAS.

An exhibition of the works of this artist was held at the Weyhe Galleries, New York, 1929. *The Dial* has from time to time reproduced linoleum cuts on Mexican subjects by Houser.

112. STREET SINGERS.

Manuel Rodriguez Lozano, an intellectual deliberately influenced by popular art, has in turn had wide influence on the younger generation of Mexican painters. He exhibited in Paris in 1926, being received with great interest. André Salmon wrote an introduction to this exhibition. Paintings of Rodriguez Lozano included in a comprehensive Mexican exhibition at the *Art Center*, in 1928, impressed American critics. See *Forma*, 1927, for reproductions.

113. CHILDREN.

Tamayo exhibited in Mexico City, 1927; at the *Art Center*, and *Weyhe Galleries*, New York, 1928. Woodcuts by him are usually on exhibit at the Weyhe Galleries. See *Forma*, no. 5, Mexico City, 1927, for article on that painter. No reproduction is published in *Idols Behind Altars* of the work of Agustín Lazo, who has, however, been of great interest to Mexican art critics. Tiles made from designs of that artist for a ballet of Carlos Chavez were exhibited at the *Art Center*, 1928. See *Forma*, 1927, for article and reproductions; also *Contemporaneos*, 1928, *Notas Sobre Lazo*, by Xavier Villaurrutia.

114. ADOLESCENT HEAD.

This head is a detail of a pencil study, a variant of the painting exhibited at the Pan-American exposition in San Francisco, where it attracted much attention. Later it was shown at the *Art Center*, 1928. For note on Pacheco and photograph of an early fresco by that artist see *Creative Art*, 1929; Anita Brenner, *Children of Revolution*.

115. DESCENT OF CHRIST TO LIMBO.

From a picture-manuscript of the Credo made for Aztecs by Indian artists under the direction of Spanish friars. Shows Mexican style adapted to new subject matter. (Humboldt collection.)

116. WOODCUT BY GUADALUPE POSADA.

117. WATER PORTERS.

Zinc-cut by Manuel Manilla.

118. MOTHER WITH CHILDREN.

Drawing by Jean Charlot, to illustrate native tale.

BIBLIOGRAPHY

Idols Behind Altars was not planned as a reference book, and for this reason the printed sources used for pre-Spanish and colonial periods are not given. Those available are to be found listed in most historical and archeological works dealing with Mexico. For pre-Spanish art, see *Maya Art,* by Herbert J. Spinden; *Mexican and Maya Art,* 116.
T. A. Joyce; *Outline of Maya Art,* by Eric Thompson, (Chicago Field Museum) and the forthcoming publication, *The Temple of the Warriors at Chichen Itzá,* by Ann Axtell Morris, Earl Morris, and Jean Charlot. (Carnegie Institution of Washington.) General pre-Spanish art, *L'art Pre-Colombien,* Basler and Brummer, Paris, 1928. See publications of the National Museum of Mexico and in *Natural History* (New York), 1928, illuminating article by Dr. George Vaillant.

FURTHER SUGGESTIONS:

British Museum Guide to the Maudsley Collection of Maya Sculpture.
Charnay Desirée, *Ancient Cities of the New World.*
Gordon, G. B. *Examples of Maya Pottery.* Philadelphia University Museum, 1925.
Gamio Manuel, *La Poblacion del Valle de Teotihuacan.*
Holmes, W. H. *Archeological Studies Among the Ancient Cities of Mexico.* Chicago, Field Columbian Museum, 1895-97.
Lothrop, S. K. *Pottery of Costa Rica and Nicaragua.* Museum of the American Indian, Heye Foundation.
Maudsley, A. P. *Biologia Centrali-Americana.* London, 1889-1902.
Peñafiel, F. *Monumentos del Arte Mexicano Antiguo.* Berlin, 1890.
Saville, M. H. *The Woodcarver's Art in Ancient Mexico,* and *Goldsmith's Art in Ancient Mexico.* Museum of the American Indian, Heye Foundation.
Seler, E. *Gesammelte Abhandlungen.* Berlin, 1902.

FOR COLONIAL ART:

Atl, Dr. (Gerardo Murillo). *Iglesias de Mexico,* and *Cúpolas Mexicanas.*

Ayres, Atlee B. *Mexican Architecture.*

Cortez, Antonio B. *Arquitectura en Mexico.* National Museum of Mexico, 1924.

Kilham, Walter. *Mexican Architecture of the Vice-Regal Period.* New York, 1927.

Mariscal, Federico. *La Patria y la Arquitectura Nacional.* Mexico City, 1915.

Revilla, Manuel. *El Arte en Mexico.* Mexico, 1893.

Romero de Terreros, M. *Las Artes Industriales en Nueva España.* Mexico, 1925.

Tablada, José Juan. *Historia del Arte en Mexico.* Mexico City, 1927.

FOR POPULAR ART:

Atl, Dr. (Gerardo Murillo). *Artes Populares de Mexico. Secretaria de Hacienda,* Mexico City, 1923-26.

See also *Mexican Folkways* for years 1926-27-28-29 and *Forma* for years 1926-27-28, and *Painted Miracles,* Anita Brenner, *The Arts,* 1929.

For general information on modern movement see Mexican number of *Survey Graphic,* April, 1924; *A Mexican Renascence,* Anita Brenner, *The Arts,* 1926; *Figures in a Mexican Rennaissance,* William Sprattling, *Scribner's,* January, 1929, and chapters on art and photographs in *Mexico and Its Heritage,* Ernest Gruening. New York, 1928.

For work of Mexican school children see monograph published by the *Secretaria de Educación Publica,* Mexico City, 1927.

117.

INDEX

118.